Painted

Bride

Quarterly

Print Annual 1

EDITOR
Marion Wrenn

MANAGING EDITOR
Kathleen Volk Miller

SENIOR EDITORS
Toni Brown
Patrick Goughary
Robin Mookerjee

Christopher Connelly
Margit Longbrake
Gregory Pardlo

CONCEPT EDITOR
Tracy Shields Moral

CONTRIBUTING EDITORS
Scott Edward Anderson
Tom Hartman
Carley Moore

Melisa Cahnmann
Major Jackson
Daniel Nester

LAYOUT EDITOR
Jason Schneiderman

FOUNDING EDITORS
Louise Simons

R. Daniel Evans

LEGAL COUNSEL
Robert Louis

Chad Rutkowski

EDITORIAL STAFF
Kazim Ali
Kim Cobb
Patricia Gavras
Matthew Longabucco
Lisa Nikolidakis

Daphne Ball
Monica Fisher
Sarah Lerow
Kara Monagle
Jason Toogood

STUDENT INTERNS
Abbe Bucholski
Alicia DeMarco
Sandy Landgraf
Erin McCool
Nicole O'Keefe
Michele Robinson
Pamela Swanson
Amy Thompson

Scott Coon
Ana Hartman
Charlene Lawler
Peter Moore
Andrew Paul
Courtney Rohan
Naima Stone
Robin Waterhouse

PAINTED BRIDE QUARTERLY
English Dept.
Armitage Hall
Rutgers University
Camden, NJ 08104

pbq.rutgers.edu or **webdelsol.com/pbq**

Cover Image: *Unsettled #6, Parson's Harbour, South-West Coast* by Scott Walden. Walden's photo essay "Unsettled" is available online (PBQ Issue #63).

PBQ is part of the Camden Online Poetry Project.

Printed by WESTCAN PRINTING GROUP Winnipeg, Manitoba

Distributed by Bernhard DeBoer Inc. and Ingram Periodicals

PBQ is a Member of the Council of Literary Magazines and Presses. PBQ is Indexed by the American Humanities Index and the Index of American Periodical Verse (Metuchen, NJ: Scarecrow Press)

Painted Bride Quarterly is published online four times a year. Unsolicited submissions are accepted year-round. Send submissions via US mail to the address above. Please include a hard copy of all submitted work, a short biographical note with phone number and e-mail, and a SASE. All critical articles should be submitted in MLA style. PBQ assumes no responsibility for submissions received without adequate return postage, packing, or proper identification labels. For more information write to the above address or visit our website.

Subscriptions for the print annual are available for $15. Libraries and Institutions $20 per year. Subscriptions cannot be forwarded. Please inform us of address changes by mail.

ISBN 0-9728565-0-1

PAINTED BRIDE QUARTERLY IS GRATEFUL FOR THE SUPPORT OF
   N–3 Oceanic
   National Endowment for the Arts
   Pennsylvania Council on the Arts

THIS BOOK WOULD NOT EXIST WITHOUT THE (MENTAL, MATERIAL, FINANCIAL) HELP OF THE FOLLOWING FOLKS. THANK YOU, THANK YOU, THANK YOU TO:
   Tim Shields and Richard "Bo" Dietl for ensuring *PBQ*'s ability to continue publishing. To Dr. Geoffrey Sill, Lisa Zeidner, and the Rutgers-Camden English Department; Deans Margaret Marsh and Daniel Hart, and Roger Dennis, Provost of Rutgers University-Camden; The Camden Online Poetry Project; Michael Neff and Webdelsol; the Khyber Pass Pub; the bands "Bigger Lovers" & "Lenola"; the Painted Bride Art Center; AWP; CLMP; New York University's Expository Writing Program; Dr. Robert "Big Bob" Donley; Soft Skull Press & the Frequency Reading Series; the Cornelia Street Café & AngeloVerga; Martha Rhodes, Michael Broder & the Ear Inn Reading Series; the Peeps; all of the Rutgers Interns; *PBQ*'s editors and editorial staff, past and present, volunteers all. We'd also like to thank *PBQ*'s Board Members: David Dondero, Stephen Dunn, Robert Louis, Cynthia Vena, Kathleen Volk Miller, Marion Wrenn, Lisa Zeidner. *PBQ*'s Mantra: "Beauty, Beauty, Freak."

This edition was designed in Quark 4.04 on a Macintosh G4.
The fonts are Goudy, Bembo and Gadget.

Marion Wrenn

Editor's Introduction: Legerdemain

"le travail qui fait vivre en nous ce qui n'existe pas" —Paul Valery

Welcome to *PBQ*'s print annual, the material apparition of our first year's worth of online issues. At first blush, it might look like five issues smashed together under a single cover: mammoth; unsubtle. With a more extended gaze, however, something else emerges.

We're a hybrid. *Painted Bride Quarterly* spent the first thirty years of its existence as a slim, perfect-bound journal. Over the last few years we moved our quarterly issues lock, stock, and barrel to the Web (complete with an online archive of the magazine's entire run). We worked hard to preserve *PBQ*, an offbeat venue for extraordinary writing, and in our drive to preserve the magazine, we recreated it. Such work is the best kind of sleight of hand.

We're now a venue that exists virtually and materially, a magazine whose use of the Web has embedded us in aesthetic and cultural discourses of access and authenticity. Put another way: our move to the Web triggered a whole set of anxieties about the legitimacy of Web publication. We've had many conversations with authors who doubted the legitimacy of the Web—for without the materiality of a book, publication didn't count, or so they felt. The online issues were like books, and not. This ambivalence revealed a deeper set of concerns. How is it that a new technology could so thoroughly banish the aura of literary art online and at the same time activate the aura of the printed word? Online, poems were lifted from specific times and places, made available in a way they had never been: thousands of people accessed the poems and fiction we included in each online issue. That's more readers than had held copies of PBQ in its entire history.

PBQ plays with cultural fears and anxieties by adopting this hybrid practice. And in that hybridity we have begun to revise the grammar of thinking about Web publication: We resist the *or* of "print or Web." We prefer unions, we prefer *and*. Instead of a Procrustean lopping of poems or essays to make this book less hefty, we opted to show you the expanse of PBQ. We decided to move all of our first year's issues in their entirety into this book to celebrate the fluidity of print and digital technologies.

Valery wrote that poetry performs the great task of thought, that it makes "live in us" that which does not exist. Writers make the absent present. So too does this annual. It renders the virtual material.

By being open to new technologies of communication, we have made the familiar strange. The book and the Web exist in a mutual embrace, mystifying and demystifying each other. While the Web and digital technology have heightened PBQ's attention to questions of production and reception, of access and aesthetics, they have also reminded us of something we forgot we knew: the simple pleasure of a book in our hands.

Or better: this book, your hands.

Enjoy.

TABLE OF CONTENTS I
Issue #63
Spring 2000

Poetry

PBAC Reading Series Thirtieth Anniversary

PBQ NYC Reading Series

Fiction

Commentary

Issue #63

TABLE OF CONTENTS II
ISSUE #64
FALL/WINTER 2000

Poetry

Fiction

Commentary

TABLE OF CONTENTS III
ISSUE #65, THE INTERNATIONAL ISSUE
SPRING 2001

Editor's Introduction

Poetry

International Section

International

Issue #65

TABLE OF CONTENTS IV
Issue #66
Autumn 2001

A Note from All of Us at *PBQ*

Poetry

Fiction

Commentary

Issue #66

TABLE OF CONTENTS V
Issue #67, The Film Issue
Winter 2001

Editor's Introduction

Poetry

Prose

Issue # 63

Spring 2000

Amy Beeder

BLANCA

She used to make him eggs with flowers.
Wild white bulbs, pearl & ivory blossoms,
beetle and night's moth-mated buds
that opened in the quick exchange of liquid
yolk for omelet. Now when he hears her name

he thinks of creamy flower buds unfolding
sour & reluctant among fiddleheads or flame
softening into fragrant oily slips
tangy secret papers, fortunes. And knows
for this one memory there are a thousand

others, moments never savored, eaten by time,
moments deflowered, bolted, lost & squandered
now faint as a spent field, memory of dark
canopy, cryptic as the alphabet of wasps.

Nate Chinen

ON THE EVE OF JOHN COLTRANE'S 70TH BIRTHDAY

Issue #63

and what is this that
what is what is this that
this that holds us
together keeps the morning
after lover the springtime
walking a fine line the
other guy the someday my
two hips the smoking on the
bus choking like the too hip
junkie the wise one the always
transcendent ultraviolet
incandescent the yes
the poet on their feet on
the sidewalks of every small
town metropolis this side of
tell me how they all came
around how they keep
from skidding free of
words can only get
worse hope lies here oh
god who moves in
music and in stillness in
motion and in
motionlessness the blues
remain long after dark
only the shape and size
comes from the next
high the round and round
tonight eternal equinox
a woman growing
older every growing older
every older every day
the chant the always the
ommm the next the next the
pursuance of a
voice a fluid cry a
song cry a song a
reaching out reaching
inside the song is you the

soaring over the bar
lines over the fat cat
smacktrap backdoor
slimehole sinnership into
and what is this that
what is what is this that
holds the psalm.

Issue #63

Denise Duhamel & Maureen Seaton

HILLBILLING AND COOING (1956)

Olive gulps spinach when a hillbilly gal
steals Popeye the Sailor away from her
and lays Swee'pea on her shoulder like sacked flour,
cooing in her Patsy Cline legato:
I'm the bitch goddess who'll break your heart. Kudzu
blooms (this episode takes place in the South)
and everyone, even Wimpy, drinks
fresh lemonade. Olive's victorious when
the spinach reaches her bunions and she kicks
the hillbilly gal in her banjo.
Popeye walks all the way home on his knees,
leaving hillbilly land like a bad cartoon. [2]

Issue #63

---

[2] The text of this poem lends itself to a device, N+7, invented by the OuLiPo (Ouvroir de Littérature Potentielle/ Workshop for Potential Literature, 1960), a Paris-based writers' group founded on the premise that "games" and formal constraints lead to artistic liberation. In N+7, the writer takes all the nouns in a chosen text, looks them up in the dictionary, and replaces them with the seventh noun after the original. In this case, the authors have chosen N+12 in honor of the twelve episodes in which Olive ate the spinach.

HIMALAYING AND COOKOUTING (N+12)

Olympian gulps spinet when a Himalayan galago (bush baby)
steals Poppycock the Saint Bernard away from her
and lays Swell Box on her shovel like sacked floweret,
cooing in her Pauper Cline legionnaire:
I'm the bitterroot who'll break your heartland. Kung fu
blooms (this epitaph takes place in the southern corn rootworm)
and everyone, even Windchill, drinks
fresh Leninism. Olympian's victorious when
the spinet reaches her buoy and she kicks
the Himalayan galago (bush baby) in her bank note.
Poppycock walks all the way home on his knickknacks,
leaving Himalayan landing field like a bad casaba.

Denise Duhamel and Maureen Seaton

Interview with a Comic Strip Diva

We sat down with Olive Oyl at her home in Chester, Illinois. We were struck by the graceful reserve with which she served us herbal tea, her quiet yet sparkling generosity.

MS: Ms. Oyl, you've been called the skinniest thing in boots. Do you find this interferes with your self-esteem?

OO: Did you ask General MacArthur that? Nancy Sinatra? Betty Boop?

DD: Are you concerned at all about America's obsession with the private lives of celebrities?

OO: I've never had sex with Clark Kent. But that doesn't mean I won't if I get the chance.

DD: Are you saying you've considered a career outside of showbiz?

OO: I am not monogamous. There are millions of monogamous people, but I am not one of them.

MS: In that case, would you like to respond to the *Inquirer*? I'm thinking especially of the front page spread with the picture of you and Bluto caught in an indiscretion.

OO: It's not as if Frank O'Hara were monogamous, right?

DD: Speaking of the New York School of Poets, do you align yourself more with them or the Beats?

OO: You can't imagine how boring it gets in all these little boxes, each strip's linear predictability.

MS: I'd heard you were a surrealist at heart.

OO: There are sardines and there are lemon trees—it depends what you're in the mood for.

DD: Are you as uncomfortable doing interviews as your publicist says?

OO: I believe in performance and page. My goal is to bust through genre restrictions—strips, 'toons, feature films.

MS: Oh, are you double-jointed?

OO: Why can't I be it all? Pen and ink legs with human hair or Meret Oppenheim's tea cup covered in fur, the way art has sex with life and vice versa.

Issue #63

OLIVE OYL CENTO

her toes are not
the lobes of autobiography
(An ingrown toenail?)
that is, a history
(An ingrown toenail?)
like Ginger Rogers in Swingtime
this: the flooding into the flooding
and shriek! shriek!
God must have a big eye to see everything
that is, a history
A shipwreck in Haven
a shape made of links, elongated
Made of untinted butter frosting: Happy Name Day, Blue Jay, staggering
Feeling like a girl

(lines in this found poem were borrowed from Robert Duncan, Kathleen Fraser, Lyn
Hejinian, Denise Levertov, Hilda Morley, Frank O'Hara, Ed Sanders, James Schuyler, Jack
Spicer, Keith Waldrop, Philip Whalen, and John Wieners)

Issue #63

Nick Flynn

RESIDUE

> *"...he somehow takes it personally, as no one has ever taken color before, simply for making the object. The color is totally expended in its realization there is no residue."*
>   —Rilke, from *Letters on Cézanne*

I move between tiny desks, I must be careful, if I ask
        about the eyes

the braided girl will erase them

& draw another balloon-shaped head over the first,
        holding her pencil like a hammer

she will color the body yellow

& the hands will be red. The shy girl
        with the cleft palate

writes about being wheeled into a machine

that takes pictures of her bones. She spells *picture* like the thing
        that holds milk

or the man who throws a baseball.
        When she reads her draft to the class

everyone talks about when they got hurt,
        I fell off my bike, my

brother got shot.... Christina's book begins,

my mother comes home & all she wants is her coffee
        & tv. She works

too much. Outside

a car crosses the gravel lot & I'm seven years old again,
        waiting up
for my mother to make it home from work. I dig a hole
        in the backyard

Issue #63

& sing a little song into it. Raven writes, *My grandmother*
        tucks me in at night,

she draws her own head balanced on a pillow,
        while her tv whispers, *yes*. Just now,

I tried to eat my orange slowly,

to sense the pulp gently untying, to savor it as if it was
        my lover's tongue, then I'm back

with this puzzle of orange skin. A boy, his desk isolated from
        the rest

asks, *is wind fast moving air*
        or something moving fast through the air?

Nick Flynn

TRICKOLOGY

Issue #63

I'm thirteen, but when I was a kid
        she'd screw a store-bought toy head,
a *water-wiggle*, onto the end of the green hose

    that made it & me go softly berserk
        twisting across the summer lawn

    as if the air itself were Valium.

            She could whisper for me to burn

& I'd turn to ash.

        A blackberry patch grew wild off the road
to the electric transformers.

    I'd fill my hat & carry them home for her
            to make a lattice pie. Now she tells me

        that she doesn't know how to bake,
        that no blackberries ever grew around us,

that I never ate pie anyway.

            Not ash,

    really, but the bright flecks rising from a burning
            house, the family outside,

        barefoot.

A Descending

Dear dark,
silent and thus as if imagined,
what do you make with the hill lines
and the crickets' songs
once you have descended?
We stand at our windows
ourselves becoming windows,
separate and hollow, neighbors
to each other and to you.
We are without breathing
as we listen for your work,
and then to our own listening,
its intricate, further dark.
You who have held and hid them both,
which is deeper, song or silence?
The walking of roads, or roads?
Or the roads without roads,
walked without walking?

Issue #63

BORN AGAIN

The first birth was easy—impossible
to come out drenched,
wishing himself a rubber stamp
or antelope, flat iron to prop ajar
the kitchen door. No choice
but a pat on the rump, this humming air—
his baby meat ripe and glowing
as though he'd just been bathed
in a tub of beet aspic.
The one philosophy: suck,
the one religion: breath.

This Wednesday, Edsel J. Mosley,
Winn Dixie's pimpled bagboy,
will smack bare feet in mud
and wade into another life—emerge
the Edsel J. Mosley
he was always meant to be. Someone else's
mother, twice as soft-thighed
as his own, waits at the river's ledge
—a towel fluttering
in her large, white hands
ready to wrap him dry.

Issue #63

Frederic Koeppel

INTRIGUING, BITTERSWEET, YET LYRICAL

Shall we mean what we say and abandon
the blush of foreshadowing? Or shall we join
the stooped gleaners in their staggered rows?
So patient, so silent and proud, as if they read
in the golden rubble at their feet the dictionaries
of grief and deliverance. May one beg your
forgiveness and still be a tiger of the mountains?
Or have I erred so often that I should not be
allowed commerce with beautiful things? I can
hear them now: "In those days, you could almost
see the halo around his head." Love of another's
body is commonplace and unbearable, a breaking
of wings in wild air, a pouring out of water from
steady hands. What have I to do with Illyria, lady,
gleaming one, glinting and glistening one, unless
you help me unloose the horses of the sea from
their deep, black stables, unless you teach me
how to grapple the bits between their massive jaws,
how to dig my bare heels into their heaving flanks
and guide them along the inaccessible shore where
ceaseless waves wrest a jagged song from every
stone.

Rick Liljegren

Issue #63

THIS IS A POEM ABOUT DEATH

It ends with the rain
on the other side of the window;
stream water folding on itself,
impressionist roses swaying like trout
swimming in place,
the house tapping its nails
against skylight.

As if this were my home,
instead of the warehouse with tin
walls, abandoned, GODS spray-painted
on the outside like a possessive
answer;

this house, where the screen door wheezes
shut, pulling me in—
I walk through rooms,
trying to steal something
from them. The bathroom mirror
slicks itself along my fingers, white
blinded by the rings hanging empty
from the shower rod.

A door takes my hand, leads me
to a room with bed marks
in the carpet, a gouge in the closet.
Outside, the wind coos
soft against the glass, saying, go ahead,
kill me. You are
my ice light, my blank
page, my Arctic circle.

Thomas David Lisk

AT THE MUSEUM
(A Pantoum)

Issue #63

1. Anger

At the museum I saw bandaged dogs
and pointed dreams. I appreciate
the generosity of the open page.
Twine fastened paddles to airless machines

and prickled reveries. I appreciate
the subtle evocations of these contrivances.
String tied wings to ground-bound machines.
I wanted to see them through a microfying glass:

made-up things that evoked subtle fears—
a pearl-grey screen trembling under a patina of dreams—
I longed to hold the scene between my eyes,
as if—why must I stumble so often on as if?

A smokey sheet rippling with thin projections,
the slide device clicks and images shift and melt
as if—why do I falter at the analogous, the hypothetical?—
a gauzy gown, the Venus of Willendorf, a full breast.

2. Lust

The film projector swallows and a picture disappears.
My eyes grab fish they cannot swallow, silver instants in the air.
An Empire shift, a fat goddess, an eloquent curve—
a cry hovers in my throat, a nestling thrush.

My eyes hook creatures they cannot quite see, trout leaping;
Aphrodite; the round, brown belly of a pregnant woman.
A sob catches in my throat, smooth fruit:
Take me, take me, free me into your world!

Venus, the visible womb of a gravid damsel,
fruit ripening in a papier maché bowl—
ravish me to let me escape the untrue visible!
In the windowless installation we danced on cedar shakes.

Bananas browning in dish of thick paper,
a birch cradle overhung with whispery oval leaves,
in the natural darkness we capered on a low roof.
The sweet smells of cut cedar rose against the fake light.

3. Lust

A baby sleeps, rocking on a tree branch
under a round quilt with big flashes of redbird red.
The scent of wood wounds waft in the incandescence.
A heart thumps, slow and reassuring as a long meal.

A small patchy comforter worked in scarlet dresses
a branch near the screened window over the sink.
The healthy core of a big creature lubbed and dubbed.
One sees so much, as if through a pirate's leather telescope.

The branch near the window over the sink is bleak,
the air trembling like a blown sheet, the bird gone.
I see so much, peering through an antique spyglass:
pills of candy cracked to jewels of painted fiberglass.

The air reveals itself in the songless snap of bedsheets.
I tell you I understand nothing, nothing but lust,
commercial candy coated with plastic to make gems.
Yesterday, yesteryear, the chew chew of cast metal pistols.

4. Anger

You see how little I understand, not even lust
who colors serene faces plaited in oily color,
a vast ten-year past, loaded toy guns
popping red ribbons of black powder caps.

Who leaps out from faces and shapes
but joy, despite the clank of nearby metal parts.
Tearing perforated rolls of gunpowder bumps,
a little cowboy then adjusts the white neck cord to his red hat.

But ignore the whumps and clangs.
Joy is not a function of imagined innocence.
A little boy adopts the garb of a righteous avenger.
No meter says this or that experience is green.

Joy is not a function of imagined innocence,
the generosity of the open page.
No meter says this or that experience is green.
At the museum I saw bandaged dogs.

Deanne Lundin

BLOSSOM SINGS AT THE HALLOWEEN BALL

Issue #63

i. *mirror*

oh it was cold in the age
of reason everyone slick as ice or
as rigid

and rage
knifed thin along blinding mirrors
honey a diet coke she said

naturally people were bitchy
dwarves dressed up like waves beached
on sand

too rich
for the heart oh dear christ not the peach
satin too amadeus and

anxious about its effect

ii. *show*

Waves. Then hush. Only the tentative whisper
as water slides under the glass, lifting,
pushing your face into place and the music
swarms towards you like bees coming home
to a burning tree. Out of your throat smoke rises
from the last place in your life
that declared its freedom.

Nobody knows you are dead. Light fixes
your face in the terrible smile of Bernini's
cupid driving the truth into Teresa as if
she could see him, eyes curled like
an evening primrose snapping shut in the light.
I've worked hard for my suffering you think, *I*
deserve it, and nothing's going to
keep me from it. And you sing.

iii. *reception*

They'd waited. And I'd seen the dark one there,
before, outside of Rage, and once
inside The Palms. O darling boys, the air

burns for us all, I said, to get them going,
since what they had in mind was clear.
No fear. I let them move in close.

It isn't far, I whispered, don't be shy.
I still don't hate him, even now—
the night whips stars along his thigh

and we're in love. He doesn't know
love's beaten him to it, chained his cries
to my voice, for love's a twisted rope—

he thinks he's free of me forever.

iv. Beaver, Utah

*My dear Charles, I don't believe we have spoken for fifteen years now, can it be so many?
but I've decided to be old, now, for a change, and act like old folks everywhere who finally stop pretending to be pleased and let their loved ones have it on the neck.*

*When I heard, I sat in the Beaver Junction straight from lunch to midnight. Ranchers,
farmers, even old Malcolm at the Arco hobbled in, rolling his one good eye appreciatively
at my shadow—they all came in to see how I was taking the news my grandson was a show
girl. I didn't take it very well. I would have flown home but then I couldn't find the plane,
as if it could be anywhere but its same old spot along the strip.*

*It wasn't shame I felt. I don't know what it was. Like when my darling Troggles died (my
shepherd-wolf, old Troglybite—that Frazer boy had shot her, "after sheep," he claimed, but
everyone knew Troggles—and the pups just on the verge of coming. She made it to the fence
before she dropped. I was digging out some onions when I saw her fall. I went straight for
my kit-bag and got those puppies out, though only two survived.*

*(Johnson offered me his bitch, who'd whelped ten days before. She wouldn't take them.) I
washed them, fed them every two hours, kept them as warm biscuits—That's what I feel,
that same enraged elation. And then*

that picture—!—silver suits you very well. I feel quite fierce, and old, and oddly like I'm

Issue #63

seventeen again. I rampaged down to the Junction like a looney, and so Lucinda's moving in (the waitress) though she'll no doubt lose her job. We've always been so quiet. Peace, tranquility, a quiet life—no more.

Nobody speaks to us, well hardly anyone, except old Johnson and the Hopi healer, who came riding up last week to tell us, "Now you know the way of clouds. When they are put together wrongly, you must speak." I don't know what the hell she meant, except that she's adrift here, too, like us. I invited her to stay but she refused. She's gone back to her trailer-farm, aglow with gro-lights. Each day I dig a little more. Each day I look out on a landscape that might as well be Mars. Absurd, I tell it. Nothing looks like that. I've made you up.

And so good-bye, dear "Blossom" (what a name! really Charles). I am too tired and confused, despite the rumors. Back to the dig. We're thinking of Australia in the spring. At least the dogs will feel at home (I hope), Ella, your own fossil, love.

from *Herbal Remedies*

EYEBRIGHT

Elsewhere, the days remove layers of doubt
The way new stars confirm our suspicion
That birth is what happens when we are out
Looking for answers. Light from the Pleistocene

Era illumines your eye in its tight fit
At the telescope. Briny little puffs
Of air from the shore leave your mouth
As stray marks of guiltless violence,

Air bleeding smoke into darkness,
Keeping you pure. It's the way bitterness

Cures. Exfoliation. Purge. Blank.
And we become Us, quick as a wink.
Sofabed. One cat. Double sink.

Issue #63

Issue #63

OUTSIDE

Couches not to be sat on, tables
you were not to set a glass down on,
drawers that were shrouded by a strict taboo,
whole rooms that were forbidden, and the ancient
tiny porcelain thing of which your mother said,
Don't you dare forget, no matter what you do,
don't go near her cup! Then when you got there,
the sense that you were being guarded like a precious
land mine that anything might set off, until
somebody spotted a cousin or dog and got rid of you:
Why don't you run outside and play?

why did these come to you as you watched
the ambulance slowly pull away from the evening
news and the mother wailing *my boy,*
my boy and the furious neighbor charging the camera,
which jumps, then jumps
to the ball scores? They didn't really have much
to say, and you think you've never seen
such grief and anger all confused, with the news,
with the weather, the parting quip, and the silhouettes
of the anchor and the sports girl gesturing
silently at each other. Such

grief and anger it goes on beyond
the zippy score, the credits, and the loud montage
of the nice parts of this city, all those
shining skyscrapers! All that
grief and anger, all confused, and now
an empty, doubtless feeling that the neighbor rocks the mother
in his arms, that there is an "increased police presence,"
that the camera crew is drinking up a storm, that
the boy blown off his stoop while you were fretting,
this evening, about the little agonies of living on
is outside now, outside everything, gone
beyond the grief and anger to a place
that isn't any better. He is not
fingering your grandmother's father's German teacup,
nor is he in your uncle's secret room

or sitting in your father's hallowed chair.
He is just gone outside, and you don't know him
from any other catastrophe of grief and anger.
He's turning from a news flash
into a metaphor, the precious thing,
never used, that lives in darkness and gets
tossed out after the wake.

Issue #63

THE LONG HAUL

A boy and girl in their early twenties are hunched together on the midnight bus from Philly to West Chester, reading (together!) —On the Road

Issue #63

Where were they going with what wind
and how were the pretty rings
of flowers to be hung on them
when they moved so fast?
The little tense things they lived with
lined the road like so many crushed spaniels.
Even the perfect heart he bragged about
was carried in a small bag
of delicate mesh, and no one was the sadder.
The moon came out full one night
in bleak Maryland and silvered the rolling
mounds of grey sand, a breeze came out
of nowhere, and there was, as they say,
nothing to stop them. And so at last
she said: This is the moon in which, this is
the road on which, this is the night when
the impossible maps we follow melt,
or they never melt. What do you say, then,
darling (and she shook him in her hands
like a kitten found by the road): shall we
close our eyes and keep on going?

For Amy Murray

Christian Nagle

TROPHIES

As long as I found no ivory,
I stood in awe of the flyblown sacks
full of impala skulls, an armory
of varnished antlers. In my socks,

shivering on the garage concrete,
I watched dust drift within light-shafts
above the shaken burlap. One slit
revealed a septum, spaces for drafts

where eyes had been. A goddam oven
on the Savannah, son. By its prongs
I hefted an entire trophy out, back in,
wondering what they do with lungs.

Once, outside Rome, you crossed our yard
to the shed with a .22. I was Reserve Wing,
unarmed, squinting to show I wasn't scared.
The sun'll stun them, you said, unblinking.

Even your wedding furniture was chaff
when, by random light shot through air-slits,
we discovered a litter of chewed effects above
star-points—the eyes of frightened rats.

Simon Perchik

*

You almost drown and what's left
from an abandoned temple wall
—on one knee carefully break loose
that shadow the dead restore
with more room, more air

—you build a trench for clams
brought back the way clouds have learned
to grasp your shoulders for water

and clam by far off clam
trembling, fitted into bottom sand
into a shell already gray and your hands
never clasp, never dry or open again.

Issue #63

M. Rebecca Ransom

SPRING

In the morning the dogs will be licking slugs
off the side of the house,
slugs that inch up the walls
before dawn, leaving thin, shiny tracks
on the grey paint.
This can't be a good sign,
you say, finding these morning feasts
disgusting, and ominous
as snakes we've seen under hay bales
in the barn, as the coyotes
that bit the legs off
our neighbor's rabbits
through the wire bottom of their cage
last week. The phone hasn't rung
in three days and you say
this clinches it: somewhere,
someone isn't telling us
more bad news.

But even the horses don't flinch,
don't snort or roll
their eyes when snake skins,
thick and heavy as purse straps,
drop into their stalls
with the flakes of alfalfa—
they push them aside with their noses
and go on chewing.
And the dogs, who eat slugs
like candy, hear coyotes at night
and howl back, making tubes of sound
spiral up past the phone lines.
All this is not ominous, I tell you,
but spring,
a wet, cool spring
when everything is feeding
on something, being fed on, or being fed.

Issue #63

Kathryn Rantala

PARADE I

Ugly art in the window,
but attention is beyond the Paradeplatz
to the high-throated boots
shrilling toward the appointed spot.
A dog circles happily.
The crowd, in one distraction,
anticipates in him.
And at the horizon,
a wind,
a self-declaring air restructuring us
the mountains,
the animals in them.
And we are fine and true and new.

Especially the animals
carved in the streets for francs
but wandering just behind
carving themselves, their bright eyes,
the short, coarse hair and
the stare and the high long legs
that know they must eventually eat something.

And when the coach finally comes
with the Burgermeister
the music
and his other daughter,
we taste it together.
It wells up.
And the carefully carved timber animals
savoring the neighborhood
grow agitated
and more frequent
in the abundant noise.

VERTIGO

I sat there, listening to the breeze,
only there was no breeze, I was inside,
the windows were closed. It was like wind
in the dry leaves, curled up stiff
like old people, when their chests have started
to long for their abdomens, they've been apart
for so many years. And their heads
have acquired an increasing curiosity about
the composition of the sidewalk; their heads
have taken it into their minds to do
research on the probable source of inspiration for Schwitters and Rauschenberg.
They want a glimpse of the many universes
Mark Tobey said he saw in paving stones.
This is how curled up those stiff, light leaves are,
curled up as my father on his last voluntary visit
to the hospital, as I walked with him down the hall,
my hand on his back, curved and bowed
as a boulder, but light as a leaf. This is how stiff
those light leaves are, still stuck to the tree,
and hissing in the breeze like corn flakes,
though it's February, and there are no leaves left
on the trees, and I am inside, there is no breeze.
I sit here, listening to the breeze hiss in the leaves
somewhere along the Occipital Ridge and I wonder
at the immensity of the canyon beneath these steep cliffs
that I don't dare look down.

Issue #63

Karen Skolfield

Issue #63

IATROGENIC SYMPTOMS

Flu epidemics kill one tenth of one percent,
a number so small it barely ends a sentence.

Doc, a hairline fracture can't begin to explain
why my knee hurts when the grandfather clock chimes ten.

By boosting the dosage of cure-all aspirin,
some patients experience the seedy side of heaven.

The Sheik of Araby is so rich that a special harem wraps
his paper cuts in silk gauze and long strands of their black hair.

Such safety in the way we number things. Two ingrown
toenails, a tonsillectomy, one true love in a lifetime maybe.

The pineal gland, once considered inactive, produces emotional longing,
changing the heart-shaped candies of Valentine's to something lumpier.

Grandmother warns that when we sneeze, the heart hiccups
and refuses to beat until someone says "bless you."

Distilled, the body's metals are worth a hundred dollars,
while a good heart can get thousands in certain black markets.

The AMA considers "bacterium" their most successful myth.
Washing cuts doesn't fight infection, but eases an inner body into the world.

Doctors call the collection of organs "harvesting"
because it's the flower and fruit of their work.

Enough silver coats the aortic valves to plate the finest
candelabra, explaining the Quaker desire to find the inner light.

Yes, the inside of the body is known to be a gloomy place.
Surgeons rejoice when the first incision opens the stomach like a window.

The last time you were turned inside out, you were a tiny bud of foetus cells,
each cell deciding whether destiny was being a nose or a hair.

For each new disease, thousands of candidates line up like Olympic hopefuls.
Even the ghost symptoms haunt in believable ways.

Non-Euclidian Logic

Everything runs on an angle. As proof, I offer
the way lips form angles of sound as we read;
the motion of flies rocketing off tables,
their simple knowledge of geometry.

I am always alert for definitive evidence:
parallel bodies eventually touch. There's the right angle,
an arm perpendicular to itself. A flagpole
and its perfect shadow. Two of these, back to back,

form a half moon which disregards the gravity
that keeps it looped around the shirtwaist of Earth.
Four right angles and we've sketched a circle.
So much depends on the circular. Four right angles,

on which even the sport of fishing relies,
a fine 2-gauge cotton thread for the angler
arcing overhead, the home-tied fly disturbing
the perfect plane of water in a flurry of ovals.

What's more disturbing: despite the title, this is all Euclidian.
I pay a yearly homage to the Greek who debunked side angle side.
Even the paper—now I see it—is cornered in angles.
And more—plaster rhombus of rooms,

a favorite overstuffed chair slouched to 110 degrees,
old walls that can no longer hide their slow
settling to a mere 87, the floor at its cheeky 180,
all the private angles that hover and bend.

And you are the finest web of atoms forming angles...
see the arrows that follow your knee's obtuse angle,
your elbow's a cute one, the fine slant of your back,
all my love simplified to mathematical proof.

Issue #63

Ruth Stone

WHEN I WAS THIRTY-FIVE YOU TOOK MY PHOTOGRAPH

I am lying full length on the grass,
turned toward you,
resting on hip and elbow,
my cheek
against the spread fingers
of my left hand.
It is mid-summer.
My breasts are pendulous,
my eyes half open;
a damp sheen of sweat
highlights my face
that is more naked
than my naked body.
My stomach is flat.
There is a fine torque
between my waist
and my hip bone.
In your dark room
where you often disappeared,
a blank in the calendar,
the film would lie in an acid bath,
the negative then scrutinized,
washed and hung, like our sheets,
with ordinary clothes pins.
Evenings, you bent over the enlarger.
Dispassionate, I consider
this photograph.
You were influenced
by Modigiliani's nudes.

CLONES ASIDE

The sheep dog is barking and biting the man.
The sheep dog thinks the man is a sheep.
The man is only trying to catch a bus.
He works as an actuary in an insurance office.
He sits all day in a small pen playing with digits.
He has the blas. It's enough to make you weep.
All this time the man's wife hears
a voice from the play pen crying "ma ma"
until she feels like a sheep.
Is the dog mistaken? All sheep are sheep
unless they are wolves in sheep's clothing.
There is no use loathing the man, the dog,
the corporate world, or the sheepish woman.
More equals more or less, I guess. And that's
the way it is, *cum grano salis*.

Issue #63

THE WAYS OF DAUGHTERS

My daughters are getting on.
They're in over their hips,
over their stretch marks.
Their debts are rising
and their faces are serious.

There are no great barns
or riding horses.
Only one of them has a washing machine.
Their old cars break
and are never fixed.

So what is this substance
that floods over them,
into which they wade
as if going out
to meet the Phoenicians?

And they have no nets
for those shifty looking sailors.
But when I look again,
my daughters are alone in their kitchens.
Each child sweats in its junior bed.

And my girls are painting their fingernails.
They are rubbing lotions
on their impatient hands. This year
they are staining their hands and feet with henna.
They lie in the sun with henna packs on their hair.

Issue #63

MALE GORILLAS

At the doughnut shop
twenty-three silverbacks
are lined up at the bar,
sitting on the stools.
It's morning coffee and trash day.
The waitress has a heavy feeling face,
considerate with carmine lipstick.
She doesn't brown my fries.
I have to stand at the counter
and insist on my order.
I take my cup of coffee to a small
inoffensive table along the wall.
At the counter the male chorus line
is lined up tight.
I look at their almost identical butts;
their buddy hunched shoulders,
the curve of their ancient spines.
They are methodically browsing
in their own territory.
This data goes into that vast
confused library, the female mind.

Issue #63

WESTERN PURDAH, INC.

Pantyhose;
lotus-foot of the west,
iron maiden of her sex,
pseudo chastity belt.

On a clothesline they present
the lower half of her
that kicks and screams in mime.
These are the blood constrictors.
Some come in plastic egg shells;
commercial embryos.

The contortions she goes through
to smooth her legs like silk,
wrestling these tubes
as her grandmother wrestled a corset;
bone-stiffened corset, ribbed
with the mouth parts of baleen whales.

Prescripted unnatural fibers
of viscous chemical milk,
strong and similar to
steel belted radial tires;
market-wise; programmed, of course,
to self-destruct, unknit, ravel.

Issue #63

Rodney Torreson

Bull Calf Stood That First Time in the Field

my head near his
as if joined at the neck
swung from some clumsy history
in hiding. How enmity
between beast and man
slept where I would pet!

Conflagrations buried in
the nubs of his horns
soon would have the error of matches
when they flared
and he would blindly swing his head,

our hearts filled with
flaming trees,
the pastures with all their polish.

Our weak trembling knees
found ecstasy in the hard ground,
in green sprigs mighty to the muzzle,
the dullest knowledge striking us
as sky baring its blue
gracious face that first time.

These were days before the itch,
when we were not given
to pawing dirt,
to the terror of our stompings,
when he was calm, clueless he'd be
the renegade of fences,
and I was mute as unbroken stone,
and together we were
the monster of sweet longing.

Issue #63

POWER LINES

are always trying to pull this world tight,
bale us with wire,
place us into a spastic nerve barn.

The power lines keep good company, hanging
about with trees, connecting
to cathedrals and their vision,
inviting to birds and their twitter.
Four lines high, they disguise
a musical staff,
only to break the view at the window.

On a barren day
they tell us that we are happy
and we believe them.
Though these body snatchers
override the heart—
weighted down by a barrage of papers,
each a stone tablet,
the power lines make a playground
of the office. Telephones
hang from our ears, pencils lose
their hulls to make a point.
They rise through the hum of the computer,
lending a false sense of brightness,
which heightens the bluster
in our fingertips,
so that at night our loving is electric.
We feed out data in our embrace
like what spare part our body wants,

until at the hospital
our hearts are hooked to suction plates
and a monitor, which takes
the last of us so there's no beat at all,
not even one last song in the heart,
nothing to glean
as the lines humor themselves,
reflect upon the heart,
under the guise of refinement
move flatly, sedately across the screen.

Issue #63

Karla Van Vliet

THE DOE

After three days on the hunt
he pulls up his white pick-up
into the yard. I hear him
from the kitchen,
truck spitting like an old man.
Hear the engine cut,
the door slam.
I finish washing my supper dishes,
dry them,
before I go to the window.

He's slipped the rope
that binds her back legs
through the barn's pulley,
has hoisted her off the truck.
Her back arched,
the slit of her belly
opens to him.
Her slender carcass
leaves a brown mark
against the red leaves
of the far hillside.
He lifts her head,
I think he means to kiss
her brown eyes shut,
then strokes the hull of her frame,
walks back to his truck,
starts it up.
At the end of the drive
he turns toward town.

I go to bed.
Late, I hear his belt buckle hit the floor,
springs grate beneath his body.
I turn my weight away
from his whiskey mouth.
He has spoiled the safety
of sleeping alone. I have learned
to fear what he calls love.

Issue #63

When I wake the light dwells
in the bent hay of the uncut field.
His body has managed its way against me.
It feels my stirring

and now has laid me on my back,
his mouth on mine,
stale taste of barley,
the fetor of iron.
His thick coarse fingers
take hold of my breast.
His nails are outlined with the blood
of his precious doe.
His other hand has entered me,
the blood of the doe has entered me.
I fracture from groin to breast bone.
He fingers my openness, my wound.
I once loved this man.
He empties me.
My body endures the cold.

Outside all that is left of the songbirds' cries
is the who who who of the mourning dove.

Leslie Williams

Issue #63

STONE

It is all of these things:

Your round, cool head

shaved to show skin;

the tumor inside,

a knotty, bitter plum;

the agate that clicks

your son's marbles

on the floor of the porch;

the ball of the pendulum

that swings

on the clock in the hall;

the chance

that skips

across the pond's

curved surface.

Issue #63

Anne Harding Woodworth

Wire Man

A man on the edge of the woods
brings in wires through dead leaves and joe-pye weed
on into the steamy interior where I think
there is life. Connection is electric

voiceful sometimes mournful
treeful, sometimes moth on the bulb.
At night, insects around me rub their wings
keeping me warm with three-syllable friction,
the back and forth of darkness.

By day, birds sing through my flow-whispers
their descant sharper and wider than a requiem solo.
Blessed baby Jesus I left you out
in the stable and that's the way I wanted it.

O Wire Man, yesterday I saw you tight-rope walk
without a parasol in heavy steel-toed boots
on high over the inner road. Balance brings
veins muscle leaves skin and earth into one body
of the most beautiful kind.

The space is heavy, moist evening
sweet air of skunk.

Herman Beavers

BODY ENGLISH (FOR M)

Start with your fears
Then we can turn
To your demons. Did you take
Sarah Vaughan for the pain?
Does *Send in the Clowns*
Mean anything to you?

Let's start with that door there.
What's behind it? No. I'd like to
Know about the howling.
It must be important, you put
That creak in the hinge to hide it.
And the way the door swung
Open? A dead give-away.

There's the hint of a glistening
When you talk about your father.
Did you know rage has a
Crystalline structure when
Observed through a microscope?

Now that's something. Even the
Naked eye can see it.

Ok. Let's talk about history.
Yes, I promise we'll get to the demons.
What about all your mistakes—
Books, maps, hypnosis?
For what you want,
Scars are better.
Leave those sharp blades over there;
With what those scabs are saying,
Only Coltrane will do.

Let's peel back the time on that one.
1978. Yes. There will be time
To talk about the demons.

Issue #63

Issue #63

But just now I noticed
Your body english.
Something about the way
You hold your
Self in the light; a
Word just beyond reach.
It's late in the hour.

Go ahead,
Sing me your demons.

Issue #63

THE JOURNEYMAN

Where does the spirit live? Inside or outside?
Things remembered, made things, things unmade?
　　　　　　　　—Seamus Heaney, "Settings"

Reflection don't happen
In mirrors; might as well
Turn your back, Take who you are
On faith. Knowing that

Consequence episcopates
Homer Plessy's Veil; a
Rhetoric of spilled blood, scorpions
Hooking their tails across your path,

You could make of your mind a fist,
But you're the child God went on
Ahead and blessed, and there are
Better devices to be styled

Out of your tooled grace; elegance
Improvised in the teeth of corporate might,
Corporate wont. I look at the bunched
Half moons arcing in your oiled back,

Your tactile song still ringing in vestibule,
Footsteps measured in the boxed light.
If it was my place, I'd tell you to
Get a grip on your hammer
And drop it down. No need to

Bristle at the sparks flying
Off the anvil, the die's cast, your
Chair's bought and paid for
Even if you don't want to sit down.

You always fathomed the eye of a needle
As the nimbus fashioned in your own employ.
If ever you walk out of this life,
Coined phrases well-spent,
Tools at parade rest, A line

Herman Beavers

Toed in the sand, folk
Milling trepidation to a fine point,
You will cross it
And take the weight.

For Howard Mitchell, 1916–99
pioneer, warrior, gentleman

Issue #63

Yusef Komunyakaa

ODE TO A SQUIRREL

Good you can't hear
The stories & jibes inside
My sleepy head, as someone
Jokes about squirrel pie

From four decades ago
Somewhere in Louisiana or Big
Thicket. Tonight, on the roof
Here in Princeton, you work

Around the clock. Early
October, back & forth
With a stash of acorns.
You tapdance on the gutter screen,

Shimmy up to the highest pitch
& overhang below a crescent moon,
& then one of those great leaps
For the same tortured branch.

ANOTHER STORY

The airport cop
unhooks his wife's bra,
telling her about a woman
named Wisteria Chang
who had stolen—kidnapped—
a little blond-headed boy
named Troy two days earlier
in Seattle, how they were
boarding a flight for Taipei,
that she had dyed the boy's hair
jet-black & dolled him up
in a Chinese outfit
made of a very-very old silk
long before the Opium Wars,
that she kept saying
He was so pretty before,
& how he once made love
to a woman like Wisteria
when he was in the marines
stationed in Okinawa.

ECLOGUE AT DAYBREAK

His unlidded eyes a wish
always coming true,
as his body slithered
from a sheath of skin
half-alive on the grass
like a final lesson on escape.
He moved only when other things
strayed beyond suspicion.
The worlds inside sleep
couldn't hold him. In an arcade
somewhere in a marketplace
he was Houdini reincarnated
in a box. Soon came the hour
he was created for: a woman,
free-footed as Isadora
in sashes, draped his body
over hers. An apprentice
placed an apple in her left hand
& lush gardens sprouted across
three canvases. Her smooth skin,
how his wedge-shaped head
lingered between her breasts,
left him drowsy. The clocks
sped up. A cruel season
fell across their pose
as they began a slow dance.
She reshaped the pattern of skulls
on his yellow skin, a deep
falling inside him when her hips
quivered & arms undulated,
stealing the pleas of prey.

Philip Levine

WHEN THE SHIFT WAS OVER

Issue #63

When the shift was over he went out
and stood under the night sky a mile
from the darkened baseball stadium
and waited for the bus. He could taste
nickel under his tongue, and when he swiped
the back of his hand across his nose
he caught the smell of hydrochloric acid.
There were clouds between him and the stars,
not ordinary ones but dark and looming,
and if the rain had begun to fall, he thought,
could it be black? Could a halo form
on those fine curls his Polish grandma
loved to brush when he was a boy, cupping
a hand under his chin? How silent
and still the world was after so much
slamming of metal on metal and the groans
of the earth giving way to the wakened fury
of the earth and the separate cries of people
together for these nights. How odd that he,
born of convicts and soldiers, of men
and women who crossed and recrossed the earth
carrying only the flag of their hopes,
should stand numbed by the weight
of a Thursday shift and raise his head
to a heaven he had never seen and sing
in a hoarse voice older than his years,
"Oh, Lordy Lord, I am, I'm coming home!"
He, who had no home and no hope, alone
on a certain night in a year of disbelief,
could sing to the ranks of closed houses
and cars, could sing as clear rain fell.

Why We Sing When We Work

Renamed Efraim after the Lord of Light, he was given
for his thirteenth birthday a small roan and pranced
in the roadway raising dust in the eyes of young mothers
whose curses, tame and traditional, did no one harm.
His brother Ismail walked at his side. A man of some years,
but merely a man, he herded the children to their safety.
Ismail dreamed of a small house at the edge of town, a view
of the distant mountains, a hillside staggered with grapes,
apple trees behind the house, their branches bowed
by dark clusters at summer's end. How little to ask for one
born too suddenly and under the wrong sign, the only brother
of he who made the sun stand still. One afternoon Efraim
dismounted to sit all that day by the waters of the river.
He neither prayed nor wept, for everything was answered.
No one remembered the year would end. Rain was gathering
in the low clouds coming in from the west, rain and more rain
until the ditches could not hold it nor the small streams
that fed the river that gave its name to our hopes, rain
that swept everything before it until the town was gone,
even the high wall that guarded plum and pear that pressed
their fruit for Efraim's delight. Hooves over great rump,
the roan was swept down the very streets it honored, its rider
and his mignons never seen again by anyone, and when spring
came back the valley greened in silence and disorder.

Issue #63

Philip Levine

THE EDGE OF HISTORY

In the basement of the two-story house on Monterey
at age eight I am plotting the next move against Franco.
I sit under an overhead light, the map before me,
studying the road ahead while my militia gathers
outside the ancient shipyards of Atarazanes to march
up the Ramblas and parade across the Plaza Catalunya
toward the old North Station. A boy, perhaps my brother,
calls my name just once. I pull the string. The light
that told me everything goes out, and for a moment
I'm in the dark. The day freezes or better say
it becomes part of late August 1936, the part that
teeters on the edge of history.
                              Now I remember.
It was not my brother, it was Herbie Lux come
to tell me that three boys had cornered my brother
in a neighbor's yard and could I come quick before
it was too late. Out on the sidewalk I fought
two boys I'd never seen before, and cried each time.
A woman in an upstairs window called the police
who never came, but her threats got us out
of her back yard. The second boy smelled as though
he'd been left out in the rain for days. He wore
a huge ring with a crest incised on it, and the blow
made my jaw pop as though I'd bitten down on a stone.
Both of us were beaten when a man who delivered ice
pulled us suddenly apart and made us shake hands.
He left a black stain where he'd circled my wrist
to push me toward the small dark-haired boy
who couldn't catch his breath through his sobs,
frightening us all. The woman came down stairs
with a glass of water and made him sit on the curb
until he was better.
                    Unstudied, the map sits
on a card table between the furnace and the coal bin,
though enough gray light seeps through the windows
to create the shadows a boy could hide in or a man
could step out of to proclaim victory if such
were the case. A month passes in the blink
of an eye, the militia stalls on the road to Madrid,

the fighting is terrible, our leader dies, shot

in the back in an open Packard. The funeral becomes
a kind of theater with two bands playing at once,
the coffin pushed forward and back up the great hill
to the final plot. Now it's September, and I rise
to dress, brush my teeth, drink old coffee, and start
for school, two defeats behind me, just one ahead.

Philip Levine

'37

Behind the Plymouth assembly plant
on East Warren, a clump
of tattered pin oaks and frail maples.
Sunday morning, late March,
the worshippers in dark groups
of two and three walked the long block
from the bus stop. Low clouds
dispersed, a watery sun rose
slowly toward 9 A.M. shedding
its light into standing pools
of stale waters. Not far off
a river ran toward another river,
not far off my father slept
his final sleep in a room
without windows. Spring punched in
right on time with iron bells
tolling from the bricked steeples,
wave after wave going out
over the acres of cars parked
in rows. I would give anything
to have February back, the perfect
winter of '37, the blanket
of snow unmelted, the dawn wind
trembling in the house. My aunt Yetta
comes back in a cab, her face
smeared, her silk hose safe
in the cracked leather purse
between her legs. Uncle Nathaniel,
not yet my uncle, rises late
but ready, knowing the nothing
he needs to know, and brushes
his teeth with beer. Outside
more snow falls on the bare branches
of the black elm, it mounds
over each link of the back fence
and buries the early thorn
of my favorite rose, a single arched
blade waiting in the nameless waste.

Issue #63

ALGECIRAS TO CUETA, 1969

We crossed in rough seas. I stayed on deck
with Teddy, my youngest who had paled
in the first minutes. All pluck, he clenched
his teeth and stared straight ahead as the waves
broke over the bow and showered us.
Suddenly the second pillar loomed
up out of the mist and I felt his hand
relax in mine, and he looked up at me
to say, "Africa." Within minutes
we docked and drove our VW bus
over the rattling wood and iron bridge
on to new land, new to us and ancient.
At the Moroccan frontier two cops
pulled an old man off a bus and took
turns kicking him and then let him climb
on the roof to throw his bags down.
"Chicago," my wife said, and we went
on to Tetuan, the Atlas Mountains,
the souks laid out in long, cropped meadows
with pennants flying at either end.
Berbers on foot or mule back streaming
from invisible huts and villages,
the tattooed women in their bright skirts
and bedecked with amber necklaces.
Meknes, Fez, where we got lost, passing
the same group of silent men three times
until I stopped and found the one who spoke
Spanish and pointed the way. "Europe,"
was all he said. I tried to pay him,
but he waved me away, a young man,
maybe a shepherd in his long robes,
his green eyes clear. He pointed again,
turned his back and spit. "We're going home,"
Teddy said, "I can smell America."

Daniel Nester

Introduction to the *PBQ* New York Reading Series

Everybody has the story of their first New York apartment. Mine involves a sublet in SoHo, in the same building where Scorsese's *After Hours* was filmed, followed by a dubiously unleased two-bedroom in Williamsburg, Brooklyn, where my rent checks would go uncashed for months, years at a time.

Both pads were humble abodes, places where I crashed after those short graduate school afternoons, belaboring being a writer in a city that is alternatively merciless and satori-inducing, especially to those of us who use line breaks, speak with music on the tongue, and wish to make no money in a time when the city became again a jazzy, rich town.

For the past few years, more of us have moved north from the Delaware Valley, going to school and working, depriving ourselves of Harry Kalas's play-by-play, Power 99's "Old School," and WWDB's "Fridays with Frank." And while we keep our connections and try to make it to Dirty Frank's as much as we can, this was the place where some of us really lived.

The *Painted Bride Quarterly* New York Reading Series, then, is our first New York apartment. It's the first place where we at the *Quarterly* hung our plants from the ceiling and said, "We're going to stay awhile; we might as well grow something while we're here."

And so for four Wednesday nights, we made our home the THEATER, a converted performance space in Williamsburg, ran by wonderful people and now inhabited by a modern dance troupe. It was part of what the THEATER called their "Wednesday Night Series," and we alternated between free jazz nights, play readings, and a "mixed bag" Wednesday.

The kick-off party for the Wednesday series was a saturnalian spectacle not unlike ancient Rome. Besides the free homemade hummus, there was an improv jazz troupe, tumblers rolling on gymnast pads, and, most infamously, a trapeze artist who did her act swinging from the rafters. To see Regie Cabico, a formidable showman himself and one of our readers, gasping, holding onto his plastic cup of wine, as two akimbo legs jut out at him, was truly a sui generis moment. To try and follow said trapeze act, as this writer did, by reading a fresh set of verse, was both a true test of will and, for me, further proof that poetry need not be held in some highfalutin regard. It's all showbiz, after all.

That was a portentous, wonderful night, and from then on, I knew our series would be a success. Some highlights: Tim Suermondt doing his best Pancho Villa voice—something like Steve Allen in drag; Chris Connelly outlining his Michigan mythology; Richard Tayson reading unflinching new work, some included in this selection; and Carley Moore hog-tying such disparate images as Picasso's wives, a talking chair, and a chorus of cats, all in the space of ten minutes.

The series was, by its design, a humble endeavor: get excellent writers in from the area and give them a comfortable place to read. Sit back on a couch. Listen. And with a two blocks' walk from the Bedford Avenue L train stop, one could do exactly that. Sometimes 40 people came, another time a baker's dozen. But for everyone there, the voices were clearly heard, the beer cold, the coffee always fresh.

I'm so happy to present these poets' work to you. Not only because the poems are excellent and goofy and poignant, but because they chronicle the nights when we *PBQ*ers up here started unpacking our suitcase, laid on our mattress and said, exhaling, "This is our home."

Brooklyn, 6/28/2000

Issue #63

César Vallejo

He sang like a gun.
He knew salt
and how to coax it from a bundle of rags with a long wooden pole.
When he laid down
he was so still children bit him.
César Vallejo's arm is dead
and so are both of the eyes that starved in the Luxembourg Gardens,
wondering at the polished brass tips on its fence's
    wrought-iron bars.
As ladies' little dogs shit around his feet,
he dreamt of snapping those bars off
to carry home to Santiago de Chuco and hand to miners as
    they emerged from the pits,
their faces white with the tungsten powder that leaked from
    straw baskets they shouldered up ladders
lashed together with strips of cloth they'd torn from their
    own pants.

MUD

I dreamt that I buried a man's arm
in a field so empty and wide
anyone who'd seen me kneeling
would've wondered if I were the broken end of a tree
or a man.

The arm was warm
and it reddened where I pressed my fingers against it.
I was sure I hadn't killed the man
but remembered holding him,
and knew his blood had left the print on my shirt.

When I woke up I thought of my father shoveling mud from a
    row of holes filled with water—
he'd hit an underground stream.
I had to steady wooden poles that shuddered and numbed my
    whole body
as my dad drove them in deep enough to stand straight.

Issue #63

Issue #63

FOG

Fog is the rain's wife.
I'm trembling not from its emptiness,
but because it is so full of what passes
    through the tongue
and the feet refuse to describe.
Fog covers the scythe in the horizon
that offers, to grass like ourselves,
the ecstasy of its edge.

Tracey Knapp

SALAMANDERS

Oh, the little hours of the night
we would tiptoe barefoot down the creaky hallway
through the porcelain white kitchen,
where the moon reflected off each tile

Then out onto the patio.
The spindly weeds made their way between
the silver slabs of slate
which we would lift up slowly
surrendering the cool skinned salamanders
into our carpal cages.

The ticklish touch of their icy fingers
the tiny tap of their toes upon our knuckles
(as if they were made of the stems of leaves)
we challenged the lizards to run away
but only gave them the other hand to dance upon.

We played until the cool night air
crept into our pajamas,
and the cold rocks numbed our feet.
Then we gently put the night creatures on the slate
the far side from their under-rock home.
They stood still, displaced, confused.

But we had already snuck discreetly
beneath our own covers
before the salamanders had slid again under the rocks.

Issue #63

DIVINE HEAD I

A thousand drawings of the same head
in film-still sequence: a flip
page cartoon. Brow moves lashes
lift from a split second shut—
maybe: a hand rising to the leaded lips
with Gideon's trumpet
playing rose petals falling.
Such divinity.

Or, just a witnessing of movement,
the mastery of musculature,
the crescendo of, maybe,
a perfect sneeze:
glazed eyes, rippling skin
around the nose, precarious cradle
of the head, the sublime rollback,
eyeballs ecstatic, turn upwards to the lid
then the final phlegm lurch
expelled in misty cascade
right off the parchment page.

Issue #63

Carley Moore

THE PHENOMENON OF ECSTASY
after Salvador Dali

If you lay the chair on its back it does not look like a woman.
If you push the chair back and remember me sitting in it,
it will remind you of a woman who was shaped by a chair.
When you sit on the chair you make the woman into
the ghost of the chair. When you leave the chair
on its back, you see the way my neck rested on
the edge of the bed. You see the way a chair that
has fallen becomes the liquid of the room.
You see the way the pushed chair lives outside of its shape.
Like the head that insists on the edge of the bed,
the fallen chair is not the reason we break.
The chair that has fallen on its side is not for you.
It is for the small kings who will use it like a carcass.
Best when warm, but best not seen.
The promise of the chair is that it will fall back
over and over again. The promise of the chair
is that it will be like my neck on the edge of the bed.
The chair is the promise of falling.
I am falling in chairs.
I am falling.
You are not the chair.

Issue #63

Tim Suermondt

Saint Augustine

There's nothing in me that's Spanish, alas.
I remember the same feeling
when 10 yr. old Tim was crushed to learn
he didn't carry the bloodline
of the great Cochise.
So much for civilization.

But, to steal from Robert Graves,
I say, Goodbye to all that
and I'm happy to do my
citizen's duty: The Flagler World

of ersatz Spanish and Arabian
(Do boys still dream of Ali Baba
and the harem girls?)
is okay with me,

and I'm not crestfallen to see
Jimmy Buffett T-shirts outnumbering
the mementos of Pirates
who once roamed these parts
(How quaint the buccaneer swords
made in Bangladesh!)

Ripley's Believe It or Not is a charm
and the fortress, the guidebook says,
is authentic. I'll hit the spaghetti plate
at Denny's and think of the 17th Century
and the superiority of all things American.
Yes, I'll have the garlic bread too.

PANCHO VILLA RETURNS HIS SUIT TO ME

"It is too big," he says
in his tough Mexican accent.
I tell him he's made a mistake
I can't help him
and I hope he won't be offended
as I ask him

why he, of all people,
would want to wear a suit.
"For my funeral," he says proudly.
"Pancho," I say, putting a hand
on his shoulder, "don't you know

you already died, a long time ago?"
"Sí," he says, "when I died then
I had no suit.
Do you understand?"
I give him the name and address

of a tailor in town.
"A nip here, a tuck there
from Applebaum and your suit
will cling to you like a glove,
or a royal bandana."

He thanks me with a "Viva"
and veers off
like destiny itself often does:
dejected, feeling naked and alone,
searching for a change of history,
a suit, a suit that fits.

Richard Tayson

Issue #63

AFTERWARDS ANTIGONE GOES TO THE WATER

When he was dead I went to the river singing.
O wind over the transparent
surface, how can I act
with my hands
broken? Sand
I kneel in, glimmering. I lose
my body each day
for an asteroid. The planets
flicker; they are not
in a pretty row. Nothing to say
of hair turned straw, eyes
plugged with dirt and staring.
Be still, I can no longer
hold you. (The one
I loved in my arms, my lips
on his crusted lips.) The scar
running the length
of his chest. And here
in the sand, his eyes
again. My life
has been but a moment
of requiring. I crush and love
in one small gesture. Nothing escapes
my vision. I lay down
and imagine my cave. Color
has no purpose in a world of dim.

VIGIL

Your face our face now
attached to sticks
held high as a mayor's face
a president's.

(You are not dead—we walk
through a sea of your faces)

Finally the pushing finally cop cars.

Your face in front of me
goes down and is torn
to shreds the way animals
tear living flesh and eat, eat.

Blonde faces crushed underfoot.
Death horses and their riders.

Good as any gun butt.
Good as any pistol-whipped.

Love, we are the species of love.

Issue #63

Michele Wolf

Issue #63

FOUND OBJECTS

I pick up the blue-striped curlicue jacket
Of a lost mollusk. My heels sink
In the sand, soggy from the runaway
Foam that slaps and slides forward again.
I pocket the shell, a lone white gull feather,
Reject trails of raggedy black brittle
Crab pincers, a grit-crusted raspberry
Dannon container, a child's chewed-up rubber thong.

Not much selection against this sundown, silvery
Cloud-shingled sky. None of the cowries—whorls
And dips and nodules, creamy white and brown—
None of the turrets, tritons, turkey wings,
That with summer's salvation
From book strap and pencil case,
Beginning with the class-wide whoop
At the final bell, so defined my life.

"She can swim, my little one, watch her swim,"
My grandmother boomed to her inner-tubed
Mah-jongg cronies, clustered around like barnacles
To a pier. Our tube was snug—for me,
My grandmother, my grandmother's breasts.
I'd slither out, a frolicking porpoise arcing up
And under and up, return to kisses and freckled,
Leathery-skinned applause. A school of white-capped
Inner tubes, we'd paddle back to shore.
Stalking the edge, I'd sift through seaweed,
Pail in hand, collecting shells.

At a splintery picnic table shaded by an umbrella
Under the palms, my grandfather played pinochle.
I'd sidle up to him. Always, he'd wink, snap
Forward his lower denture with his tongue,
Evoking my practiced yelp. The others would chortle
And wheeze and ask me to marry them. I'd sit
Quietly, stacking towers of tottering chips.
After the game, two sweat-drenched sleepwalkers,
We'd head for the luncheonette, order

My grandfather's cherry soda and my butter-pecan
Cone, numbing cold against the socketed gap
Where I waited for top teeth. A revived windup
Toy, I'd ride right and left on the red vinyl stool.

I'd sit in the tub on top of a half-inch-high
Accumulation of beach, previously plastered to me,
Inside my suit, in the most unlikely places.
The aroma of pot roast mingled with Dial,
Breck, Vitalis, Listerine, as my grandmother,
The aproned Ethel Merman of West Bahama Drive,
Bellowed a coloratura "Seventy-six Trombones"
And dashed more paprika into the pot.
My grandfather snoozed in front of the television,
The *Hollywood Sun-Tattler* on his lap.
Dinner over, on the back porch, against
A streaky cobalt and apricot sky,
The scent of gardenias and ripening mangos,
And the sputtering putt-putt-putt of the sprinklers,
The three of us praised and sorted shells.

On a different beach, at the close of a day,
I still scavenge the shore, combing the sand
For what has been taken away, and what has been
Tossed back, looking to the sea
For a salt-sticky seven-year-old—honey tanned,
Her corkscrew ponytails wagging—a bikinied
Torpedo crashing into the water
With a wild-splatter belly-flop splash,
Walking à la handstand, diving
Under a wave, so as not to be
Tumbled to shore, rising to the surface
To wait for the next breaker, bobbing.

Reprinted from Conversations During Sleep, *by Michele Wolf,* © *1998 Michele Wolf,
published by Anhinga Press and winner of the Anhinga Prize for Poetry*

Issue #63

Rita Welty Bourke

The Leaning Volvo

Issue #63

The distinctive sound of the Volvo broadcasts news of its arrival. Jane Halsey Christianson looks up from her cutting board perched over the kitchen sink.

She watches the car roll down the gravel driveway, noticing that it lists slightly to one side. It dips a fender into the muddy waters of a chuckhole, drags its frame and other body parts up the other side, and proceeds into the parking area behind the house. Dripping dirty water, the car dies with a grateful sigh.

But not quite. Like some old reliquary unwilling to give up its saintly treasure, the Volvo strains and groans and then rights itself as Lieutenant Colonel Halen Christianson removes himself from the driver's seat.

Jane's husband, self-proclaimed genetic savior of the Halsey family, has come home: home from his weekly trip to the Payless Grocery Store; home to little Jane, twenty-five years a wife, twenty-four a mother, forty-two on the planet.

Jane stuffs carrot scrapings into the garbage disposal and turns on the switch. While the disposal grinds its meal, she washes and dries her hands.

Halen Christianson stands for a moment by the side of the Volvo, surveying tattered seat covers, worn floor mats, rubbish-strewn center cavity. Then he slams the door. "Janie Sue," he calls, looking toward the trim ranch house. "Come out here and give me a hand."

She slips on old mules, tightens the tie on her terry wrap, and heads out to where he waits. The coiled spring pulls the screen door shut behind her as she descends the wooden stairs. She winces when her feet hit the sharp stones in the driveway and wishes she'd taken time to grab her work shoes.

Hale leans against the Volvo, tapping out a drum beat on its roof. All his life, some sixty-odd years, he has looked much as he looks now: heavy-jowled; white-haired; oily-skinned. Even in childhood. Had Jane been around when he was born, she believes she could have picked him out of a crowded hospital nursery.

Ten years ago he began to shrink. Like a post-menopausal woman, he started losing height, a half-inch, then an inch at a time. The disks running down his back ground against one another, disintegrating, powdering into splinters that tortured him day and night, and finally dissolving, leaving bone to rub against bone. Hale has lost three full inches so far, though he still claims his teenage height of six-foot four.

Now he lumbers around to the back of the car, raises the trunk lid, and picks up two bags of groceries.

"Jane Halsey," he calls again. "Come on out and help with the groceries."

Jane is right behind him. "I'm here," she says. She picks up the remaining sacks and follows Hale into the house.

* * *

"You're killing me, Janie Sue," Hale used to tell her. "You're killing me with your cooking."

"You don't have to eat it, if you don't want it," she would reply. "No one's forcing you."

Jane empties the Payless grocery sacks onto the kitchen counter. She shoves frozen rib eyes, whole chickens, and hash browns into the freezer. She stacks canned soup and vegetables on the pantry shelf. She picks up a box of Raisin Bran and stops, thinking of her mother who lies in Green Acres Nursing Home, her bed rails covered with lambswool. Above her mother's head is a wedding picture: Teresa Marie Halsey as a bride, white dress pulled up discreetly so she could see the stairs she was about to descend; flash of white thigh from a gust of wind that blew across the porch and billowed up under her dress. This instant recorded by the photographer would become the family's favorite wedding photo. Six years ago Jane had Quik-tacked the picture to the wall above her mother's bed. She'd wanted to remind the nursing staff that her mother had once been young and beautiful. Now Jane slides the Raisin Bran into the cupboard and closes the door.

She picks up a container of Soft Scrub. "Jesus Christ, Jane, can't you at least clean the bathtub once in a while?" She remembers that snippet of conversation from years ago: eight-year-old Nina running into the kitchen, crying; "Mommie, what's pubic hair? Daddy says there's pubic hair in the bathtub."

Jane brushed her fingertips across her daughter's forehead. "Nothing, honey. You aren't responsible. There are lots of grownups in this house."

At the time, there were. Hale and Hank and Brent all lived at home. And Jane. Now there are only Hale and Jane.

Jane had borne two sons and was carrying her third child before she found a way around her pastor's prohibitions and her husband's demands. Her last baby, the only girl, she thought she didn't want, until a few months after Nina was born. Then Jane began to understand that she finally had an ally in the house.

Jane's oldest boy, Hank, has gone to a pauper's grave. The boy was twenty-one when he died. Hale declined to pay for the funeral. The government would do it, he said. He knew about the government; he'd served twenty years.

Jane had wanted her son buried in one of the plots reserved for the two of them. Somewhere she'd heard of the European practice of putting husband and wife in the same plot; the first one to die went deep, the second one on top. But Hale refused, and Jane didn't argue. She understood that her son, in death, needed to be as far away from his father as he had been in life.

Brent is gone, too. First to Seattle, then to parts unknown. Maybe Alaska. Maybe Canada. Maybe the South Seas.

Nina lives ten miles away, but it might as well be ten thousand. She never calls. They rarely talk.

It's down to Jane and Hale.

*   *   *

"You're killing me, Janie Sue," Hale repeats later that evening. He slides a chunk of macadamia jam cake onto his plate. The cake sops up the grease from the fried chicken, milk from the burnt-flour gravy.

And you killed my son, she says silently. Eat up, Hale. Have another helping.

It is a thought she has only recently allowed into her mind, though she has felt it, deep inside, for a long time.

The awful picture of Hank, dead beneath the living room window, flashes across her brain, and Jane looks out into the darkness of the backyard. If the picture comes in the daytime, she often looks directly into the sun, knowing she is ruining her eye-sight, but knowing, too, that it will burn the image out of her mind. The trade-off is worth it, Jane believes.

When dinner is done, Hale sits in the living room and reads the newspaper. Since their son died, Jane never goes in there if she can help it. She can't walk into the room without looking out the side window. From the window she can see the lawn, though she can't actually see the spot where she found her son. It is beneath the window, close to the house.

She'd come home from work early one night, and something made her walk around to the side of the house. She never knew what: an uneasy feeling; a broken branch on the tulip tree; a bit of debris on the fresh-mown grass. Maybe it was simply the moon, poised above the ridge of the distant mountains, inviting her to come close, to stay for a while. What she found was what was left of her first-born child. Hank Christianson.

Next spring she will work the flowerbed, if she can stand to do it. Pull out the weeds, sweep away the spider webs on the outside of the window. Plant some holly-hocks, maybe. Something that will grow tall. Cover the whole side of the house. Maybe.

*   *   *

Dinner over, dishes washed and set to drain in the sink, Jane dresses for her job as night clerk at the Newbern Holiday Inn. In her vanity mirror she catches a glimpse of the girl she used to be, before she married Hale. She moves close, wanting to con-nect with the lost nineteen-year-old, but the image fades. She applies heavy make-up and tries out the smile she'll use until quitting time.

She hears Hale call out to her as she closes the back door. "Jane Halsey," he calls. She tiptoes across the darkened porch and down the stairs, wondering why it is always Jane Halsey, and never Jane Christianson.

Abandoning stealth when she reaches the landing, Jane hurries to the car, gets in, revs the engine. She zooms out the driveway, laying down a trail of blue smoke.

There's nothing wrong with the engine, Hale says. The automatic choke causes her to burn a little oil when she first starts up.

Some hard, underneath part of the Volvo scrapes against the edge of the chuck-hole, and Jane feels a sense of satisfaction. Take that, you piece of junk.

The Volvo drives differently when Jane is at the wheel. On the narrow road

Issue #63

heading toward Dyersburg, Tennessee, she pulls the seat forward and leans back. She has to spread her legs wide and stretch in order to depress the accelerator. The car was built for long-legged Swedes, she once told Hale.

Volvos are the finest vehicles on the road, he responded.

This bit of information has become, over the years, his standard response to any comment she makes about the car. One day she plans a comeback. She can feel the words rising up inside her.

Maybe for you, Hale, but not for me. Or: So? Does that mean I have to drive one? Does it matter that I hate this car? That Hank drove it the day he died? Suppose the best doesn't suit me? Suppose I want less than the best?

She glances at the dashboard clock, then presses hard on the accelerator. She's doing fifty-five when she heads into the S curve at Harpers Mill. She hugs the inside, wrong side of the road on the left hand turn, then slides into the gravel on the right. She flies over the bridge at Monarch Gap, feeling a sweet pain in her stomach when the car momentarily leaves the road. At Fulton Run she tests her driving skill; the bridge walls are waist high, Hale's waist, that is, and she stays close to the wall, expecting to feel the kiss of concrete in the steering wheel. On the way home she'll try to shave the whiskers off the other side of the Volvo.

The car doesn't list, like when Hale drives it. Still, Jane dreams of owning some sleek, sporty thing. A Thunderbird, maybe. Or a Celica. She pulls into the parking lot at the Holiday Inn, unbuckles the ill-fitting seat belt, and sits for a moment. She listens to the creaking, settling sounds of the car and wishes she had something else to drive. The Volvo seems like an old Edsel to her, though they quit making them years ago. Like the Edsel it is old and heavy, and it has that awful front grill. Volvo. Vulva. Too close.

They make the damn things to go two hundred, two hundred and fifty thousand miles. There are Volvos on the road with half a million miles on their odometers. Hale says he intends to drive it until it falls apart; Jane believes he aims to set a new mileage record.

She looks down the row of cars parked in front of the side-by-side rooms. A yellow Miata catches her eye. The color reminds her of the goldfinch who visits her bird feeder in the summertime. But even with its black convertible cap laid back and its passenger compartment open to the sky, it is too small for Hale. He wouldn't fit.

But the yellow bird speaks to her.

*　*　*

Behind the counter at the Holiday Inn, Jane works mechanically, checking guests in, giving out keys and directions, suggesting restaurants and auto routes, late night drug stores and liquor marts. At eight o'clock her coworker, Mr. Tatum, plugs his time card into the machine, sets it back in its pocket and leaves. By nine o'clock the hotel is full, Jane flips the switch that illuminates the "No Vacancy" sign.

There is the crackle of ice dropping into the bin of the ice machine, the hum of air conditioners, the pulsing music of some TV drama. Thursday night: E.R. Sirens wail, tires squeal, nurses and doctors yell for stretchers, medical equipment, personnel. When the phone rings Jane picks it up without looking away from the television screen.

She hears nothing on the other end, and she drops the phone back into its cradle. She wonders if it was Hale, checking up on her. When the phone rings again, Jane picks it up and holds it to her ear, but does not speak.

"Is Peachy there?" The voice is far away, muffled.

"Peachy?" Jane isn't sure she heard correctly. "Brent? Is that you?" She hears the click of the disconnect.

Peachy. Brent's childhood name for his grandmother, Teresa Halsey. Yes, Peachy is alive, Jane could have said. But was it really Brent who was calling? And is Teresa Halsey really alive? The point is arguable.

Jane's mother lies in her woolen bed. She wears diapers. She eats through a hole in her stomach, food hypodermically injected. The point is certainly arguable.

In the years since Brent disappeared, there have been several calls Jane suspects were from him. This is the first time he has ever spoken. She wonders if he's in trouble. She feels a pull from this lost son.

She thinks of the Christmas and birthday presents stored on the closet shelf in Brent's old room—the room he once shared with Hank. He was gone for three years before she stopped buying gifts for him.

Mother's Days are the worst. On that second Sunday in May Jane stays close to the phone, waiting for it to ring, praying that Brent will call.

He never has. Her sons are lost to her. And even Nina is gone.

* * *

Jane takes a detour on her way home from her job. She drives the Volvo into town, past Haverty's Furniture Store, the Exxon, the Seven-Eleven. She stops in front of Harper's Used Cars. It is nearly two A.M.

Floodlights illuminate the car lot. The summer crop of night-flying insects disperses the light, and the air is heavy with mist. Jane looks at the parked cars, their front ends aimed at the street, their prices chalked on their windshields. She'd like something small. Maybe red.

Maybe she'll frost her hair. Ash yellow, like the Miata at the hotel. Or maybe, just maybe, she'll go red.

When she was young her hair had gleamed with copper highlights. Hale was willing to take on the red in her hair. After all his years in the military, it wasn't something he couldn't handle.

He had come to save her, he let it be known, from a drab life with one of the local dullards she'd let take her to proms and movies. Together they would have beautiful children who were strong and would grow in his image and one day make their country proud. As he had.

Issue #63

Jane had planned to go to nursing school. But there was Hale, wanting her, needing her, promising a good, solid life together. On the day he proposed she looked at that snapshot of her mother, Teresa in her wedding dress. It reminded Jane of the picture of Marilyn Monroe from *The Seven Year Itch*: Marilyn with her dress blown up by a blast of air from a subway vent, a teasing, oh-you-bad-boy look on her face.

Life with Hale seemed to hold such promise. But after Hank was born, and then Brent, it all dissolved. The little cherub boys she delivered were more Jane than Hale. They trembled when their father came into a room, and he hated that. Little sissies, he called them. It was as if he expected grown sons to leap from her womb and declare themselves ready to do his bidding. A boy who spent his free time composing love songs on his guitar, as Hank did, was not to be tolerated. A boy, like Brent, who refused to share Hale's hunting trips, refused to watch the skinning and gutting of a deer, was worse than no boy at all.

Jane has given up wondering what she did wrong, what she could have done differently. She suspects some ancient, mythological, Oedipal thing was at work, but it was so far beneath the everyday flow of life, she has no desire to try to figure it out. And no patience. She feels no connection with her past life. Those first years of marriage were lived by someone else. The girl, Jane Halsey, is as gone as Marilyn in the publicity shot or Teresa in the wedding picture.

* * *

The Volvo rocks gently with the idling of the engine, and Jane wonders how it would like the drive to Alaska. Up the Al-Can Highway, all the way to Anchorage. Gravel road, she's heard, but you can do fifty miles an hour. Fly away like a goldfinch in winter.

Maybe she can find Brent. Maybe he needs her. She would like to know that he has warm winter clothing, and enough to eat. She would at least like to know he is okay.

Hank is safe in his grave. Nina has her lover and needs no one else. All three of Jane's children have been able to get away, and she envies them that.

She would like to visit her mother one last time and try to explain. But what difference would it make? In this quiet morning hour, with the mist nearly as thick as rain, it seems easier to send postcards from stops along the way. Let the nurses tack them up on the wall beside the leggy wedding picture.

Cracker Barrel has lovely maps. Simple ones, showing major highways and interstates, rivers, borders, and the locations of their restaurants.

She looks at the odometer. Mileage 85,798. She knows it is actually 185,798. Will it make 250,000? It's early summer. Jane wonders if she could get there before dark. Alaskan dark, that is, which lasts twenty-four hours a day. The days get shorter and shorter after the equinox, until the sun disappears completely, leaving only a tinge of gold spilling over the horizon as the sun circles the globe, rotating around the lower forty-eight.

Issue #63

The faint, faraway sound of a train brings her back. She puts the car into gear and eases away from the curb, executing a U-turn in the deserted street. She heads toward home, crossing the bridge at Fulton Run, slowing as she nears Harpers Mill. She glances at her wristwatch, then at the dashboard.

Lit like an airplane cockpit, the dash displays tachometer, oil pressure gauge, speedometer, and various internationally marked lights and warning signals Jane has never quite figured out. The clock, centered beneath the rear view mirror, reads a digital 2:19 A.M. She's right on time. The nightly ritual is in place.

The City of New Orleans, on its long, overnight haul from the Gulf of Mexico to Chicago, is due to barrel through Newbern in exactly five minutes. It left the Amtrak station in New Orleans at 2:15 P.M., about the time Jane was taking her macadamia jam cake out of the oven.

The train headed north, boring through Louisiana, Alabama, Mississippi, and into Tennessee, plowing through delta country, pulling its load north, drifting farther and farther from the great river that divides the country. All the while it spewed black smoke into the air, some to settle on cities it passed through: Slidell; Hammond; McComb; Brookhaven; Hazelhurst; Jackson; Yazoo City; Greenwood; Memphis; Dyersburg; and some to waft down on the white blooms in the cotton fields along the way.

Jane cracks the car window and listens for the wail of the train. When she hears it again she inches forward, stopping thirty feet shy of the crossing. She sits in the Volvo, focusing on the curving tracks. When the train comes into view she waits for it to line up with the grove of cedar trees, then the railroad tool shed, then the Overhaltzer barn. The nose of the locomotive is one windshield inch past the farmhouse when she jams the accelerator to the floor. The car hesitates, then bursts forward toward the tracks.

The tachometer flies into the danger zone, odometer climbing nearly as fast. Zero to sixty in six seconds, Jane thinks, counting off the numbers in her mind. She feels the jolt of the railroad tracks, catches a whiff of diesel fuel, can nearly taste the surge of adrenaline.

She makes it across. Whistle clean. As she has every night. So far. But tonight something is different. She glances at the dashboard; the oil pressure gauge trembles inside its round, yellow-lit face. The needle wobbles, then starts a steady descent, like a Grand Canyon sunset. Down, down, down, it goes, heading for horizontal flat.

Jane instantly knows what has happened. A rail has slipped loose from its spikes, risen up out of its bed and punctured her oil pan.

She grips the steering wheel, knowing that for tonight, at least, her choices have narrowed. Home is three miles away. She watches the needle, thinking about the unlikely possibility the odometer will ever turn two hundred thousand, let alone a quarter of a mil. She wonders if Hale will try to find another Volvo, if this one dies, as it surely will.

The road is deserted. Lights from farmhouses dot the surrounding countryside, but none are close to the highway. She hears a faint, clicking noise that gets louder

Issue #63

with each passing mile. She turns on the radio, finds a country station, and tries to ignore the sound. Home is so close.

*   *   *

Jane pulls into the driveway of the little ranch house, and her headlights sweep across the flowerbed where she found Hank, her first-born son, his face blown away by a shotgun blast. He'd sat among her flowers that last day of his life.

She parks the Volvo in its accustomed place behind the house, gets out and slams the door. When she steps away from the car she can feel the heat of the overheated engine spreading into the night. The noise of the motor, a clunking sound, continues.

He needs a car like this, she thinks, rubbing her breast where the seat belt has cut into it. He needed strong sons. And he needs a strong woman. Some great, big-boned, bovine woman who can sling great arms around him. Jane was never enough. Never could love him, like he needed to be loved. She's served him for twenty-five years. But no more.

She walks into the house, into the living room. It feels cold. She switches on the light and notices the spider webs laced across the window. Tomorrow she will get a broom and sweep them away.

She has choices. There's money she's saved from her job and hidden away. Enough for a car of her own. She has maybe half a life yet to live. She turns out the light and goes into the bedroom.

Hale is asleep, his body curled oddly. Beneath the sheet he looks small, smaller than ever before. She undresses and climbs in beside him, careful to stay to her side of the bed.

And in its parking space behind the house, the Volvo lets go of its last few drops of blackened oil.

Nikki Macdonald

SHARING THE MUSE: A COLLABORATIVE VOICE EMERGES

Issue #63

In 1997, when I first caught up with Denise Duhamel and Maureen Seaton to discuss their then newly released collaborative manuscript, Exquisite Politics, *Maureen was living in Chicago and teaching poetry there, and Denise was living and writing in New York City. Then Maureen went to Ragdale and Denise went to Spain, and neither one had a telephone. This time I want to discuss their latest collaborative effort,* Oyl, *a collection of poems about the cartoon character Olive Oyl. Frankly, I am nervous. Maureen is in Chicago—now Artist-in-Residence at Columbia College—and unreachable by phone, while Denise is teaching at the University of Pittsburgh, and I have no idea how to find her. I resort to e-mailing both of them, and in a day, like magic, all questions are answered. Now I know their secret.*

Duhamel and Seaton understand the drawbacks of long-distance communication better than most. The two met in the summer of 1987, when Denise was housesitting for a friend in Tarrytown, New York. In 1990 they began to share poems and collaborate on others, what Maureen refers to as "stroking each other artistically." Since then, they've never lived in the same city at the same time, though they've corresponded by fax, e-mail, phone, and letter. There are also the occasional visits (lately it happens every June).

At first they wrote for their own enjoyment, then they began to submit to magazines. Calling attention to their work has been a challenge; one publisher called the act of two poets writing together "oxymoronic." Duhamel and Seaton began to think there might not be an audience for their collaborative work until encouragement finally came from a few literary magazines (*Mid-American Review*, *Prairie Schooner*, and *Indiana Review* among them).

Exploring Foreign Territory

Is collaboration foreign to poetry? If the answer is yes, then there are exceptions, of course. The New York School is one of them. John Ashbery and Kenneth Koch worked together on joint projects. Ashbery wrote *A Nest of Ninnies* with James Schuyler. Frank O'Hara, who collaborated with painter Larry Rivers, among others, wrote with people simply because he preferred a social act to a solitary one. W. H. Auden collaborated on plays with Christopher Isherwood. Today David Shapiro even writes with his young son. But writing poetry and prose is regarded *primarily* as a solitary act. And it is surprisingly foreign territory for women to collaborate on poetry. The pioneering collaborative efforts of Olga Broumas (with Jane Miller and, more recently, with T. Begley) have inspired the work of Duhamel and Seaton. Broumas's subject matter, that of feminist kinship and sexuality, resonates in much of Duhamel and Seaton's individual work. In their first collaborative book, *Exquisite*

Politics (Tia Chucha, 1997), issues of feminist kinship interact with those of sexual identification to form images of societal and spiritual abandonment. In *Oyl* (Pearl Editions, 2000), their latest manuscript, there are similar issues of sexual identification, isolation, abandonment, and fulfillment—a continuation of the first book, but this time there is a strong feminist role model in Olive Oyl.

Duhamel and Seaton are no strangers to the topic of gender, especially that of womanhood. Its complexities reach into their work farther back than they'd like to admit. Denise is the author of five books of poetry and numerous chapbooks. Her most recent book is *The Star-Spangled Banner* (Southern Illinois, 1999, winner of the Crab Orchard Award in Poetry). Before that came *Kinky* (Orchises, 1997), a collection of poems about Barbie. In *Kinky*, as in each of her books (*Girl Soldier* [Garden Street, 1996], *The Woman with Two Vaginas* [Salmon Run, 1995], and *Smile!* [Warm Spring, 1993]), Duhamel confronts the barriers placed on women in America (male oppression, stifled sexuality, preoccupation with physical beauty) armed with her greatest weapon, her sense of humor. With poem titles ranging from "How to Rid Yourself of the Jealousy You Feel about Your Lover's Best Friend Who Is the Same Sex as You Are" to "As If Lovers, by Virtue of What They Are Called, Are More Attractive Than Husbands or Wives or How," Duhamel creates her own complexities. In "A First-Love Poem," she writes, "He's Sleeping Beauty and I am the Prince," calling the reader's attention to role reversal, to things not being what they seem. Men give birth; soldiers wear lipstick; Barbie is bisexual. The characters in Duhamel's poems don't just struggle with gender, they toss it on its head.

In her third book of poems, *Furious Cooking* (winner of the Iowa Prize for Poetry and the 1996 Lambda Award), Maureen Seaton sets ablaze the myth of women's domestic roles and responsibilities in male-female relationships. She calls the book risky. Some may call it refreshing. In the title poem she writes, "It's the kind of cooking where before you begin / you dump the old beef stew down the toilet . . ." On a personal level, Seaton has experienced that kind of spiritual upheaval. Ten years ago *she* became a controversial subject when she left the heterosexual world. Since then she has received an NEA fellowship and an Illinois Arts Council grant, as well as having written three prize-winning books of poetry: *Fear of Subways* (Eighth Mountain, 1991), *The Sea Among the Cupboards* (New Rivers, 1992), and the aforementioned *Furious Cooking* (University of Iowa, 1996). Seaton's fourth book of poems, *Little Ice Age*, is forthcoming (Invisible Cities, 2000).

Sometimes, Seaton admits, her work is interpreted as angry. But there is more to it than anger; Seaton's energy is electrifying. One reason for this? She deals with passionate issues—feminism, agnosticism, homosexuality. Seaton approaches her audience like an investigator on the trail of the truth. She searches for reasons, "There we are, week after week, filling the pews / handing men the reins. What do we expect?" By confronting the intimacies and complexities of women's relationships and exploring gender stereotypes, Seaton seeks to discover truths that are as much a surprise to her as they are to her readers.

When the two poets merge, the result is inspired and often explosive. *Exquisite Politics* explores bisexuality and homosexuality with a brassy defiance. A third voice

Issue #63

emerges throughout the book, one that cannot be attributed solely to either poet. Denise and Maureen define this third voice or "created voice" in the introduction as "a voice that is at the same time both of us and neither of us, the mysterious voice that sings between us." An earth mother speaks, flamboyant and formidable. The poets agree, the first book is a wild child. "This voice of ours feels restless, goofy, shrill—basically unbecoming to a woman," Maureen says. "It was easier for us to be unbecoming together."

In *Oyl*, the second manuscript, the poets' voice is more formal, more defined. "As wild as our first child is, this second seems almost dignified," Seaton explains. The poets followed formal techniques in *Oyl*, along with some interesting twists, such as incorporating "exquisite corpse," the surrealistic parlor game played by André Breton and the French visual artists of the 1930s and 1940s (as well as by the New York School poets in the 1950s and 1960s), with the formal aspects of a sestina or a villanelle.

In this case, exquisite corpse is played when each writer writes two lines on paper, then folds the paper so that the other writer only sees the second line. The result is a surprise. Duhamel and Seaton grew so familiar with the game that they imposed mandatory rhyme schemes and limits, thus adding an element of skill to the already existing element of surprise. Duhamel claims that the result of combining exquisite corpse and a formal technique helps them to be "less didactic" in *Oyl* than they were in *Exquisite Politics*. "When playing exquisite corpse, anything can happen and any agenda must be given up," says Duhamel. In *Oyl*, the poets also chose to borrow from the ideas of the OuLiPo, or Ouvroir de Littérature Potentielle (Workshop for Potential Literature), a Paris-based assembly of writers and mathematicians formed in 1960 whose goal is to discover what use mathematical structures might have in writing. Seaton describes the process:

> Strict prescriptions/restrictions are created and fulfilled. N+7 is a better-known example in which the writer looks up all the nouns of a piece in the dictionary, counts down seven nouns, then fills in the new words. We decided on N+12 because there are, in existence, twelve cartoon episodes in which Olive ate spinach. We gave each poem twelve lines. The idea of writing a poem in OuLiPo style came up early in the manuscript. It was the "O" that attracted us.

There are a number of "N+12" poems in *Oyl*, including "Popeye's Fix-It Shop," where "Olive kicks the greasy toolbox aside, / stomps over carburetors and spark plugs / and pokes her men into teary submission." Olive Oyl becomes the embodiment of feminism. Unlike Barbie (who Duhamel wrote an entire book about), Olive Oyl never changes her clothes. She is a role model that is at once clumsy and powerful, awkward and beautiful.

A cento, or patchwork poem, is a collage of existing lines of poetry. Duhamel and Seaton employ centos in order to collaborate with each other as well as with the included poets. As in *Exquisite Politics*, a third or "created voice" emerges within the formal poems found in *Oyl*, and this voice seems to sing. In "Olive Oyl Cento," a compilation of voices from *Norton's Postmodern Anthology*, Duhamel and Seaton collected phrases that they admired, pooled them, and played exquisite corpse on e-mail. Seaton describes the end result, a melding of those voices, as "a small anthology of its own, and, in a way, homage to the quoted poets."

Sharing the Muse

Have Duhamel and Seaton ever written with anyone else? A few years ago Duhamel worked with the visual artist Susan Shatter on a series of paintings Shatter had already completed. They didn't write and paint in the same room, nor did they provide each other with inspiration or input during the process. Although it was very different from the collaborative method used with Seaton, it still brought Duhamel creative fulfillment. The poems were "unlike any other poems I've ever written—either by myself or with Maureen." Duhamel describes the poems as short, lyric poems (a form she seldom, if ever, uses), poems that would have never come to fruition had they been done solo. "That, I think, is the power of collaboration—not knowing where another person's work is going to take your own, but being willing to go for the ride anyway."

"I've worked in a kind of 'spiritual' collaboration with my lover and partner," Seaton says. "We shared space, vision—it was wonderful, empowering." Seaton wrote the poems that eventually would become *Fear of Subways*, while her partner, an artist and wood sculptor, created a body of work around the themes of race and gender. The two fed off of each other's energy. Seaton believes her second book would not have developed without her partner's influence. Though Seaton has done "spiritual" collaboration, as well as some collaborative work with her students, she has come to the realization that "Denise and [she] have something extraordinarily rare."

The process of writing with a partner requires the shared intimacy and trust of any good relationship. "Sometimes I think women are well suited to the intimacy it demands," Seaton says. She also surmises that most writers would rather work alone for one specific reason: Why bend for a human when the muse is already kicking our butts? Duhamel attributes her ability to work with Seaton to the basic feminist "ethic of balance," a woman's innate ability to sense another woman's needs. "It's vital that collaborators have the right partners, partners they can trust," she says, "Partners who are respectful of the process agreed upon by the two writers before they begin."

Collaboration is "not for every writer, nor should it be," Seaton says. "There is no moral, social, or spiritual imperative to collaborate with another poet," she explains, although she encourages other writers to try it and come to their own conclusions. Perhaps those who do will delight in both *Oyl* and *Exquisite Politics* and want to read more collaborative endeavors.

This leads to another question about the process of collaboration. How were rules established? How did they know when to stop writing the poem? Ground rules and parameters were crucial. "It was easy to decide beforehand that the poem would have 36 lines (or 18 couplets), or that it would be a 14-line sonnet," Seaton explains, "Or that we'd both free-write for five minutes, ten minutes, whatever." Seaton says the length of a particular poem was predetermined, then revised if it went too long or too short. Closure was a "felt thing," as it is in a writer's individual work. When cutting and pasting their work together, the poets discovered there were often pieces of poem scattered across the cutting room floor. They also worked in forms, exploring sonnets, sestinas, and prose poems. Duhamel found the sonnet to be the most liberating to work on with Seaton because Duhamel is reluctant to explore the form on her own. She refers to the voice in the *Exquisite Politics* sonnets as "wild, irreverent, and even a little mean-spirited," a voice both writers are unaccustomed to hearing in their own work.

Only once in each manuscript do the poets choose to reveal their individual identities. In "Baby Democrats," a stanzaic prose poem in *Exquisite Politics*, the author places her initials at the beginning of each stanza. The writers chose to do it this way to avoid confusion. "It dated and polarized us quickly," Seaton explains, "We thought the book might benefit from a small opening in the curtain to reveal the puppeteers, so to speak." "Baby Democrats" not only reveals the age difference between the "puppeteers" (fourteen years) but also provides the reader an opportunity to hear two distinct voices. Reminiscing about the political and social events that took place during their respective childhoods, Duhamel and Seaton cover topics such as Kennedy's assassination and Watergate. In "Interview with a Comic Strip Diva," included in *Oyl*, Duhamel and Seaton reveal their identities by posing questions to Olive Oyl. They wrote "a bunch of questions and a bunch of answers" (in Olive's voice) that didn't have anything to do with each other," Duhamel says. They questioned each other and tried to fit the answers, cutting and pasting as necessary. The outcome is an amusing mixture of voices.

The Thing about Politics

"Politics comes along when you least expect it" is the first line of "Exquisite Independent." In modern America, sex and gender are political. These are the "exquisite politics" confronted and explored in both *Exquisite Politics* and *Oyl*. Was this intentional, writing books about politics in such a politically conscious time? "I don't think we were originally conscious of the politics of the poems," says Seaton, "But that's the thing about politics. It's everywhere." Someone debating with someone, someone winning, someone losing, someone throwing weight around, someone pushing back. Politics are on the playground and in the pulpit. And everybody knows that politics can be controversial; Duhamel will attest to that. After *The Woman with Two Vaginas* won the Salmon Run Poetry Prize, it was censored by the Canadian government, condemned for being "something other than art."

"Litany of the Fathers," a poem modeled after the Roman Catholic litany prayer, is included in *Exquisite Politics*, although the authors entertained the notion of leaving it out. "I spent three months thinking about it," Seaton writes, "Finally, Denise and I . . .decided to include it." Seaton explains that the poem might be criticized for its "obvious lack of subtlety and therefore, to certain critics of poetry, its lack of artistic merit." The poem is a mantra, an incantation that summons members of the male species to account for their actions (or lack thereof). "*Hear us*," the poets chant, "*Pay us back.*" The poem focuses on man's disregard for women and children, as well as for himself. Critics might find fault with the poem's seemingly ferocious attack on men, but the writers are willing to stand behind their work. "Writing it was no problem," Seaton explains, "We wrote it because it felt appropriate to put the litany into the world." Questioning the appropriateness of certain poems prior to publication is an important issue for Duhamel and Seaton. It is clear they don't censor themselves but approach their work by questioning how it will affect the feelings of others. Duhamel says she thought long and hard about whether or not a potentially offensive poem should be included in the book, and even contemplated editing or removing it. "Certainly Coleridge wouldn't approve of it for its see-through, white-hot anger," Seaton explains, "But that's OK . . .sometimes you just get tired of biting your own tongue."

"What Are Homosexuals For?" is a prose poem in *Exquisite Politics*. It is an essay of sorts, inspired by the questions raised in a chapter of Andrew Sullivan's book, *Virtually Normal*. Sullivan attempts to justify the function of homosexuals in a society for which the primary purpose is to procreate. In an attempt to answer the question, Duhamel and Seaton began to free-write, copying down every aspect of the topic that occurred to them. This exercise led to cutting and pasting pieces into a discovered whole, welcoming "any resulting conflicts and confusion." The third voice is not conjured in this poem, but the narrator does provide an interesting, albeit humorous, dichotomy. Stereotypical notions about homosexuals go side by side with analytical definitions of "butches" and "femmes." "What Are Homosexuals For?" has powerful statements to make about the latter part of the twentieth century, as in the end of stanza six: "I know what homosexuals in the nineties were for— those sadly dutiful worker ants employed as pall bearers."

In "The Origin of Olive Oyl" (included in *Oyl*), Duhamel and Seaton redefine the creation of Popeye. Though the reader might find the idea scandalous, the poem makes it difficult to resist. They write, "Olive, it is said, created him when she slipped / on a slimy spinach leaf and landed on a pipe." The poem also explores Olive Oyl's sexuality in lines like "Orzo, Ooze, Oulipo— / as though the whole world were one big O!" Certainly the "O" or orgasm is used frequently in the poem. There is even a footnote at the end of this line, a reference to Frank O'Hara's favorite form of punctuation, the exclamation point.

Bigger Umbrellas

Neither *Oyl* nor *Exquisite Politics* is entirely political gender-based poems. Characters experience love and loss, anger and release, disappointment and liberation. There

Issue #63

are those who lose the battle against obesity, abusive parents, witches, drag queens, and same-sex marriages. There are butches and femmes, princesses and communists. Among all the mischief and chaos that transpires, there are, thankfully, no happy endings.

What message do they hope to get across to their readers through their collaborative efforts? "I hope [the books] will give them a sense of their oddly singular yet connected place in an odd, enormous universe," Seaton says, "And a new look at the feminine." Duhamel hopes the books give readers a good laugh and an openmindedness they might not have had before.

"It seems to me that if poets want to retain any of their dwindling readership, poetry had better start becoming a little more entertaining," Duhamel says. Certainly Duhamel and Seaton have seen to that in *Oyl* and *Exquisite Politics*, which encourage readers to laugh at society's icons, at what we deem important and heroic. Duhamel believes today's readers have a shorter attention span than readers of yesteryear due to the onslaught of electronic media. "I have hope for poetry for that very reason, its brevity and beauty," she explains.

"I like new definitions and bigger umbrellas," Seaton writes in a recent fax. There seems to be plenty of space under the ever-broadening creative "umbrella" to include serious collaborative efforts like *Oyl* and *Exquisite Politics*. Hemingway once said, "Writing, at its best, is a lonely life." Duhamel and Seaton are the first to admit that distance can be painful and, at the same time, crucial to the creative process, yet they continue to face the obstacles of everyday life to till fallow ground.

Although it was difficult in the beginning, they have received much admiration for their collaborative work. David Lehman, author of *The Last Avant-garde: The Making of the New York School of Poets*, describes the two poets as "having so much fun with the language it rubs off on the reader." He writes, "They're funny and they're smart and they're fast." In the alliterative poem "The Origin of Olive Oyl," the poets write, "Only Olive owned ostentatious orgasms; / the puerile position of pomp belonged to Popeye." Here Lehman sees the allusion to John Ashbery's famous Popeye sestina. "So clearly they know their legacy, where they're coming from," he writes, "And they're proving how much vitality there is in collaboration as an avant-garde ideal and a New York School tradition."

If one wasn't familiar with the determination of Duhamel and Seaton, one might wonder if this is the end of their collaborative efforts. They assure me, the answer is no. The next challenge? To complete a collaborative novel, which they have already started to write. Long-distance, of course.

Scott Edward Anderson

Windfall: New and Selected Poems
Maggie Anderson
Pitt Poetry Series, $12.95 paperback
ISBN 0-8229-5719-1

Issue #63

Maggie Anderson's new collection, *Windfall*, brings together a selection of polished fruits from her three previous books with a group of less ripened poems of more recent harvest. The danger in any volume of "new and selected poems" is that weak poems stand out.

In her most successful poems, Anderson writes with a clarity and force of purpose that is both powerful and self-assured. Often, she tries to make sense of the tension that arises in love, loss, and circumstance. In her poem "Daphne" Anderson reckons with unrequited love,

> Daphne studies her lover's face.
>
> Eyes, nose, a few wrinkles.
> Here's a spot like a seashell.
>
> "You need something I can't give you,"
> the lover says smiling.
>
> Lacking, Daphne shudders. What could it be?
> What could it be?
> She swoons at her lover, "I'm sorry, I'm sorry."

Elsewhere, as in "Empirical," she realizes that much in the world is beyond her control and that it's sometimes better just to let go:

> I lie down to wait for the river.
> What I love about sorrow is its capacity
> for metaphor, how sadness makes things
> resemble each other. To the river, my body
> is just a stone.

She gives in to the river and the river takes her, but while she lies there staring at "clouds the way I saw them as a child," her vision is not clouded, never obscures what she sees around her.

What Anderson describes most clearly are the mining and mill towns of her own life in West Virginia, Ohio, and Pennsylvania, and the changes affecting the people in those communities. This, from "Closed Mill":

Issue #63

> Wall by wall,
> they are tearing this structure down.
> Probably we are not going to say
> too much about it, having as we do
> this beautiful reserve, like roses.

Lives and places in transition are a recurring concern. The poet is an unflinching witness with a sensitive and empathetic worldview. In many ways, she seems to be saying, these lives could be hers.

In the new poems, however, Anderson strays too far from her worldview. Perhaps only the "Black Dog" poems come close to achieving her more characteristic knife-edge vision. And if the last poem in the collection, "These Greens," with its mixture of prose and poetry, hints at an intriguing new direction for the poet, one wishes she had developed its devices further.

Her new poems seem unfinished, half-thoughts on their way to becoming poems, which sounds cruel, but pronouncements such as "Didn't say it right, said it dumb, / or some would say sweet, with an accent, / but wrong nonetheless" belie a self-consciousness and hurried lack of craft that is discomfiting in such an accomplished poet. Much like the lights in that closed mill, the power seems to have gone out in her most recent work.

Nowhere among the new poems can one find such haunting images as:

> they sealed up
> forty miners in a fire. The men who had come
> to help tried and tried to get down to them,
> but it was a big fire and there was danger,
> so they had to turn around
> and shovel them back in. All night long
> they stood outside with useless picks and axes
> in their hands, just staring at the drift mouth.
> ("Long Story")

One of the values of a "selected poems" is that older work is resurrected and published again, perhaps long after it is out of print. Despite the flawed new poems, *Windfall* contains the best of Maggie Anderson's work thus far. We follow her in these poems, as we follow the narrator in her poem "Caving": "We roll in the grass like dogs to get the muck off, / eat the flowers, fondle the tree bark, / shed dank bandages, / kneel in the weeds, / breathe."

30 Years of the Painted Bride Reading Series: Interviews with Gill Ott and Major Jackson

This year marks the thirtieth anniversary of the *Painted Bride Quarterly*'s stepsister the Painted Bride Art Center (as some of you may know, we share a name but we are separate non-profit entities). To celebrate, the *Quarterly* thought it would be a good idea to take a closer look at the fine work the Art Center has done, particularly in bringing poets and writers to Philadelphia to read in its remarkable reading series.

Issue #63

What started out as a celebration quickly turned into an exploration—of aesthetics, economics, chance, and community. We discovered alchemists among the Bride's poetry curators. Behind the scenes at the Bride has been a long line of curators whose aesthetics and passion have inflected the reading series held there. These curators have helped create a treasure of the most ephemeral kind: a world-class reading series. Despite the powers of videotape, once the readers have read, the special magic of writer/audience/word/voice disappears. We hope here to document what goes into the work of curating: part inspiration, part intuition, and part secret knowledge. Though we would love to have talked to all of the curators who served the Bride, we chose curators Gil Ott (from the Bride's early years) and Major Jackson (who ran the series during the nineties) to share their thinking on the subject of curating, community, and the pleasures of poetry.

*　　*　　*

Gil Ott

PBQ: How did your personal aesthetics (what is good poetry, what good poetry does/sounds like/looks like) inform your curatorial choices?

Gil Ott: Not too much. You've got to realize when I was curating: the late seventies and early eighties. My own aesthetics were formative, but more so, the task at the time was to build a community. There was great, enormous talent in Philadelphia with very few venues to hear it. Each new venue comes with a new way of encountering the art, with the concomitant social aspects. I wanted to build a series that tapped this impressive pool of local poets and gave the public as many ways as possible to participate. I helped put together the Active Poets Theater at the Bride on South Street, an informal salon that met weekly and that evolved to publish a journal called the *Plum Series*. I also coordinated a weekly poetry radio program on WXPN, back in the day when the station was community oriented. Since I was also publishing my own journal, called *Paper Air*, at the time, I wanted to promote alternative publishing in Philadelphia, so I organized two small press book fairs at the Bride. These were very successful. My first actual reading series was held at Myles Pettengill's Middle Earth Books, and was aesthetically eclectic. Eleanor Wilner one week, Sonia Sanchez the next—many really

Issue #63

great "local" poets who are still among us. I went on to curate the series at the Painted Bride in Old City and continued to respond to the need for breadth and inclusion.

In answer to your question: I think I consciously suppressed my own aesthetic impulses for the perceived greater good of building community. This is not an altogether bad thing, but I did become frustrated at the lack of intellectual and aesthetic dialogue that is generated by a reading series, which tends to be more promotional and bottom-line oriented. By the mid-eighties, I was out of poetry curating (save for my own Singing Horse Press) entirely.

PBQ: What effect did curating the series have on your writing? Or on your way of thinking about poetry?

Gil Ott: The aim of presenting is seamlessness. There's an illusion, a magic that exists between the artist on the stage and the audience, and while one concern of mid- to late-twentieth-century performance has been to question and play with that relationship, it remains crucial. Where the curator benefits most is in the events that surround the organizing of the reading: the enhanced contact with writers s/he admires.

But perhaps your question is about the differences between the written/published poem and the performed one. While it's easy to say that these two exist on a continuum, they really are very different things. Writing/reading, these are more private than the public reading, which brings with it its own set of conventions and possibilities for invention. These differences are now so pronounced that it's difficult for many to speak of the conventionally published poem and, say, the slam poem in the same breath. Poetry is perhaps the most flexible of arts, because it is the most basic. It seeps into every new crack. Poets collaborate in every conceivable artistic discipline; we have poetry on buses, on the Internet, in the schools. And it all remains poetry so long as it refers back to its foundations: the heart and mind, which are combined in the body, which yearns for community.

PBQ: What do you say about the interaction of the audience and the poet and the Bride (art center—and magazine)? How did the readings build your audience, build community? What effect do you think poetry readings have?

Gil Ott: Philadelphia is very lucky to have the Bride (mag and Center). Both are class acts, with high production values, informed curating/editing, rich history, and independence (by which I mean non-academic). The alternative arts movement, with its government subsidies, which grew in the seventies and eighties, was damaged by the NEA censorship wars of the eighties. Many cities lost their Painted Brides. The *Quarterly* has been a consistent ambassador to other cultural hubs for Philadelphia's emerging arts in ways that the Art Center alone could not be.

I do not think that poetry readings have much impact. If they did, they'd be better attended. For the most part, they are historical, a sort of "reading into the record"—and promotional. But a place like the Painted Bride, which has the longest running poetry series in Philadelphia, gains cumulative substance. Occasions like Etheridge Knight's residency there in the mid-eighties, or the spontaneous reading of *The Satanic Verses*, with nearly 100 writers in attendance, when Rushdie's fatwa was announced—these are events which could only have happened at the Painted Bride. We have needed a Painted Bride to serve as a flashpoint for the community.

PBQ: Who were your favorite readers, favorite poems? Put another way, what event was most memorable to you?

Gil Ott: Going back to your first question, about how curating informed my aesthetics, I organized two events at the Bride that were seminal to me personally. One was a week-long residency by the wonderful and influential poet and publisher Rosmarie Waldrop. A surprising number of poets (about 20) signed up for her workshops, and she was a very generous presence to have around. Early on I was influenced by (and I still listen very closely to) the poet John Taggart. I even dedicated an issue of *Paper Air* to his work. That issue was the first publication of his long work "Peace on Earth," a prayer of sorts for Vietnam and our war there. I remember that I was so moved by the poem that I read it aloud, all 40 pages, on South Street in front of the Bride, in full, Whitmanic voice. I was surprised when I brought John to the Bride to read it, and his voice was soft, hypnotic, not at all what I'd assumed.

PBQ: Would you consider curating an art?

Gil Ott: Well, of course, curating can be approached as an art. For something to be an art, the putative artist has to approach it humbly, with an open mind and a willingness to be fully involved, to understand silence, to suggest when appropriate, and to respond when appropriate. Most curators don't manage this, because the "form" of the reading comes with many constraints and demands. The appeal of an art form lies in its ability to support the artist's freedom. Curating is more dialogical.

Editing is too, though its substance is more directly the creative act.

* * *

Major Jackson

PBQ: How did your personal aesthetics inform your curatorial choices?

Major Jackson: Aesthetics are a great deal more fluid than what we are used to thinking. Some of the writers I was introduced to earlier in my life I simply did not appreciate. When I came to the Bride as first an intern, and then Finance Director, curating kind of fell into my lap after Lamont [Steptoe] decided to leave for various reasons. The Bride gave me free rein to do whatever I wanted, as long as it was financially solvent.

What I'm trying to say is that I stepped to the job with a sense of arrogance, naivete, and an air of the impresario. My first programs wholly reflected my influences, my taste—performative and socially-relevant—unapologetically did not have much range. A key component of my vision as a curator was to provide an artistic forum for underrepresented voices. I also wanted to open up and strip down the elite veneer of the Bride so that certain populations in Philadelphia could enter and not feel like art or its venues were alien to them. So, my first reading featured Amiri Baraka and The Roots (formerly Square Roots) and the Bride was packed: literary types, college students, old-guard activists, and Philly's hip-hop community. It was an amazing evening! It represented all of my worlds, the spaces I then occupied; however, it was a poetry reading and tons of people were there, something like 250 or more, which made the Bride happy since they had not seen that kind of attendance in a long time for poetry.

Fortunately, if you live with a particular aesthetic for too long (or anything for that matter), you tire of it; you desire something new. Additionally, I was reading and writing myself, broadening my grasp of contemporary writers and techniques but also familiarizing myself with the community of local poets in Philadelphia. (That's how Word UP!: City-Wide Poetry Fest came to being.) But I can honestly point to meeting Thomas Sayers Ellis and members of the Dark Room Collective as a turning point. I booked the Dark Room Collective to read in Philly. Afterwards, we became friends and a whole host of writers opened up to me. Too many to mention. Okay, a few: Bob Kaufman, Seamus Heaney (Thomas and Kevin Young had studied with him), Sam Allen, Clarence Major, the experimental community of writers that surrounded Brown University's Keith and Rosmarie Waldrop, Peter Gizzi and others.

All of this to say, aesthetics evolve. I still believe art administrators and curators should consciously seek out the underrepresented voices of our diverse communities. I still am attracted to socially relevant poetry, particularly when the critique is substantive and some element of the poetry is being pushed, is at stake, as if the volume were turned up, artistically speaking of course.

PBQ: What effect did curating the series have on your own writing? Or on your way of thinking about poetry?

Major Jackson: I'm not sure if it impacted much. However, it did heighten my appreciation for language and its use(s) in society. It's a privileged and sacred space; no other moment in our lives do we gather to honor its importance than when we attend a poetry reading. I am still struck to awe whenever I listen to a poet, young or old, emerging or established. The idea of active listening, being engaged by another's understanding of the world or dread or sense of fragmented reality, which is then rendered in this wonderful artifice of language and shared communally, excites me greatly. The music of thought and feeling, the life-rhythm embodied in the cadence of the voice (marked time, if I may), empowers, fortifies, and reaffirms who we are. I read somewhere that all poetry aspires to song, and songs are about praise, even songs of lament. So, my hope as a curator is that the audience walks away with their humanity intact and ringing loudly in their ears.

I am lying. Of course curating impacted my writing but much later in my tenure. I tend to be a zealous kind of person. If I discover or am introduced to a writer, I consume their work, their corpus. I believe in imitation, in poetry as an art, a craft to be studied. (This gets me into a lot of trouble.) After reading a poet's entire work, I want to physically hear them. Of course, I did not go through this process with everyone. But, this is how I honor them.

I majored in accounting as an undergrad at Temple University. Curating was my means of catching up and I've learned a great deal about writing. Levine taught me about narrative movement in a poem; Sharon Olds taught me how to anchor a single, vibrant image in a poem. John Yau's wit and sense of humor is underappreciated. Elizabeth Alexander is heir to Michael Harper's project of creating open-ended myths through historical figures. One could learn much about lyricism couched inside a narrative frame by reading Garrett Hongo. I could go on and tell you what I've learned from most of the writers who read at the Bride while I was curating.

PBQ: Who were your favorite readers? What were your favorite poems?

Major Jackson: That's a tough one. Most of the poets who gave successful readings at the Bride are not necessarily performative, the benchmark for a "good" poetry reading these days. I especially enjoy poets who do not rely on the dynamics of the stage but rather create a propulsive and redemptive space for the audience to leap into and to be swept away. I am thinking of Mark Doty's "Mercy on Broadway," Marie Howe's "Kissing," Yusef Komunyakaa's "Anodyne." Yusef often gives us a suite without much prefacing; you know, his presentation is seamless where each poem reveals even through all of the artifice an emotional center that is both familiar and alluring. Two days before Yusef first read at the Bride, another Louisianan artist performed, trumpeter Terrence Blanchard. He played the soundtrack to Spike Lee's movie X, "The Malcolm X Suite." After hearing both of them, in close proximity, I gathered the nature of Komunyakaa's appeal. Levine struck me as avuncular with all of his stories and hilarity; but once he begins you understand it is a means of buttressing the absurdity in the lives of the people of whom he writes. I've also found this to be the case with Gerald Stern who is one of the most tender human beings I've met on the page and in life.

PBQ: What were some of the most memorable events you recall from your time at the Bride?

Major Jackson: In 1997, I left the Bride to attend graduate school at University of Oregon. I returned that fall for a reading, my only featured reading at the Bride, with

Issue #63

Issue #63

Sharon Olds. I arrived and Sharon offered to read first; I laughed.

Most memorable event? Gwendolyn Brooks sitting at a table in the Bride's cafe, signing books and talking, at length, to everyone that came out that beautiful Sunday evening—at least 250 people. Her reading lasted about 45 minutes; her one-to-one conversations went on for two hours. Crazy, right? Again, think about this in comparison to all the hype about Web sites and e-mail discussions.

In 1993, Audre Lorde died. I never met her, but I read her amazing poems of love and resistance. "Coal" particularly comes to mind. I decided to have a memorial reading. Half of the poetry and candle event was programmed with the help of Aisha Simmons and Jordan Keith and the other half was free-styled. So many people came out, brothers and sisters, lesbians and heterosexuals, gays and students, mothers and fathers. Essex Hemphill was still alive and gave a moving reading. There was a video presentation. Afterwards, we drank wine, ate bread, talked, folks brought fruit and water. All poetry events should be so festive.

PBQ: What do you think or feel about the interaction between the audience and the poet and the Bride (art center—and magazine)? Could you say something about the effect of a reading series and the art of curating?

Major Jackson: Not only am I a zealot, I tend to be a naive idealist. The first City-Wide Poetry Reading had as its aim fund-raising money to be split among the cafe reading series and small presses that sent poets to read on their behalf. I wanted poets who read nightly in Philadelphia to be compensated, even if it amounted to nothing more than $20. Philadelphia, like many medium-to-large cities in the early to mid nineties, was barraged with a ton of poetry readings. Everyone walked away with $18.50. More importantly, the event brought everyone together; that kind of communal appreciation for poetry is always electrifying. Have you ever attended the Dodge Poetry Festival? It's almost like church... well a little more cultist. I do not use that word pejoratively either. This country has a robotic-like drive for industry, technology, money, sports and competition. It saddens me when mega-mergers and mere Dow numbers become our headline news as if there was something courageous and heroic about it all. So, to attend poetry readings or festivals, large and small, reawakens my belief in humanity's capacity to enrich and to feed that part of us—if it's not dead yet—that wonders and looks on in awe at the miracle of existence.

Even if I only attend one reading per year or crack open one page of the *PBQ* per month, there is something extraordinarily edifying that no cell phone could come close to providing. Charge me with comparing apples to oranges, but to answer your question, this is the impact of poetry readings, of literary journals, of art.

Issue # 6 4

Fall/Winter 2000

Raphael Allison

THE IDEA OF ONE PICTURE

The woman does not move. Her idea moves.
In a series of ripples, quickly and with supreme
assurance, derivative light expends itself, the idea

of light. She is gathering her scarf into fleshy folds
of yellow-white twill, slowly flagging its own unclocked
motion. There were many pictures to make this one,

as they say Flaubert read 1,500 novels to produce just one.
So this chance argues against chance, and the moment
that was perfect was perfect only by chance, the one-ant-chance

on the hill. One picture is the idea of one picture, though
there are negatives stuffed in envelopes that say
one picture is a lucky dance in a moony crook of field.

Issue #64

Priscilla Atkins

LIKE A LILY

At night, I long to recline
like Sarah Bernhardt
in the shape of a coffin,
the way I imagine
after a magnificent performance
of *Hamlet*, she climbed
into the significance of roses,
then lay down exhausted
in her silk-lined bed.
Each elusive moment liquefying
into one last murmuring spoonful,
the whole world dissolving—
even taxes, their slender ledger lines
collapsing.
Every furious space patiently filled:
no room left for Wonder,
or Worry. No room
to ponder prevention, or intervention.
Religion. Children.
Just the narrow
unknowing
filling, and filling
with a single white blossom.

Issue #64

WAR ROMANCE

How his eyes dilate at the famous pictures.
Death yanked and slapped
into pleasing compositions.
The quickening in his buttocks and groin
when he beholds the arching spine
of the man-child slain on the field
under Seminary Ridge.
Gut in air, head forced back,
legs delicately spread:
a baby fighting the diaper,
in extremis, erotic, dead.

He's fingered the facts,
thumbed through books
the size of family albums.
Salivated over generals strutting
in front of airy tents:
uniformed men posed in camp chairs,
circles of men conferring.
Muscle and haunch
rippling under dusty trees.

He's in love with numbers.
Names of battles.
A litany of hindsight reflections
he can confidently recite.
Like the shiny drops placed
in a newborn's eyes,
the photographer's silver gelatin
has spilled into his blood.
A liquid dream. He falls and falls.
Green apples float through morning air,
and the slender limbs of boys
who left them hanging there.

Issue #64

John Bargowski

SUPERING AT 206 OGDEN AVENUE

Zero weather, expect Bill bent
  over half the night shoveling
coal into the mouth of the great
  furnace pumping steam and hot
water to the thirty apartments
  in 206, and if your sink or toilet
backed up you'd probably find
  him in his bermuda shorts
and fireman boots wading
  through six inches of shit-
filled graywater, maybe planning
  which street sewer he'd dump
the new litter a stray bitch
  dropped behind the coal bin.
And when a tenant moved in from Jackson
  Avenue or the Greenville section
you could depend on Bill
  to set out poisoned potato halves
under your sink and refill
  the paper dishes of laced cornmeal.
You called him on the nights
  the Steinmetz twins in 4b chased
each other down with six-inch steak
  knives, or Margie Klederman banged
her shell-shocked husband's
  head on the bedroom wall,
expecting Bill to take
  the steps two at a time
the way he did when Eddie McDermott
  was called into General Foods
at one or two in the morning
  and Eddie's wife would tap
her code onto the steam pipes,
  Bill rolling out of bed
on the good chance when she undid
  the deadbolt lock and loosed
the short chain, she'd
  be wearing the same red
and black crushed velvet bra

Issue #64

and lace panties he'd unpinned
from her tangled clothesline
a dozen times before.

Issue #64

Wendy Barker

Through

layers of rock the softer
dirt collects, fountains with moist
leaves of mint, scilla, purple
hyacinth, and primula.

*

Boundaries, margins, hedgerows.
Maintaining separate fields.
But the leaves, branches, white hair
of roots press beyond fences.

*

The clouds have woven countries.
Rain falls here and somewhere else
you might be moving, your feet
touching the same earth as mine.

Issue #64

Eric Birkholz

DREAMING THE LAST DAYS

Our umbrellas withered like sugar in the light snow,
and the avenue glittered, splintering at the Flatiron
and curtained any further north.

Manhattan was another prefecture of Honshu,
redrawn by the sober hand of Hiroshige,
the light a mere hunger for light.

It was the humbled gray Apple
of January when the storms root
and the city settles into itself like a turtle.

We were walking hand-in-hand,
open-faced to the sting of the wind
though there was none: alone and the gods

of each other's solitude, as Rilke saw:
angel-protectors where each knew
only the other is true.

Issue #64

Bruce Bond

THE O AT THE END OF THE WORLD

Tonight I take refuge in the *Tibetan*
Book of Living and Dying and, if only
for the moment, enter the curious skin

of someone I never was or could be.
I too want to believe, to imagine,
as believers do, every face at birth

is a rock on fire, falling earthward.
I want to think some flash of arrival,
a flame in the first white shock of milk,

burns away each former life, if not at once
then slowly, over years, throwing back
the ash of what we said, how we said it.

If I'm a fool for the unbreakable
cyphers of stars, opening their designs
to the smoke of prayers and fathers' bodies,

I admit, I have my own expectations
I pinned up there like a child's drawing
full of anger: all that ancient light

approaching; there are times I read I fade
like paper, turning in a stranger's hand.
What I remember is a book buried

in the book I'm in. Now most every night
every page I turn I open a door
in Whittier, California: a window

shades the lamp on a table, its jar of pens,
a terror as still as a glass of water.
And just opposite the wall, a bed

where word by word my father's mind is
brimming like a bin of leaves. The child
in his head coughs up her Rorschach of blood,

and he pities himself, as she does, bewildered
by the nameless daughter who visits, her stealth-
talk of one day's weather, that moving of lips.

Who wouldn't look under each lost word—
revive, revive; dying is a fuel that way—
who wouldn't write the story that takes us

there and back, flaming into ourselves,
fighting heaven with heaven, until nothing
too would be our birthright: the closing palms
of a book, welling up with white light.

Issue #64

Grant Clauser

The Taxidermist's Daughter

The workshop smells of chemicals
and wood, a hint of fur and the sound
of wild running through tall grass.

I watch him peel the skin from deer,
polish bear claws and fix the flaws
of careless shots in the body of a running fox.

But best I like to touch the birds,
the pheasant caught in flight, eyes
turned toward field and shining like a ribbon

or the wood duck gently landing
on a farmer's marsh, wings turned down
for slow descent, water parting at its feet.

And when the lights are out,
all the glassy eyes of fish turn cold
and hold the moon like lanterns

burning from the bottom of a lake,
my father's hands alive in animal dreams,
all spinning surely to the sea.

Issue #64

Christopher Connelly

ORPHEUS

He was a god, he didn't need Eurydice.
It doesn't matter that the lavender honey of his
   too-perfect love hardened,
or that he saw the sun from pure darkness.
But don't hate Orpheus,
praise him for the space that his failure left between love and the world.
That singing means nothing without death
is the truth he dragged for us out of the mouth of the cave.

Issue #64

Samuel Exler

WINTER COVERS THE NATION

It's time to be alone, solitary
As light upon the snow;
Snow comes down to warn me Whitman is dead,
And the wounded boys lie uncared for on hospital cots;
Snow reminds me how much it costs
To blow up a city, and how Einstein longed
For a reasonable god. Icicles hang
From the drainpipe. The oil furnace
Rumbles below. The president speaks, snow
Lies over the fields, and the Indians
In full retreat, march north though the Dakotas.

Issue #64

Jeffrey Franklin

Boundaries of Seeing
for Judy

The temptation is to watch the clouds,
      swollen with moonlight, drift
    across the night sky, a migrating

herd of leviathans, but if
      you lie spread open on the earth
    long enough and focus

between them, you may see
      the clouds slow, the obsidian
    depth behind them ease

into motion, and sense yourself,
      in a parallel gesture, begin
    to accelerate, until like

the twin runners of a dogsled,
      you and the night sky
    are reeling along the luminous track

of frozen cloud. Once,
      white men trundled a projector
    over the tundra, as only

white men would do,
      and splashed a movie across
    the igloo's breath-sheened wall:

black-and-white people
      raced to and fro, made
    overblown gestures to make up

for the lack of sound. What
      did they see, the Eskimos,
    polite enough to feign a chuckle

Issue #64

when the visitors slapped their knees
     and, when the film came
    flapping to a halt, to praise

the shifting abstract patterns,
     how with such slow grace
    they drifted and swam

across the igloo's starry dome
     like the breath of the Aurora,
    they said,

in the cupped hands of the night sky.

Issue #64

Martin Galvin

The Silence of Eggs

He never told anyone at the monastery
How he talked to the chickens as he took
The warm eggs from under them,
How he forgave their beaks, their sharp
Reminders of the privileges of motherhood.
He never even told the tree he came to
For its murmuring shade to wipe his brow
Of the Iowa summer. His best friend
Kept the bees, was becoming one himself,
Talked to the queen, he once confessed,
In bee, the sweet melodics of a love
That made nothing of the hive but sense.

Once when he was forty-five his sister came
From the East to visit him. She was allowed
To sit with him at meals but not to talk to anyone,
To listen while they ate, listen and meditate
On the scripture the senior reader chose.
She told her children how the Trappists' teeth
Scraped as they tried to chew the broth,
How the rosary beads sounded like rattlesnakes,
How she was afraid the whole time she was there
Of what she had become, how far she'd gone
Away from this holy silence, so far that she heard
The rattle of the bones each time her brother walked.

We got a crate of freshfed, handpacked eggs
From the monastery every couple months
During the war. The cardboard cups we kids used
To save our favorite stones could take an egg from here
To Timbuktu and back again my older brother bragged
Who otherwise had nothing much to do with miracles.
Every week my mother cracked a half a dozen open
To scramble us our Sunday eggs, she'd listen hard
For the silence that came tumbling out. Best part
Of the week, she'd say. That silence. Safe
In her own kitchen, among her gang of galoots
Who found in noise the harmonies of being young,
She would hide the silences of the eggs away

So she could have it with her afternoon tea.
She sometimes said when we were gone
She'd take the cloth, tuck herself inside a shell,
Not say another word till evening broke.

Michael Graber

I. A Primer on Quilting an Adulterous Scene

Weave the high tones of conversation

into a quilt, still threadbare

where the wind has taken your loose hair.

The silence is too much not to mention.

Just sew what is hard to say—

the tilted face of wild children, our

frozen spouses, lonely as dying stars

whose lights barely flicker after day.

Go inseam with a faith you've lost since youth

like a girl who runs through glass to follow a bird

and stops, noticing blood stains on the floor.

Unstitch the untrue—the hearts, the kissing booth—

and gather images you've naturally earned . . .

spilt wine on denim, a motel door.

II. Further Instructions on Quilting:
A Lesson for the Visionary

When a callus blooms from an exploded blister

and basic stitches write themselves as learned,

then fall to folly. Your license is earned.

The world settles in original desire—a letter

sent home, not a poem stolen

at a high price from the faith of your husband.

The art will seem a cinch, natural as sand,

when you think of instinct as invention.

Then, form shouts like a sinner at revival

who allows reason to die and emotion rule

the trust that he'll wake above water.

Excesses sink to the bed of the baptismal

lake. Dive to the watery bottom, your school

where experience hardens your shaky finger.

Issue #64

Issue #64

SMOKE

is always second-hand. Always a distant spiral,
a curling sign. Even if we breathe it,
we keep only vestiges, carbon particles freed
from wood or leaves, spinning into our ignorant lungs. My grandfather,
an acre away, stirred a black pot spidered
over an open fire,
and no one can tell me

what he mixed or even if I dreamed it. (I remember the screened-in porch,
mud pies, a gourd dipper in a granite bowl;
I remember purple vetch,
its tickle infinitely preferable to the cobwebs and the dark and the stench
not even lime could cover.) He'd wanted to be a lawyer
but became a drunk instead. Or so I am told. I never saw him

drink. Never saw him hit. My mother
has his toolbox, and his hammer in it. She keeps his chalkline
(lead weight on blue string to mark the cut) and his spirit
level (splintered wood and oily bubbles)
atop his chest. I have a picture—he's carving
ham on the woodstove, I'm standing on a chair beside him, wearing red plaid and crinoline—
and my mother's word
that he favored me. I don't remember

his voice. I never held the books he read, double-helixed in the smoke-
house. My mother said "snakes" so I could not turn
the pages, see his words, know what he knew, match my fingerprints
to his. I never saw the rugs he braided,
couldn't ravel them, thumb denim and plaid flannel, read
the flat twist, the tight coils
he'd wound himself. I don't know if it hurt

him to slaughter hogs, to open their throats with a butcher
knife while my mother cowered in the house, fingers in her ears, blocking
sound. Never knew his recipe for smoking hams. No way to know if he spoke
before he died, pulled over on the mapled vein of country road,
breathing blood while October burned.

Michael Hudson

ME AND YOU IN *THE GUINNESS BOOK OF WORLD RECORDS*

While you held your breath the longest and fell without
a parachute the farthest, a distant

church bell dragged its broken foot across
our last Sunday

morning together. And all through breakfast,

the Heaviest Man in the World scraped his eggy fork
across a greasy plate, making a sound

like the oldest documented parrot (bald, blind and
demented) stropping his

ragged break against the bars of an unnecessary cage.

Issue #64

AFTER THE SIRENS

Trace me with chalk
So I know where I end
And where the asphalt
Begins. Draw around
My edges, closely, in white.
Show where I'm small and
Where I'm not.

On your crisp sheets,
Touch me with fingers
Rough and dry around
My ankles, past my hips,
Across my wrists so
I know they exist.

When I've been carried
Away, let there be a trace
Of me to prove I was
Really here, that my body
Lay here, breathless.

Issue #64

Wayne Miller

A Year in the Present Tense

I. Summer

Walking across a golf course at night,
I stop to pick up a tee, a thin white funnel
planted in the grass. Or perhaps

the smallest ear trumpet ever made,
I can hear the nervous laughter
of teenagers drinking on the seventh green,

and I can hear the silence ten years ago,
when I stumbled onto a couple making love
in the cupped hand

of a sandtrap. *Please don't step on my glasses*
was all the girl said
as I hurried past their crumpled clothes.

From this slight rise,
I can see the moonlit arcs of the sprinklers
as they sputter around on a flat stretch of greens,

then collapse at the tap of a timer.

The vista from a boat
stranded in a reflecting pool,

the silent, planar emptiness
of a man-made lake.
Faint window lights on the shore,

a thin line of trees
that I keep moving toward, walking on water,
whispering apologies into my hand.

II. Fall on Prospect Street

A flattened paper bag

Issue #64

among the leaves in the gutter.

The road is held together
by seams of tar.

Children at play,
silhouettes on yellow.

The cars move so slowly
you could walk with them.

Mrs. Anderson comes out
to light her Jack-O-Lantern,

her wrap-around porch
like an empty stage.

She's told me thirty times
I look like her son.

We wave across our yards,
leaves falling between us.

Drag another tarpful
to the curb, Mr. Finke,

a long shadow
chasing your footsteps.

III. Christmas Eve

Snow falling at a hard slant,
the sidewalks lined with candlelit
paper bags. Soft light

like a flashlight under a bedsheet,
the muffled drone
of the pastor's sermon

behind the closed doors
of the First Presbyterian Church.
Houses roughly sketched

Issue #64

in lights, thin branches
of dogwoods and elms
strung in Rorschach patterns.

Down by Worthington Street,
a bag catches fire,
burns away in a few seconds

leaving just the candle,
which somehow keeps burning
against the falling snow.

I imagine my parents
wrapping presents
after I drifted to sleep

fifteen years ago,—
bayberry candles, the tinkling
of Christmas ornaments

as the dog laps
the green preserving water.
The breath hanging

inside each glass ball
is still the same sealed breath
as the year I was born.

And now the church lets out,
the street filling
with the organ's steady voice,

the quiet conversations
of people finding their cars
covered with snow.

IV. *Spring*

Inside your body,
someone is squeezing
the soundless accordion of your lungs.

Issue #64

Sunlight enters the room
through the ribs of the venetian blinds.

Cars splash last night's rainwater
beneath the window.

Your lips part as if
to say something, then close again.

The striped square of sunlight
sits at the end of the bed
like a child we haven't had,

escaping to our room
from her nightmares. Slowly,
she moves into the space between us,

then climbs the wall,
spreading as she dissolves.

I whisper in your ear
Time to wake up, time to wake up,

as the paper boy chucks his bundle of headlines
with a thud onto the doorstep.

Issue #64

Kristy Nielsen

Waiting to Be Rescued

In the suburbs a man
kills another snake, chopping it
with a hoe
in front of the neighbors.

I bend over
in the field nearby
in the long grass, open, crawling
toward something
to finger my senses awake.

In the suburbs sun shines.
Snakes return, men
take up shovels and gleaming hoes.

If my father crawled
up the driveway in the shape of a snake
who would kill it?
There it is, the knowledge
that some knowledge is unsafe
even in my fragile hands, careful as I am.

In the suburbs, sun shines again.
Fathers wait with shovels. Daughters
find danger in fields and ditches,
every opening another snake hole.

9:30 P.M.

"No, I don't feel that he's with me," I say
although I'm winning at cards
and a warm breeze blows the hair
from my face. Though the cat who likes no one
sleeps in my lap and mosquitoes reject
my blood tonight. I play the winking Jack

of Spades and take the trick. The chair
is dead, the pillow, the Queen
of Hearts. He's become an apocryphal man.

When I touch myself I cannot pretend.
The unfinished feeling
of a clock striking half past: I wait still
for that final chime, the hours counted
neatly in rhythm, leading somewhere.

Issue #64

BARKING

I planted lettuce while the farmer plowed something.
There was a loud whirring. I put each leaf in the ground
and dumped old rainwater over them. I became filthy.
The dog found me and sniffed thoroughly. I let him.
Then the whirring stopped and the farmer went into the woods
with a small wooden pipe. The dog looked at me and became
frightened, and began barking as if I had offended him
in the darkest of ways. The bark was incriminating, ripe
with anger, tearful. He listed his troubles while I rocked
squatting on my feet. He barked until he was hoarse, until
I felt my eyes search the back of my head.

It was dark. I lay down in the lettuce. Where was the farmer?
I lay there until I began to bark, and I barked until I knew something.
I barked to a lower place, where the dog's brown eyes closed
and together we entered a field of voices.

Planting the Baby

Several children are walking in their swimming suits
toward the red barn. A naked fat man sits on the roof.

The sun is in patches and without sufficient legs.
Nothing is rooted down, not these tall flowers,
not this piece of paper in the wind.
These children appear to touch the earth,
but it is difficult to know for sure.

It is important to know that the youngest,
the baby, was lost this morning.
They played with it in the cornfield.
Then they ran away, and now
no one knows where it is.
When it is found, it will be burnt.
Or maybe it will not be there at all.

The children have run away from home.
They can't cry anymore. They walk up and down
the hills. They do not touch or speak.
They are not trying to make this difficult.
It just is.

One child begins to cry again,
and soon they are all crying. Another
hits its head repeatedly with the heel of a hand.
Perhaps it thinks that the baby
is lodged inside, and could exit the ear.

When dusk comes, a strange man takes
them gently into the barn.
They may or may not be crying now.
They are tired.
He hold them carefully to the ground,
where goodness surely lives, or has lived.
He beds them down
in a nest made of his hair.

They sleep as the plants have slept
for thousands and thousands of years.

Issue #64

Winter in Iowa

I cheer myself up by creating a system for getting things done.
I pull the pipe from your hand and fling it through the window.
I explain to you the difference between helping and taking
while you are unfolding yourself in my hand, an unfolding
that takes place nightly. Every night we talk about things that smell like the river.
Every morning we take and eat someone else's eggs
in the few bright hours we are given. We remember the pavement
as the grave distance it has become, and it remembers us.

You bring me the juice before you put your glasses on.
I happily hand you the gladiolas. There is no give and take here,
there is no helping. He means transport; you want to take the heaviness
from your eyes and put it somewhere inside me. Take is another journey for us,
one whose destination is another heaviness that I will have to remove.
The removal must take place here in the darkness,
and we are both so tired of it being dark.

Giving is something that happens with everyone else; it is something
being set down gently with you in mind. Giving is the placement of a journey
or a gracious watering, the way one hand waters another in a dry spell.

Kyoko Uchida

DRIVING LESSONS

Issue #64

1.
Following August across New Mexico borders
into rain so fast grinding glass and asphalt,
I lose the white markings where the lanes go,
numbers on road signs, arrows. I can't see
the other cars or hear them. I'm negotiating
windshield wipers, still learning to shift;
weaving stupidly through Gallup, missing
interchanges, overpasses, merging or gone.
On impulse I'd stop anywhere, this itinerary
for leaving: inches-thick sheets of water
sweep sideways, edges running together like
paint, until the car merely drifts in some
general direction: There. East. Forward.
My knuckles pale, a dull itch where
my arm has gone numb. He says, *Try to stay
on the road. Watch where the pavement ends.*

2.
Later, the terrain emerges
vertical and edged. Cliff sides wall in
broken shades of rust and flushed
magenta, ribboned stark for miles. He says,
Here. Look on your left. I'll hold the wheel.
Instead I turn to watch his face: the low
sunk slope of cheekbone; the vein-travelled
throat; eyes steady grey on the road.
A loose fist has the steering wheel
near the bottom, keeps it in place,
his shoulder leaning in a little, toward me.
Left, he says. *Look to your left.*

3.
The mistake is in learning the clutch on
his car, packed with my belongings, everything
I am taking with me, and him.
The car runs difficult under the weight,
slow climbing even the slighter grades,

the two-lane highway near Kansas.
Through dust-blown towns where it turns
Main Street or Central, I avoid stop signs and
lights; I have trouble stopping then
gearing into first, never know
how much to give, or where it catches.

The next time I'm in third with too much
distance on a late yellow light, I run it,
his voice sharp against the windshield where
I see it turn red. Someone honks,
but I can't stop here and stall again,
not now, I have to get on with it, this
driving myself away from where he lives.
It shouldn't be that difficult or slow.
Past the town's end, I'm speeding now, too,
tears dripping like rock into my lap, and
ignoring for the next mile his voice,
weary, yielding: *Pull over. I'll drive.*

SNOWPRINTS

Gravity, too, grows thick with snow,
accumulates inch by inch,
but the sensation is of flying.

I am moving over white space as it
takes itself up, the storm lifting east and
fast about my ankles, in my pockets
where my hands are tucked with change.
I'm running out of milk, out of time
in open snowlit streets; and retracing
two blocks home from the store,
I can't find my own footprints
where I've just been. Not erased but
filled in, the way absences fill.
It takes no time, as if snow
fell more quickly there.
Where all winter I saw nothing, branches
brighten like stitches of lace.
Something had been there: leaves, or
the yellow clutch of bird feet, balloons.
In the crease of my coat, the pressure of
hands, an embrace. We leave no evidence.
I could lose my way easily, the path
no longer familiar, untravelled,
stranger for having been here before.
We answer the same distances, each time the first.

Issue #64

COMPULSORY FIGURES

I want to ask you: in those classrooms still
new to you, do they sit waiting, their hands
folded clean, like rows of
faceless daughters? In my dream
my nails are trimmed and I hold the pen
correctly. There are hundreds of us, all
anxious for equations, answers to questions
we do not know to ask.

I want to ask you: do you give them
what you've refused me these
open-handed years, slow
compulsory figures to begin with,
simple formulas to work? Or is there
among them the daughter you've
always wanted, the one who speaks clearly,
unafraid, who knows to grow up
on her own? Without surprise, without
expectations, how could I have
impressed you, where could I
finally stop? In my dream you
never arrive. I will be there, always in
the back, long after the room goes
empty. For you are
in my teachers' distances, in their
forgetting my name.

Joe Wenderoth

FROM LETTERS TO WENDY'S

> The following letters were written on postage-paid "Tell Us About Your Visit" cards found in Wendy's fast-food restaurant. They are excerpted from a series of more than 340 letters written over about a year's time.

December 14, 1996

I always feel like someone at Wendy's is going to *help me change*. It's so hard to really change— most of the time I don't even think of it as a possibility. At Wendy's, though, especially when I've ordered and I know that good people are working hard to bring me what I deserve, I know I *can* change. I can become something truly special, like an escaped death-row inmate or a twelve-year-old prostitute.

January 25, 1997

Light is hectic. That's obvious, and it should tell us something. *Where we are* is inimical to us. We have overlooked the plain facts too long. How many times will we allow ourselves to be betrayed? It isn't as though *where we are* has given itself to us— we have taken it! Do not believe otherwise! A *home* should be like Wendy's: discreet, impersonal, practical, and altogether unholy.

January 29, 1997

Could it be that everything that *is* is just a funny after-taste? That brings us to the terrible question of what is funny. Certainly the body hanging down or bobbing is funny, and perhaps too any sounds associated with the noticing of it. But those sounds— that's a different kind of funny. And those sounds get stuck on themselves eventually. Then a meal with no funny after-taste seems absolutely necessary.

September 12, 1996

I seek respite from tolerance, in every sense. Stop giving me what I want! Say to me, "This has gone far enough!" Put me under arrest, take me to the other side of the register! Take me back into the manager's tiny office and explain to me the gross error of my design! Manage me! To manage— what is that? *To not let be.*

February 19, 1997

Nodding, bleeding out as steadily as anyone ever, the go-getters uphold their migration. Sometimes it's even beautiful— their freedom from thought and their vigilant impulse to nestle further in to the flock. Lord, let them nestle well— do not leave one behind! Let them pass, squawking, drifting blankly in their beautiful rows— let them find that warm nest far away and breed and die. And let their brood return to us as welcome criminals.

September 25, 1996

A woman with twins today, aged five or six. Almost perfect replicas. They sit eating, staring off now and then into the mid-air realm, the not-eating realm. They stare out knowing that their mother is there. They stare out from the good of eating. I want to ask them: *is that good already not good enough? And do you understand already that there is something more original than a mother?*

Issue #64

Jennifer Swender

JUMP

That she does not jump in means she jumps in many times. True, these jumps are in her head and therefore not real, but that doesn't make them feel less. There is the one where she underestimates the edge of the rocks, lands stiff-legged like a doll in unexpectedly shallow water and timbers into the hold like a falling tree. There is one that starts the same way, but in which the rocks are slimier. Upon hitting them, she slides in feet first, heel bruised and shocked. There is the chance of aiming correctly for the deep center of water, but not coming back up.

There are smaller possibilities, too: that she will gasp out too loud, come up coughing and spitting, breathing water, not dangerously, but sloppily. She can imagine being surprised by the cold to the extent that an unplanned noise emerges from her body, a groan or squeal that she doesn't want the stranger to hear.

There are also irrational scenarios. The bottom of the swimming hole is not rocks, but huge fingers reaching up to grab and drag her down, or worse, brushing against her teasingly. She imagines a dark and predictable-looking creature rising with her, smiling, green and murky.

She sits on a rock and dangles her toes in the water, starts lowering herself in. "That's just torturing yourself," says the stranger. "It's too cold for that."

She's aware of the bottom of her swimsuit, and how, when she stretches her leg into the water, the edge of it rides up and over her hip bone, crossing a limit both back and front. She pulls her leg back and slides a finger under the elastic to pull it down. She wonders if the stranger has seen. But he's climbed to a higher point up in the rocks. "Right from here," he is saying. "You have to jump from here."

And he does. He comes up. "It's not bad once you get in," he shouts. She smiles. This is what I do, she thinks. She is up to her shins.

The sun is hot and flat on her shoulders. A line of sweat appears in the crease of her waist. She imagines letting herself slip and float, being relieved of the heat. A fly insists on landing on her elbow. The feel of her own hair on her shoulder makes her slap at it.

In front of her, the stranger floats on the backs of his shoulders, arms stretched out to his sides. Every few minutes he lets himself drop, brings his arms overhead. His fingertips are the last thing she sees. Then he's back again, thrashing and threatening to splash her if she doesn't jump in.

"How deep is it in there?" she wants to ask. "Did you touch the bottom?" She has other questions about the formation of the rocks, about the changes in the current, but she's not sure which to ask. The stranger keeps floating and looking up at the sky.

She crouches down and sits on a rock just under the surface. Her legs hang over the drop into where the water gets deep. She is up to her waist.

"That's just dragging it out," the stranger says. He swims to the ledge, pulls him-

Issue #64

self out, scrambles up the rocks and readies himself to jump again.

She leans forward to dip a hand, up to the wrist, up to the elbow. She considers the cold, wet glove. Then, a slight shift, a possibility. A sliver of a drop that feels like falling down in a dream, before sensing the absence of floor, before waking up. There's dry breath in her lungs. She catches herself, pulls back.

The stranger pops up, shaking limbs and hooting, like a hybrid of wet dog and owl. She, too, shakes her wet arm, as if at certain moments everything must be wrung out. There's a painful-looking flick of his neck. He seems satisfied. He's floating again.

"What are you thinking about?" the stranger asks. She appreciates his upfrontedness. She doesn't answer.

"Sorry," he says, and submerges. She watches him move away, like a fish in a tank, his body long, shimmering and far. He pulls himself up, swings legs around, walks away.

She's experimenting cupping water in her hands, letting it fall over her shoulders to see what it would feel like. He's on his way back up the rocks. She starts to want to tell him something, but he's already jumped in.

Major Walter Long

> It has always seemed to me that I had to answer questions which fate had posed to my forefathers, and which had not yet been answered, or as if I had to complete, or perhaps continue, things which previous ages had left unfinished.
>
> —Carl Jung, *Memories, Dreams, Reflections*

I am thinking about you, Walter Long, demented Granddad, polite to a fault, always inquiring (after greeting us with extreme courtesy), Who are these nice people? When you last knew yourself, old grandfather, you had been a writer for 40 or 50 years. You had been a reporter for the Philadelphia *Bulletin*, in its day the largest circulating newspaper in Philadelphia. You had written a novel. Walter Long, in your wildest imaginings, in your worst terrors, did you dream it would come to this?

That your decades of writing would be entirely expunged? That your sentences, compositions, words, newspaper articles, recorded thoughts would be unobtainable even on scratchy microfilm, even in some carton forgotten in attic or archive? Though I am your granddaughter, Walter Long, I have never seen your handwriting, nor a typed page of your writing, nor a column of newsprint written by you, a reporter who ended up on the Metropolitan page with no byline. Major Long, I have spent days in newspaper archives looking for your name.

The few crumbs I learned about you when I was a girl growing up during the long night of your dementia had to do with your disappointments. The greatest disappointment of your life was that you did not get to report the sinking of the *Lusitania*. Or was it the *Titanic*? You did report the Lindbergh case. At least, someone thought so, because it is recorded in your 1966 obituary. But—this week, on the telephone, my father, your son, tells me that the greatest disappointment in your life was not getting to report the Lindbergh case.

Of your lucidity, I remember only how you took us kids out to the barn to see the gleaming black buggy that no longer had a horse to pull it. This was in 1948, the year you retired to a gentleman's farm in Bucks County. Not long after that, your mind was gone. You no longer knew your own son, much less the child I was, the writer I would become.

A Philadelphia reporter, you must have known the brick and cobble of old Philadelphia as well as you knew the contours of your own tall thin body. I remember cobblestone streets and stone houses, shutters, slate, the cracked Liberty Bell. I remember a stone statue of that other writer, Ben Franklin. We would drive to see you —not you, truly, in your dementia—but your wife Nan, my Scottish grandmother. We would drive north from Maryland and stop in Philadelphia. We would linger for hours in Leary's Bookstore, its three floors stuffed and sagging with used books. Or wander the Philadelphia Art Museum, its majestic Beaux Arts grandeur on a hilltop overlooking the Schuylkill River.

You inherited Philadelphia from your own grandfather. He too was a writer.

Issue #64

Colonel Stephen Winslow edited the *Philadelphia Commercial List* and was known as "the grand old man in the newspaper life of Philadelphia." Walter Long, you were 23 when Stephen Winslow died. I imagine him mentoring you, introducing you about town, arranging for you your first job. Colonel Winslow worked and socialized right up to the end. Upon his death in 1907, one of several glowing obituaries declared, "He was the oldest reporter in the city, and it may be that he was the best liked." As for you, you went senile 16 years before your own body gave out. You died unknown even to yourself, and went to your grave forgotten.

Upon your death, they discarded your novel. "He wrote a novel," my father told me many years later. "It wasn't very good, and we didn't keep it."

Last year my aunt, your daughter, sent me every extant relic pertaining to you or to my grandmother, practically nothing. But the little package included an undated clipping from the Philadelphia *Bulletin*, which features you. The photograph shows a balding, thin-faced, bespectacled man smiling brightly. This clipping doubles what I know about you:

Walter Long.The Zoning Board of Adjustment goes into sesssion.hearing pro and con on whether a new apartment site shall be approved.News is being made.and Walter Long's there.accurately recording the builder's arguments, the opponents' vigorous stand.For 15 years Walter Long has been one of the Bulletin's experts in municipal affairs.He roams the City Hall annex.drops in daily on the Board of Health.keeps tabs on the Department of Supplies and Purchases.and distinguishes himself with his detailed reporting of the City Housing Rent Commission Hearings.

Not the *Titanic*. Not the Lindbergh case. But there you are.

I have a photograph of you looking up from your writing desk with its inclined surface. In your right hand you hold a dip pen. Perhaps the pen has a metal nib shaped like the Eiffel Tower or like a pointing finger, like the antique dip pens advertised in the *Levenger's Catalog of Tools for Serious Writers*. I imagine on your desk a fine leather-cornered blotter, an inkpot, fine paper, perhaps a cream-colored sheet with a linen finish. Perhaps in the lamplight you are working on your novel, writing scene after scene. It makes you happy to think of people reading the very words you are writing. Your handwriting is round, neat, and straight, as befits a scholar raised in the Age of Penmanship.

You smile to yourself and sip the cup of English tea that Nan your wife has brought to hand. You write easily into the night, a war story perhaps, full of romance. Perhaps you are thinking of your own war, the Great War, the Battle of Champagne. There, during the week of October 2-10, 1918, you "remained at exposed post and by.constant presence kept up the distribution of ammunition in a well regulated manner." For this you received the French Croix de Guerre with a bronze star. Perhaps the heroine of your novel resembles your first wife, a girl who died at 22 of tuberculosis.

"Whoever she was, she was of no significance," my 85-year-old aunt, your daughter, tells me. This first wife of yours, Walter Long, nobody remembers her name.

I see you there, old grandfather, writing in the lamplight with your gold-nibbed

Issue #64

dip pen. The inkpot, the nib, the draw of the black ink, pleases you tonight. It is late summer, and the moon is out. Your wife has long since gone to bed. Tonight your characters—let's call them Oliver Winslow and Hannah Olson—begin to fall in love. One of them has tuberculosis, but they don't know that yet, and they are completely happy.

Issue #65

Spring/Summer 2001

International

Marion Wrenn

Palimpsests: Editor's Introduction to *PBQ* 65

I had a dream of becoming an explorer
—Tomas Transtromer, *PBQ* 40/41, 1990

Ten years ago *PBQ* published its first Translation Issue. A double issue, thick and perfect-bound, the magazine is adorned with the late Ellen Powell Tiberino's elegant sketches. Flowing figural line drawings surround work by Tomas Transtromer, Ingeborg Bachman, Jose Agustin Goytisolo, Bei Dao, and more. In thinking about our new international supplement, I held that book in my hand, felt its binding resist and give, and remembered the history of *PBQ*.

We'd published an interview with Transtromer. Responding to a question about his "interior interest" and "outward perception," Transtromer said,

> That probably is the way inspiration works for me—the feeling of being in two places at the same time . . . Or of being aware that you are in a place that seems very close but that actually every thing is open. Well this is vague, but it has to do with the whole inspiration that makes a poem for me. (34)

Transtromer searches for a way to name the ephemeral, mysterious process of his craft, the way his imagination works. In doing so he names for me the way *PBQ Online* works. Not only do the poems and essays collected here open up space in the confines of what tends to get published in literary magazines (see the International Supplement's intro for more on this), these pages create the illusion of expanded space and time. Read slowly. Re-read. Return to these amidst the bustle of your day, your instant messenger, your bookmarked pages. With our electronic transformation, we too are in two places at once, riding the edges of the past and present, opening up the tight space of print publication with the breadth and possibilities of e-publishing.

No good story of transformation is complete without a haunting. *PBQ Online* has a ghost: the 30-year-old spirit of its print version. How could it be otherwise? Though digital technology radically shifts the ways in which we read and write, the new technology is deeply inflected by print culture. The effect is uncanny. Though page numbers might have disappeared, residual features (like a table of contents, for example) remain. We are a book, and not. We are the book's ghost, present and absent at once. Online, the book (dis)appears. You can sense its presence here in *PBQ*'s second translation issue, and we plan to make the apparition stay with an electronic archive of the complete run of the magazine, presented in such a way that you can see what the actual print magazines looked like. In this way we will document the work of the past within (and through) the technology of the present.

Our new electronic form has allowed us to continue to do what I would argue (and have, often) is the best work writers can do for other writers. As a print publication we were forever thwarted by the cost of making the magazine. On too many occasions we had wonderful issues parked and idling as we scratched together the funds to go to press. Such concerns have eased with our digital reconfiguration.

Now that the magazine is seen by more readers and users (30,000 unique visitors with our first online issue), we have morphed from the coveted (and occasionally cursed) prize of poetry aficionados to a role as passionate and curious gatekeepers. There are writers behind the veil of *PBQ*, a collective of editors who have created what Mike Neff of Webdelsol described as the "Knights of the Roundtable." It's an apt moniker. Fancy this: knights, veils, and . . . a vellum map, scarce and valuable (since paper—a Chinese invention—had yet to be adopted by Europeans). Imagine it scraped and re-inscribed with a new territory, suggesting a new journey. Even as we chart the new path, old boundaries and legends surface. Nothing is ever completely erased. The new preserves the old; the old resides within the new.

Concurrent with our launch as an online magazine, *PBQ* found a new home. *PBQ* has recently affiliated with Rutgers University, Camden. It is no secret that the magazine was run for years out of the kitchens and car trunks of generous editors. Though guerrilla independence has a certain sexiness, we too often found ourselves in desperate straits, too preoccupied with where to hold the next meeting (Dirty Frank's or a local pizza parlor) to make good on plans for a reading series, themed issues, or workshops. By partnering with the Rutgers, *PBQ* has joined a team of magazines housed under the newly conceived Camden Online Poetry Project (COPP). We now have a permanent home and offices, a battalion of interns, and the pleasantly uncanny feeling of coming home (*PBQ*'s editorial board has long been made up of a number of Rutgers-Camden alum). We've become a spatial and virtual palimpsest. We are in two places at once.

For a 30-something nonprofit independent literary magazine we have made two radical choices: electronic transformation and university affiliation. Their effects overlap. We are exploring the limits and possibilities of online publication even as we re-imagine the possibilities of *PBQ*; by affiliating with the university *PBQ* finds itself at the center of a growing community of scholars, students, and creative writers. We've found both stability and the charged atmosphere of inspired thinking in Camden, where *PBQ* has become a teaching tool for the English department at Rutgers. Students are competitively selected for internships with COPP, where, through *PBQ*, they learn the ropes of running a literary magazine. It seems we've made a Möbius strip of our "map": we've turned a print quarterly into an online magazine; our online form allows us to teach and train aspiring editors. Our transformation brings us back to our starting place: preserving *PBQ*.

This play of images lingers with me as I think about the ways in which digital technology "reinvents" print publication. With our third electronic issue, we've become the explorers I've long dreamt we'd be. No longer bound by the silken ties of debt and deadlines we incurred as a (homeless) print publication, we are free to range and collect, design and desire (although they seem the quotidian practice of editors, these are luxuries hard fought and won by *PBQ*). Look for special featured sections driven by specific editors in forthcoming issues (beginning with Chris Connelly's work here).

Upcoming features include a film section, a section dedicated to the haiku of

Nick Virgilio, an aesthetics issue, a pedagogy issue, a fiction issue. Look too for *PBQ*'s first annual print anthology, containing our first Web issues.

But look first here: *PBQ* 65.

Raphael Allison

FROND

In the snowed-in flowerpots
sporting wizard hats
a frond, green shoulders
stiff against the old, frozen dirt
emerges, misinformed.

The little green bishop's tendril
rigid near the stem-cuff
slumps to the white crust.

It is an old mistake:
here, but not now.

The weather report says:
"more snow."

International

Molly Bendall

CHARMED

Off the ragged hull of
                    a ship a gleam stepped.
A bit of a springy step. It danced on top

of the water. What were my intentions once?

                    How I seduced him till we bled.
And found his errand was living-cold but possible.

There I was zipping around so I reeled him

                    in. The gleam wants to show
me, project a little document on the beach.

Would I take a vow like that again?

                    I can clip and prune
                    the fruit trees so easily
and I love their tangle, their
maze of laughter,

                    almost too hysterical.

Sticky fruit, cut my lip. The shore widens,

                    my collections wait and stir around
the gleam, its song.

Issue #65

ISLAND CALL

No season I've seen. Lightly the algae and I drift.
                    We resemble each other.
      Until a flat fish came hovering,

told me to stop behaving like
                a fugitive.
Note that I'll accept letters in the hollowed out

                branch near the wing-shaped ledge.
I swear the current changes,
                    pushes its teeth
toward the back of the island, haunting me. Whatever befalls

          me, I'll dance with it, train it
to yearn with me. But I'll dismiss

those who come encumbered with fruits and soothe-talks
         and too many
generous directions.

Molly Bendall

STITCHES

I think the man I didn't give change to
               lurks near my cruising rock.

Although I'm shucking and peeling—so busy,
  there's no plot to untangle
from the scratchy earth.
              Nuts in-between the lines of heaven.

          Urchins parade the whole month around, and
new months I've taken to measuring in loaves.

              I call out that new sound
as they wax and wane.
                Bones are for needles,
      sticks are to chew, and with my scallop brooch,

             I'm aloft and singing.

He marked an attitude of mine—paranoid sorrow.

  It eddies in lame laps.
             And I shelve them all as
I cut smoothly the vacancies here.

Issue #65

Over Sleep

The long reason of his life pours out—
slender-drool-string. But I've built

this canopy. Yes, the

shipwrecked girl left for dead.

Not as haunted as you'd like to think— Lone tribeswoman,
          wrecked, leader of an expedition, survives alone.

                    And I'm nudged by
          the tumbles of sand.
                         I was meant to appear.

Cannibal, well, yes. That's how I get closer,
                         just believing
it. I have plates and knives, and, oh yeah, I have

moods—out here anything can lead me astray.

INSURANCE MAN 1947

Silas, you might not be here come April.
Ain't none of us ever promised tomorrow.
If you died right sudden, you'd need a will.

That way you control who gets your nickel
when you gone. Get your ducks in a row,
Silas. You might not be here come April.

Yeah, your policy's up-to-date and we'll
pay, say, if you lose an arm at the elbow
at the mill, but if you die, you'll need a will.

Double pay for accidental deaths? We still
have you down for that. Folks won't need to borrow.
Silas, you might not be here come April.

Being alive is enough to get you killed.
Did you hear about them folks up in Monroe?
If they hang you from a tree, you'll need a will.

Your folks won't have to worry about a meal
with this insurance when that day of sorrow
comes. Silas, you might not be here come April.
If you died right sudden, you'd need a will.

Issue #65

Nightmare 1947

If they hang you from a tree, you'll need a will.
Ain't none of us ever promised tomorrow.
Silas, you might not be here come April.

An echo loosed from the mouth of Zekial,
the insurance man—blacker than tomorrow.
If they hang you from a tree, you'll need a will.

Crackers in their best Sunday apparel—
hate frenzied, sweaty faces flushed, skin sallow.
Silas, you might not be here next April.

Community men each with a broken bottle grin
cutting their faces like a welt.
If we hang you, you'll need a coffin.

Surrounded under an oak, Silas prays.
Their cold sharp fingers slice off his ears and nose—
keepsakes. *Silas, you won't be here next April.*

Hanging until the convulsions stop, Silas drops
free into his bed awakened by the cock's crow.
After we hang you, they'll put you in a hole.
Silas, you won't be here next April.

Sandra Kohler

THE POND

Why does a man decide to build a pond
on the land of a house he's planning
to sell, a Vermont schoolhouse? Too ashamed
of this decision to tell his wife of forty years,
he calls the contractor, hires him,
commits himself, his shame equaled
by his insistent will: this pond must be.

He should dig the pond himself: fire
the contractor, send away the bulldozer,
the backhoe, begin to spade the thin hard
dirt of Vermont farmland covering the ribs
of stone underneath the way skin covers
an old stringy horse. The pond will come
from the belly of the farm, the loose bowl
of its pelvis. Earth under the hard dry soil
will turn muddy, dense, not friable, still
hostile to the spade, studded with rocks.
It will take days to get down to water.

This man needs to take days. He needs
to sweat in the hot thin October sunlight,
the days that start in cold fog, burning off
slowly, then getting hotter and hotter;
his body, cold in the morning, moving slowly,
by noon hitting a rhythm he puts aside,
sitting down, his back against a tree, to eat
bread, to drink. Then in the short afternoon,
four hot hours, sweating and bending,
his body finding something he thought
it had lost. He must sweat it out
of himself, create the pond, digging it
out of the earth, out of his body.

Issue #65

Kelly Le Fave

PROPHECY

That morning, people in the next house

all the way to the badlands will grab

somebody's wrist. Momentous instant! Each

will scan another's eyes; at last love

will be nothing but concord and proximity,

its slope greased on the spot. And you, everybody's

bundle, rose rising in your cheeks at the touch

of a stranger. That morning, you will stand

between silence and breathing: endless *once upons*

opening their veins. That morning will quiver

with capillaries, each cell slipping from blue

into red, anticipating your sigh.

A monstrous quiet will tremble in thresholds

all down your street; you will know it one day

by the way it dwells lightly, the way evening

will sparkle in your eyes when you know it is evening

and beginning to fade. And whose hand will it be

that presses your ribs the first time? Who will

remember when you ask? Tranquility

gives us the word's pleasure, but not its flesh;

yours will be a life languishing

in crisis. You will never be tall.

Ethan Paquin

LAUGHTER IS X, LAUGHTER IS Y

I.

I had to get there quick to see it:
Harry's pursuit for the perfect umbrella,

the graying myriads plying the naiads
at Flought Beach for dimes and ice nuggets

(which spell the flume of hot dough and frankfurter
almost enough to keep the bikiniads pleasant),

thongs re-routing the glances of   a. Hopper
                                           b. Rockwell
                                           c. Winslow

                               [it is said that, depending on their infirmity,
                               many of them choose to "go by" their last names]

; those becapped men we've known to frequent the strip,
where they claim there's nothing to top the sensation
                                    of denture cream *down there.*

II.

Well, I told some old friend the story,
mailed it to him, I think; I even affixed an Expressionist poster-replica—
I do not think it was Lautrec—
of an absinthe bottle—it was not Degas, either—
half-drunk
; the cigars stood out, though
; every dapper gent gripped one professionally,
somewhat confidently, even the casual observer might add.

III.

There are simply the old men with gray back hair walking the plankstrips at
    Flought Beach,

men who "fought wars and strained their backs lifting hay bales and wielded the
    mute tools of a generation,"

who ever reflect on that shaky spell:

when Maman's whisper splayed the air, the Gospel in the pantry louder than
    hearts recently aneurysed;
when grass tracked in by Father would ever live as a chalk on the wind.

IV.

(His response, an extraneous letter I called A Maiming)

I hung the Expressionist absinthe bottle next to the typewriter.
I was told Lautrec by the passive voice of the Apartment C2 bank-teller
...or is she the surgeon?
Well, anyway, I was glad to know we still have the same taste in art,
but the question remains: will we ever break bread again,
sup on the primrose <vin> again?

V.

Laughter is X,
Laughter is Y.
Laughter is in their faces, is it?
Well, what do any of us really know about their faces?

There is a grove in Oregon that supplies walking canes for 90.3% of Americans.
There is a grove further north, in Alberta, that supplies canes for 79% of
    Canadians.
The grove is the loudest grove you've ever seen.

On Flought Beach, I was struck by their dim eyes holding firm on mine,
their stares like cats underfoot, like night studying decomposition—
because it's born bandaged and scratches at all of us, underneath.

Laughter is X, laughter is Y?
Everyone's given up on that now, all umbrellae are folded
for the eve. Look the tide is out—even God has given up.

Joanna C. Scott

FIRE

...Manila, the eighties

Here, when the dead come back
to ease unruliness of soul,
the atmosphere becomes so charged
the slightest spark can set off
one of those unexplained
unexplainable
sudden upward rushings,
like a surge of anger,
like the hotel on the esplanade
that burned for two weeks straight
before they put it out.

Or like our house, one moment
somnolent in afternoon's
slow buzz, maid's half-dozing
over chopping boards and knives,
the little temple bird,
black head snugged down
into its own red breast,
swinging in its bamboo cage.
Comes the brush behind,
one maid turning to the other,
hair rising on her arms
and nothing there,
just knowledge of the dead.

—*What's that? What's that?*

Perhaps it was the sharp
slice of the knives, perhaps
the bird's stained breast
that closed the circuit
late that afternoon. Although
it could have been something
more. Perhaps a revelation
of how culpable we are
in our own miseries,
how they drag us back

Issue #65

and back into ourselves
where we nose about
for a new way to have done it,
giving off the vulcan whiff of hell,
the soul's conducive cry.

—*Hush. It's nothing. Nothing.*

And then the temple bird looks up
to see the wall exploding out,
the fiery revenant advancing.

Sean Singer

Loss

There is loss in the world. I don't feel awful because lost people
Took part of me. But because I can no longer give to them.
He is in a coffin in a church in Chicago, or she is dating someone new
And singing Schumann.

Great Tumblers of the Universe have done things: make me feel needed,
Give me someone to embrace by a yellow barn, or,
In an eastbound cattle train, let me reach through the metal grate
To get at the delicious wet snow.

Brian Teare

DANGEROUS KITCHEN

Divorce proceedings : getting mother on the cross-town bus. Two hours early to make sure—"Don't rush me, cherubs. They can't start without the wife."—bath, hat, shoes, good wool suit, matching calfskin gloves. To the curb to wait.

After she left, we changed what we could : we cleaned.

After an afternoon's eternity of lye, bleach and scalding water that left our hands' pink peeling at the cuticles, after the green sponges doused a thousand times, our arms like derricks pumping dirt from linoleum, after the unused counters scoured, stubble like ants rinsed from sticky porcelain, after his old underwear ripped into dustrags, after buckets brought full from the garden hose boiled on the stove, sudsy hair pulled in long sopped strings from the drains :

the white. The dangerous kitchen.

When the last bus dropped her back changed in name only, we went to bed, she to her books. But every night that week after, lights out,

we played kitchen creatures, drew high the burners' blue crowns for the dark to regale itself, donned the domestic drag of aprons and oven mitts.

We gave ourselves to the knives. On the wall

drying in a line like split fish : streetlight cloven on gleaming flanks of serration, sequins bluing in schools. To cut, in our hands, the bread knives split their one infinitive. Pressed against skin, left red waning crescents : months dull. We remembered every weekend father cutting nothing,

sharpening-stone moist with oil, imitated with our voices the slow high slice-slicing of the blade, back-and-forth of the body against the stone a thrust almost a rocking,

a man's lullaby : mothering the blade.

Christopher Connelly

INTRODUCTION TO INTERNATIONAL POETRY SUPPLEMENT

Don't mistake *Painted Bride Quarterly*'s "International Poetry Supplement" for another friendly exhibition of the exotic species of poetry that flourish in other countries. Instead, think of it as a kick aimed at contemporary American poetry's corpulent ass. Years of inbreeding have produced a surfeit of lazy poems that are either too hermetic to be understood or larded with homely anecdotes that pant for readers' sympathy. I want to wrench poets' attention away from their own cliques and direct it toward some brave writers working outside the atomized world of American poetry—poets whose work points out paths to rejuvenation.

There may be more "poets" now than ever before, but their tendency to write for their own "schools" or scenes has diminished the art's influence on American culture. Politicians, intellectuals, journalists, and even fiction writers and essayists readily avow that they read little poetry and neither understand nor like what they read. Despite a glut of new volumes of poetry, newspapers and general interest magazines rarely review new poetry and almost never publish articles on even the best contemporary poets. What flourishes instead are hordes of widely ignored literary magazines, university-sponsored journals, micropresses, and webzines, all devoted to publishing the work of their editors, friends of their editors, and others who subscribe to their particular theories.

What unites the work of the writers featured in this supplement isn't an aesthetic program, or an academic affiliation, but boldness. If you have gotten used to the competent but dull work that clogs many literary magazines, you may be startled by the chances these poets take. Their poems are driven by strong feelings rather than the desire to fit into a particular tradition or "school." Instead of endless chains of allusions or in-group references, you will find an array of original images—proof that these poets intend to reach as large an audience as possible.

* * *

Nearly two years ago, when *PBQ* first decided to publish an international poetry supplement, senior editor Daniel Nester and I immediately decided that we needed to talk to Bob Holman, the American poet most committed to bringing vivid, living poetry (and, in particular, international poetry) to a mass audience. While other poets bitched impotently about the power of the media, Bob had the guts to put poetry on television, liberating it from its academic ghetto. His widely praised (and just as roundly condemned for its allegedly "slick" production values) PBS series television *The United States of Poetry* was the biggest invasion of the airwaves poets have ever staged. Millions watched as poems were read, shouted, and sung by rock stars, Nobel laureates, and complete unknowns.

For more than three years, I worked with Bob and co-producer Josh Blum on an even more ambitious follow-up project called *The World of Poetry*, a multimedia exploration of the eclectic, eccentric, or simply overlooked poetry created in countries throughout the world. The goal was to put together a series of episodes focusing on a specific theme, language, or region of the world. These programs would then both be broadcast on television and also stored digitally, along with supplemental audio and visual footage, at The World of Poetry Web site.

Bob's interest in international poetry has led him to the work of the griot poets of West Africa, which he discusses at length in this supplement's featured interview. His playful transcription of griot Papa Susso's song "How Kora Was Born" illustrates how open, accessible, and fresh poetry remains when in touch with its oral roots. In his own work, with lines like:

> Through the mandhara of your eyes,
>> dear Poet
> I see each second of eternity pass, frame-
>> by-frame, over Sana'a
> A Shadow constantly seeking its Object

from the poem "On Changing the Past," Bob concentrates on evoking intensely subjective, inner states. The otherworldy imagery and frequent repetition of enigmatic words and phrases create an almost incantatory mood that represents an exciting departure from his generally more outward-looking work.

Chinese poet Yang Lian's own intensive investigation of inner states and explorations into the nature of his native language have yielded equally exciting results. His essay "In the Timeless Air" provides a potent reminder of the crucial role that translated poetry played in the formulation of modernism. Lian points out that it was Ezra Pound's study of classical Chinese poetry that inspired the "early Imagism that revolutionized the expression of the English language." He claims that Pound, in spite of an incomplete understanding of the Chinese language, intuitively grasped the essential difference between "synchronic," "timeless," Chinese poetry, with its juxtapositions of images and actions that all exist simultaneously, and "diachronic," Western poetry and its linear arguments and strictly ordered series of events. Lian argues that this discovery inspired Pound to try to create synchronic poetry in English, and that these attempts culminated with *The Cantos*. But in Lian's opinion, Pound's work only truly achieved the synchronicity he had worked towards for years with the recent translation of his masterpiece into Chinese. Interestingly, the Chinese version of *The Cantos* has in turn influenced a number of contemporary Chinese poets, including Lian.

Lian's own poetry combines the dislocations found in *The Cantos* with a passionate surrealism. Remarkably, for a poet dedicated to creating strikingly original images (he claims that one of his foremost goals is to avoid repeating himself), Lian's poems are full of emotion. In lines like:

> I have accepted any place
> in a corner of this village   there is snow
> the snow has small crystal balconies

Issue #65

> *and towers   twilight sniffs the station*
> *a daughter studding the glass with stars*
> *tree monsters posting up night outside   water*
> *locking the door tight   destination infinite black*
> *enchanting as the womb mother once used*

from the poem "Notes of a Blissful Ghost," Lian conveys the strange combination of disorientation and exhilaration that comes from living in exile from his native language and culture. (Since the crackdown in Tiananmen Square, Lian has been unwelcome in China because of his involvement with the Democracy Movement.) When I read Lian's poetry, I don't feel that he intends to shock, annoy, or outsmart his audience (as I do when reading the work of too many "avant-garde" American poets) but is instead making every effort to communicate utterly unique and specific feelings and observations.

Danish poet Katrine Guldager's work at first seems more earthbound than Lian's dark, dense poems. "It happens, of course, that you get a flat, that you will have to get by with one that's too high:" Guldager writes at the beginning of "Crash" and drops us in the middle of the street next to a bike with a flat—a situation that we all recognize. It is not until she reminds us of the "strange inklings" in our hands, the "accidents hanging in the wind," and the "small stones that you hide under your skin" that we realize how unfamiliar we are with the everyday world we unthinkingly inhabit.

> *There's earth and asphalt and a city: There's a city on top of the earth: There's a city*
> *on a city, there's asphalt on top of asphalt, earth above earth, and there's no way getting*
> *down to it, or around it, that's how it's always been:*

she writes a few lines later, and confronts us squarely with the sordidness of the world we have made for ourselves. But the relentless repetitions suggest that the narrator feels something more than frustration. As she bores deeper and deeper beneath the street, Katrine actually seems thrilled to have penetrated to the utter arbitrariness that underlies our seemingly well-ordered world. And she doesn't brood over her discovery, but allows an unexpected, almost perverse, sense of delight to glow beneath the grim, angry imagery. Her willingness to confront the world's ugliness without feeling sorry for herself only reminds me how much gloomy self-pity could be banished from similarly anecdotal or narrative American poetry.

*   *   *

And that is the extent of the work that I can take credit for bringing to *PBQ*; the rest of the poetry in this supplement came either through the efforts of other editors or though good luck. *PBQ* senior editor Greg Pardlo's translations of Danish poet Niels Lyngsø's "constellation" poems provide the supplement with a dose of formal experimentation that it otherwise lacks. I don't know if I have ever come across a more effective visual device than the wonderfully simple, yet subtle, idea of spreading groups of words across the page at distances that determine their "gravitational influence" upon the rest of the poem. Lyngsø's work is certainly livelier than most of the poems created by a return to conventional forms.

Yet for me, it is these poems' essential and elemental subject matter that brings the conceit to life. Lines like:

bent body in a temple of meat	I cannot	There is flesh beneath bark
	wrest me free	which in large flakes
for The apple falls	but perhaps new seeds	fall from branches and lie plainly
sour and green		throbbing bluish-purple film
and hard as heav		with a mold of white

are full of wonder and dread. These powerful feelings allow the unconventional arrangement of the text to deepen and intensify the poems' effect, rather than simply exist as an end in itself.

Greg also brought us the playful yet cerebral work of Jacques Roubaud, as translated by Professor Richard Sieburth and Françoise Gramet. Poems "I." and "II." from *Six Little Logical Pieces* parody Gertrude Stein–style, high modernist poetry through repetition and delicately skewed logic. Roubaud takes his experiment so far that it goes beyond wit and raises troubling questions about language's transparency and about our ability to truly communicate with each other.

Daniel Nester brought to my attention Matthew Zapruder and Allan J. Sorkin's translations of Romanian poetry. I immediately admired Zapruder's ability to put across in English the earthy intensity of lines like "Her teeth had all fallen out. She was still beautiful. / She had hips made of gulfs, and she swayed bluely," in Eugen Jebeleanu's poem "Venus XX." In Nora Iuga's poetry there is a similar vitality, along with some violently surrealistic imagery that Sorkin renders lucidly and deliciously, in passages like:

> hey you gellu naum shouted at me you buried woman
> then he shoved a handful of leaves down my throat
> what a green agony just imagine
> > what a green agony.

*   *   *

And then there is Rilke. Annie Boutelle's brilliantly clear, unfussy translations of four of Rilke's *New Poems* allow us to re-examine the inexhaustible work of the poet who, at the beginning of the last century, showed how powerful lyric poetry could be. By demanding that we go beyond melancholy and longing and learn to really see the things of the world, Rilke taught us to write short, intense poems that addressed largest of themes. I only regret that so few poets have followed his example. In the early twenty-first century's myopic poetry scene, it is rare to find poets (like those featured in this issue) bold enough to contemplate a call out to the hierarchies of angels.

Christopher Connelly

INTERVIEW WITH BOB HOLMAN
GRIOTS, GESTURAL POEMS, AND GIVING OFF SPARKS:
BOB HOLMAN TEACHES *PBQ* HOW TO PUT THE ENGLISH ON THE WORD

If you have paid attention to poetry at all during the last twenty years, you have probably heard of Bob Holman, who has long been the neglected art's most tireless advocate. He is the author of seven books of poetry and the editor of two anthologies, including *Aloud: Voices from the Nuyorican Poets' Café*, winner of the 1994 National Book Critics Circle Award. On his 1998 compact disc, *In with the Out Crowd*, Bob performs his poems with the support of such acclaimed musicians as former MC5 Guitarist Wayne Kramer and Bob Neuwirth. In 1998 he was commissioned to create a poem for the Frankfurt Book Festival's fiftieth anniversary, and then, with a group of fellow poets, performed "The Semicento" at a dinner for 4,000 commemorating the event. He is perhaps best known as the founding co-director for the revitalized Nuyorican Poets Café where, from 1989–1996, he served as master of ceremonies for many nights of tumultuous poetry slams. In 1996, he co-founded now defunct Mouth Almighty Records, the only poetry CD label to ever gain distribution by a major label.

Bob is also a pioneer in bringing poetry to television. In 1985, his first poetry video, "sweat'n'sex'n'politics," was introduced by Lou Reed at the Public Theater. He went on to produce more than 50 "Poetry Spots" for WNYC-TV that helped to earn the series three Emmys between 1986 and 1994. Since 1999 he has worked with Josh Blum, the President and Executive Producer of Washington Square Films and Arts, to produce the breakthrough PBS poetry video programs *Words in Your Face* and *The United States of Poetry*. Since 1997 he and Blum have been at work on *USOP*'s follow-up project, *The World of Poetry*.

In 1998, Bob was appointed visiting professor in writing at Bard College, where he teaches a course called *Exploding Text: Poetry in Performance*.

One warm afternoon this past September, I talked with Bob about griots, Panic DJ, American Sign Language poets, and Bob's long-running affair with the television camera.

[As I step out of the elevator and into Bob's office (which doubles as the front room of the Tribeca loft apartment he shares with his wife and two teenage daughters) I see him walking toward me, plucking the strings of an unusual-looking instrument.]   —CC

Painted Bride Quarterly: So what's the name of this instrument?

Holman: It's called a molo. It's from Gambia—I got it from my griot, Papa Susso, Al Haji Bunka Susso. I spent 16 hours with him yesterday. It was unbelievable. We went up to Bard to pick up his son, who I helped to bring over here. He's 15 years old. We picked him up in Poughkeepsie, where he's crashed with Papa's other son, and took him over to Bard, where I teach, and where Al Hassan gave his first American performance. He's been in the country for two weeks.

PBQ: So both the father and the son are griots?

Holman: Yeah, you know it's not necessary anymore that the griots come from the griot families—of which there are four or five, traditionally, in Western Africa. But still it's a very strong tradition to pass it on. The way that it works now is that if you come from a griot family you might become one, but at the least you have the skills—maybe you've leaned to play the kora—even if you don't become a full-fledged griot.

But at the same time, people born in other families are also becoming griots now, as art begins to take its place in a griot world and changes what had been pretty much just a functional position—there wasn't any real separation to what an artist does…you know you've got your job in the culture like everybody else. Which happens to be where I would like…what I'm trying to do.

A lot of what's happening in the U.S., you could follow the same models in Africa as well. It used to be that the griots were attached to the kings, queens, chiefs of the tribes. They no longer are, mainly because there is no such thing anymore, by and large. The countries are ruled by political governments now, and while some politicians do hire griots for various events, they work on a contractual basis now—$1000 for a praise song, or whatever the rate for that day.

So what you have is that people of the upper caste and of the ruling class, who might have become a chief before, now they become a griot, and so things are…it's really breaking down—though the kids up in my class at Bard were aghast when I told them this, because they saw it as a breakdown in the oral tradition, but, in fact, it's simply changing with the times. You know, it is just a different world, and being able to get the words out on a CD instead of a live performance changes things. And griots are not blind. They see this very well. Although, for example, the molo is still primarily used [pauses and plays a riff on the instrument's thick nylon strings] for seeing the future.

PBQ: So its notes inspire visions?

Holman: Yeah, yeah. [Still plucking strings] I try to play it as much as possible. [Stops playing and lays the molo on the table in front of me.] Anyway, I can play the kora too.

[Walks over the corner of the room and picks up a much larger instrument, its neck made from what looks like a broomstick that is stuck into a large dried-out gourd half. A piece of hide is stretched over the open front of the gourd. Its strings, like the molo's, are thick nylon strands, all of them colored bright blue.]

The kora is a much more powerful instrument. It's got twenty-one strings.

[Sits with the kora in his lap and begins playing, producing tones similar to those of a guitar, although more hollow, unsteady, and haunted sounding.]

You push these braided cow hides up and down to change the tunings. It used to be braided antelopes' skin that was used for the strings, but now you get plastic fishing line. And the cow skin is attached to the calabash with carpet tacks—thumb tacks. It's a homemade instrument. [Strikes a wobbly, slightly out-of-tune-sounding chord.]

PBQ: It's an interesting combination of the natural and industrial trash—kind of improvised. So how would you characterize what a griot does? Are they poets—sort of court poets?

Holman: I'd say that the closest thing to a griot we have would probably be a poet, in that griots are involved in the artful representation of language, although they're generally—it's more or less done with music, a few tribes no music, some tribes a musician and a griot together—the griot provides only the words, and there's a musician that accompanies him. And in most tribes there is a person who plays an instrument while also doing one of a number of other jobs. He's a genealogist, who keeps the history of the tribe, as well as the keeper of the oral traditions, which includes the epics, which are memorized, and sometimes even updated. Those are the griot's main jobs. But then there are many, many other jobs, such as composing the praise songs that I mentioned, and then there's giving advice to the chiefs, and there's settling disputes, primarily because the griots know the genealogy, so they know what people's relatives have done in similar situations—the griots just lay that on them. Also there are naming ceremonies, circumcision ceremonies, weddings—you know they do do weddings.

PBQ: And for each of these ceremonies a griot would be hired?

Holman: Exactly. It's almost as if an event can't take place unless there's a poet there to document it and participate in it. Which would be a real job for us poets in the West. It would give us a social purpose. But what they don't do is sit around and wait for the muse to come and tell them what to write about.

PBQ: They're commissioned.

Holman: Yeah, they work on commission.

PBQ: That leads me to another question. Why do you think that most Americans, most Westerners, don't believe that poets have a purpose? Especially since, some would argue, there are as many, if not more, people writing poetry than ever before. But outside of those who write it, no one reads it, or pays much attention to it.

Issue #65

Holman: Well, you know, our studies of it tend to follow poetry's lineage back to Europe and not back to Africa, and our studies only travel back as far as the book. We think of Homer as being a great writer, even though there were no books when Homer spoke the poems. So one problem is opening up the definition to poetry's oral roots and its international roots, because the United States is an international country. And the population's changing now and our education should be aware of that and change too.

There are other reasons…we have this extraordinary Bill of Rights that gives us freedom of speech—but it's not worth so much if you can't be heard. And while people have been able to write what they want to, I think that the people in power have been unwilling to let the crazies have a chance to be heard—the poet on the street corner, the poet of a village or town. Was the town crier a poet? You know, you could see how this person—it's hard to find the news in poetry, but not if there's a town crier out there shouting out, you know, about what happened in Concord last night…trying to get that shot to make it all the way around the world.

I think that poets have also bought into the definition of being off on the sidelines, you know, as a safe place to be and a place…where you can make a living now, as a poet, is by teaching poetry, and so there you are. It makes sense that poets would gravitate to a place where they can write. Now, though, those definitions are being challenged. I think that's happening at the same time that the definition of a poem is being—is up for grabs—and that the media that present poetry has also gone through such extraordinary changes.

PBQ: Was that part of the inspiration behind first *The United States of Poetry* and now *The World of Poetry*—to let the town criers of the world be heard by taking advantage of new media?

Holman: [Laughing] You're good. Let me interview you! You didn't need me for this. Well you know the story is that in the early 80s—coming out of the commune and all, I knew that television was the enemy of poetry… was killing poetry. I created a character called "Panic DJ" who urged everyone to throw their televisions out the window, though he did say it would be helpful if you were on the television that you were throwing out the window.

But that was sort of a dream until I was approached by a TV producer, Danny O'Neal, at WNYC, who wanted to film poets in their kitchens, and he asked would I help him make contact with poets so he could get into their kitchens, and it took me about two seconds to sell out. I realized that I was giving my readings at St. Mark's Poetry Project and other places to the same 30 people, and they were the world's greatest listeners. Every year I read I had to read new poems, and I'd have to read 45 minutes worth so you could get your two dollars' worth.

Then I saw how you could reach, really reach, a mass audience, and the purpose is more to turn on people to what poetry is than to present them with any standardized message. There's plenty of content in poetry, and that's why the Internet and cable stations love us, up to a point. But the idea is for everybody to use their voice. To jump out to what an art can do for your own life, and to say it, and to not have to follow anybody else's lead.

PBQ: And at that point—I think you've told me this story before—you met Josh Blum, right?

Holman: Yeah. Well, you know, I got involved in the re-opening of the Nuyorican Poet's Café, and it took off like a rocket—it was just that moment when multi-culti was starting to step into the news and here was a multi-culti scene based on an art heretofore moribund, where the artists themselves, and not their handlers, were making it happen. It was young and it was angry, and it was loud, and it was funny, and it had the full ironies of the poetry slam as an engine. So one of the things that happened is Josh Blum walked in the door and came up to me and said, "Hey, this oughta be on television," and we've worked together now for ten years, and done a bunch of TV work.

And now we're in the process of buying a building together, which will then become the home of a poetry club, as well as a home for Washington Square Films and Arts. It'll be a nice place for poets from around the world to read, and hang out, and not have to always be in United Nation's tea parties—to find their American audience.

PBQ: And you'll put on a program of readings?

Holman: The idea would be…to have it be a business—how can the club (which I'll be in charge of) pay for itself with poetry as a centerpiece? How can it retain the spontaneity that is at the core of what poetry can do best, while it goes through the seemingly inevitable institutionalization process. In other words, if a guy just drops by, which everybody does in New York, at one time or another, there's got to be space for them to read at the Bowery Poetry Club.

[The phone on the desk rings for the first of a several times during the course of the interview, and Bob excuses himself to answer it. After a conversation about setting up some kind of poetry slam, Bob hangs up and rolls his chair back over the table, snatching yet another instrument from his desk on the way over. He settles back in next to me and begins playing a sort of miniature version of the kora he had played earlier.]

PBQ: So what's this instrument?

Holman: It's called a continu. It's got four strings. [Repeatedly picks out a bluesy-sounding riff that culminates in a twangingly dissonant "plonk."]

PBQ: Those fishing line strings and the cowhide sounding board really make an

Issue #65

unusual sound.

Holman: Yeah, you can really see how the banjo came out of these things. Even the way the strings are.

[Holds the continu up to his eye and peers through the steep arch made by strings above the body of the instrument.]

PBQ: So to get back to poetry, at the beginning of the 20th century, poets like T.S. Eliot, Ezra Pound, and Wallace Stevens became interested in European poetry because they believed that American and English poetry was bogged down in the Victorian era. Did you have a similar sense when you started working on *The World of Poetry*—that American poetry needed revitalization?

Holman: Again my work just follows from the type of poetry that I do and that I love. As long as you're gonna do a reading, why not bring all your faculties—whatever you do—to it. I've never been intimidated by language—it's always seemed to me to be a functional love machine. It really just goes out there and grabs people. So you want to put the English on the word as much as you can. So, wherever that led me—it goes to the conversational poetics of Frank O'Hara, it goes to the body-as-poem of the Dadaists, and it certainly goes to the utilization of music and melody with poetry that comes from Sappho, and from the griots, and hip-hop.

It's also to do with the belief in the power that language can have, if you give in to it. A poet like Alice Notley who…this semester at Bard I'm teaching the epic, as envisioned by the griots and by Alice Notley in her book *The Mysteries of Small Houses*, which is a poetry autobiography and the opposite of what the griots do. It's very personal, and yet the power of language is there, for me, every bit as much as in hearing Papa Susso in a class performance. My students, thank God, disagree with me. They'll go one way or the other, but they refuse to go both, which is the way it ought to be.

PBQ: So Alice Notley's book is kind of a personal epic?

Holman: Well, yeah. It's huge and personal. So the first assignment for my students was to write an epic of their life. And they came in saying "Gee, this was a hard assignment. We had to do it in a week." To write an epic in a week is not the easiest thing to do—so I gave 'em another week. [Laughs.]

PBQ: And that was enough? It took nearly four hundred years for the ancient Greeks to get down the *The Iliad*.

Holman: Well, you know, I hauled out the Fagles translations for Papa Susso [reaches up to one of his bookshelves and pulls down hardcover editions of *The Iliad* and *The Odyssey*] and said, "Here's our epic. *The Odyssey*, for example here is [pauses to flip to the final pages of *The Odyssey*] fiiiive hundred, and ah, thirty-five . . . and forty-one pages long, including footnotes."

I said, "How long is your longest epic," and he said, "Long!" [Laughs] And I said, "Yeah, but how long?" He thought for a second and said, "Two days." [Both laughing] O, ho, ho! Wow! Yeah! Well, how long do you think it would take Homer to do it—*The Iliad*, *The Odyssey*, the whole thing. It might take a few days. It's just the way you think about it. We think of books, or poems, in terms of pages—Papa Susso thinks of his work in terms of time.

I asked him yesterday if he would do, in class—I've heard the great traditional songs he does—jeliya is one, and Ala-Lake is another—he's teaching me these songs. I said, "Why don't you do the genealogy of the Sisko tribe here?" He says, "Not in the classroom." I said, "What's the deal?" and he said, "It doesn't go here. I'm not gonna do it." Which is great. He said, "You can come to the Gambia and I'll definitely do the genealogy of the Sisko tribe. I do it a lot there."

PBQ: "The Gambia"?

Holman: That's the country Papa Susso's comes from. One of the smallest countries in the world. It's just a little finger around the River Gambia, right in the middle of Senegal. It's the craziest country—they're completely surrounded by Senegal, and then the Atlantic Ocean, and West Africa. A teeny, tiny country, but what a concentration of arts. About a million, 1.2 million people—that's it—and of course they speak eight languages there.

PBQ: Eight languages!

Holman: [With mock disapproval] Of which Papa Susso can only speak seven.

PBQ: That's amazing. But are most of the griot songs that he does in one particular language?

Holman: He does them in the language of his people, the Mandinke, but there are versions of the bigger pieces, like the Sundiata epic, the Askia Mohammed epic, in other languages. But they have basically the same form. But there are some pieces that are simply available in a single language. And Papa Susso does not perform in any other language than Mandinke, because they are his people. He even likes it if you call him a jali, which is the Mandinke word for griot. The world "griot" itself does not belong to any single tribe. It's simply a pan-African word—some people say French, but that's really in dispute—for that position in any tribe. It's kind of a generic word, and some people take umbrage at the use of the word "griot," but the griots I've met have not taken umbrage. So I use the word *griot*—apologies to those who...you know.

PBQ: You've done a lot with poetry written in other languages and poetry written on the margins of American culture—when was the first time poetry written in some other language, or from some other country, really caught your attention?

Holman: Well, I can remember very clearly the first time my brain exploded over this idea. I was doing a gig at Rochester for Writers and Books, they called it the "Bridge Festival," and American Sign Language poets were performing on the same bill as hearing poets, and the poems were being translated into these other languages. It was the first time when I was really able to work with my signer—at this time I was doing the Panic DJ show and wearing this crazy jacket with question marks all over it. Well, I brought a jacket for my signer, and I taught him some steps, and he was signing along with me and moving along with me—it was a great little vaudeville turn.

In fact, it was that night that I was talking with Peter Cook and Kenny Lerner, who make up this group called "Flying Words"—Peter was in *The United States of Poetry*, the last poet filmed for the show. And we were talking...I was blown away by these guys' work, you know—how word as gesture, word as sound, how Peter's soundings, how Kenny's translations were of a poetic variety rather than as an interlinear. How Lerner was able to build on Cook's gesture—the drama that was going on in front of you, visually—and drop in sound cues that were more than a translation of the gesture into some kind of English equivalent.

PBQ: So what were the translations from?

Holman: ASL [American Sign Language]. In this case, Kenny is a hearing poet and Peter is a deaf poet, and they would collaborate, or as they say, "barter" poems together. Peter would perform them in sign, and he is an extremely gifted poet of sign, and then Kenny would be the soundtrack, which would translate the—it's more like a soundtrack than it is a translation. So that's the way that they worked, and I just thought it was the most—they still stand out in my mind as just...what do they call it...a meme—is that what they call the smallest element of information? Or maybe it's the opposite of a meme—maybe they're the biggest element, you know a dyno, or whatever it is. It was blowin' my mind that here was a poem that I was watching that couldn't be in a book. It had to be performed for you to read it.

So that night at the poetry bash, over the poetry beers, I was talking directly to Peter with Kenny in the middle translating for me, although Peter is very adept at lip reading—we were doing pretty good working with or without Kenny. I was saying, "You know, your act is so good you oughta take it on the road and do it on the performance art circuit," because at that time—the mid-eighties—performance art was the hot ticket, and there was a whole network that you could get on to do that. And what they were doing could be seen as performance art, or theater, or poetry. And Peter said to me, "What are you talking about? You can't do that." And I said, "Why not?" and he said, "Because we're poets."

International

So here I am out there espousing what poetry is about and should be, and here's a guy who's coming back to me and saying, you know, "Fuck you. I can't get on the performance art circuit. I'm a poet, man." And then it just drove home to me, how it's the poets ourselves who keep redefining what poetry is, and it just sold me again on other languages being the key to acknowledging where the poet is in a culture. By growing up in U.S. poetics we always see a poem in a certain way, and the reason why the poem is not effective here is because we don't see these other ways, and once we do—it's not like we gotta make it up, other cultures have different ways of seeing a poem, and if we follow those leads we can get light to the poem.

PBQ: There are people who say that a poem can't be translated. I would guess that you're not a person who believes this.

Holman: Oh, yeah. I'm in for use, but I understand the idea—one of my good buddies, Ed Foster, at Talisman [Press], believes that the poem exists only on the piece of paper the poet wrote it on, made the corrections on, and that is the poem—you've got to see the process through, not watch it be fancified onto 24-weight paper with embossed typeface. Well, you know, he's just as loony as I am. And any course in between is fine with me, too. Which is why I can say that I think that what you see in *The United States of Poetry* are poems, not video poems, no more than you'd say "book poem" or "page poem"—although you've got to call it a "video poem" now or people look at you like you forgot to say "video." It's about getting the director and the poet to collaborate on an image track that is going to illuminate the poem in this other medium. Why do you want to do that? Because it's there. Because people are at home watching television, because…I think the collaboration on poems helps to open them up to other hearings—and that's a good thing in my opinion. And for poets ourselves, it opens us up to other possibilities for language.

PBQ: What would you say to critics who claim that poems written with a mind to performance sometimes lack the complexity and depth—I mean, have you seen any performance poem "Wastelands," or is it not really fair to compare?

Holman: Oh, I definitely think there are performance poem "Wastelands." I think Patricia Smith has written a bunch of performance poem "Wastelands." I think that the Dallas Slam Team [the poetry slam team, coached by Holman, that represented New York City at the National Poetry Slam championships held in Dallas in 1997] did a poem called "Superhero Poet, Baby" that is a performance "Wasteland."

But I also think that the statement that when writing performance poems you don't get…that you won't go for the depth you do for a text poem, is true. Because I don't think that you write performance poems—you write poems, and later on people tell you what they are. I don't know how many poets see words on paper, or see words inscribed in the air, or see, as Hannah Weiner did, words inscribed on peoples' foreheads, and then write them down. For me, in general, I hear the words. The word is in my mind, but not the text of the word. It comes to mind, and then I write it down and it becomes a text.

Every poem is a performance poem…to teach performance poetry you should always use poems that are impossible to perform—you should use John Ashbery. I teach Alice Notley because in order to perform a poem well you have to…a true performance is simply a close reading physicalized. A poem gives off sparks in every direction, and some of those directions are into the public eye. And if you follow those sparks—which are coming from you, just as when you read a poem you are writing the poem—the old postmodern saw—so when you perform a poem you're bringing to light—sparking—those aspects that your physicalizations can make of the poem. And the American Sign Language poets, again, are the people that most show that—the poem only exists in the performance because it is in a language that does not have sounds and texts as components. It's a gestural language.

[The phone rings again and Bob slides over to answer. He begins another conversation about the poetry slam. Thinking I've recorded enough and unsure whether he'll finish his call before I have to return to work, I gather my notes to leave. As I'm about to stand up Bob hangs up and begins to talk to me about something called "Poetry SlamJam 2000," a poetry "Olympiad marathon" that will be held at Elizabeth Irwin High School in Manhattan.]

…which I think is such a great setting because slams should be for kids. It's when you've got so much hormones that poetry just has to break out, like pimples. And I really think that if there were poetry slam leagues—if you could letter in poetry— you could begin making a case for poets getting as much money as the athletes get. You could get poetry books and computers and teachers, you could get coaches and all that stuff. Poetry SlamJam 2000 will have a youth slam, a college slam, a pull-down sellout, which is where if you like a poem you have to put money in a bucket to vote—put your money where your mouth is! And the winner is the guy who gets the most money. And the prize is that you get the money!

PBQ: That may be the only time in history when it is the best poet who gets paid.

Holman: Well, it's not the best poet—boy, that's for sure! The best poet always loses! We all know that! But what will be great is that you'll get the absolute dollar value of a poem. That's October 28th if any of your readers are in the neighborhood. I should say that's the year 2000, by the way. This interview will probably come out in 2002. [Laughs.]

[I explain to Bob that PBQ is now a webzine, and reassure him that it actually will be published quarterly and will be out by 2001.]

Holman: Let me tell you what happened with Papa Susso when I said we could make a lot of money if he would just do an epic in English—he really can speak great English. It's the language of the Gambia, the official language. So he does the epic, and I write it down, make it into a poem, and then we'd make a lot of money. And he said that was a "terrible idea." So I said, "How about this for an idea. You just go ahead and sing in Mandinke and I'll write down what I think you're saying, and then I'll perform it back with you, with the both of us performing—you doing what you normally do, and I'll read what I think you're saying, and that'll be our performance." And he said "That sounds good." That's what we came up with—so far we've done one. [Laughs.]

PBQ: We read and watched and listened to a lot of poets when we were research-ing for *The World of Poetry*, and I'm sure you've seen a lot more since then. What's some of the most exciting work you've come across?

Holman: I still think that the work we did at that reading series [the "World of Poetry Reading Series," which ran the fall of 1997 through the winter of 1999 at venues throughout New York City], which was done by our bootstraps and off the cuff, was so exciting for small audiences. Getting to know [Cambodian poet and sur-vivor of the Khmer Rouge's killing fields] U Sam Oeur, getting behind those poems with him—now he's an American but he's from Cambodia—all these things break down. Also Cecilia [Vicuña, Chilean poet, performer, filmmaker, and visual artist]. I still think Cecilia's entry into *The World of Poetry* database shows how creative one can be while working with the web and poetry. And she is—as the ASL poets are to poetry—one whose work can't be unraveled until you can follow the hyperlinks.

And as long as we're on those guys, I want to mention Frank Lima, who is a U.S. poet—getting to know Frank helped set up the cover story for *Poets and Writers* mag-azine last month. I sort of put together this new form of investigative poetics, based on Ed Sander's work, where I took interviews with him and I laid them out—laid each little thread as a poem, and then made the through-line to put it together. I'm very happy with it.

But you know, going to Eritrea and meeting the African poets really opened my eyes.

PBQ: Was this connected with Charles Cantalupo [poet, professor at Penn State University, and translator of African poetry]?

Holman: Yeah, it was Charles Cantalupo's thing. And I met poets from all over Africa—poets and academics—and really got to the roots of one of the goals of *The World of Poetry*, which is to document and preserve endangered languages. And to watch the languages being pulled back from the brink, like what's happening in Eritrea, where there are nine languages—for three and a half million people—and every single language is the basis of a school where kids can go learn in their native tongues—until sixth grade, when everything switches to English. But it does get you started.

PBQ: And what about his conference [a pan-African gathering of poets and critics in Asmara, Eritrea called "Against All Odds: African Languages and Literature into the 21st Century" that Cantalupo co-chaired]?

Holman: That's where I went. That's where I met Papa Susso. That's where I met Thomas Hale, who wrote the world's greatest book on griots. This is the book, which I'm teaching this year, if you want a way in to the world of the griots.

PBQ: I'd wondered if the conference was actually going to come off, because of the war between Ethiopia and Eritrea.

Holman: There was a war at the time, but we luckily hit a moment when it wasn't hot. But a month later it got hot and people I knew were displaced and…it's just the saddest story.

Afterward, I went across the Red Sea, and then into Yemen where I hung out with the poet laureate, with whom I went to "chews." The way their social calendar works is not through cocktail parties—because it's a Muslim country—but through "chews," because people chew khat. It's this mild amphetamine-like leaf…

[Bob's phone rings yet again. As he begins his third conversation of the day about "SlamJam 2000," calling out a list of poets for the person at the other end of the line to get in touch with, I wave goodbye and leave.]

International

Bob Holman

How Kora Was Born
as sung by Papa Susso to Bob Holman

This story begins long long long long ago
So long ago that it was a place not a time
There was a man
He was so alone
The only person he could talk to was Africa
Luckily there was a tree nearby
Even more luckily behind that tree
That's where his partner was hiding
All the sun and all the water were condensed
Into a single tiny block
Which the man planted in the sandy soil
He blew and he blew on that spot
Each time he blew he thought he heard something
What he was hearing was of course his partner singing
The man didn't even know what singing was
Because he could only talk
He couldn't sing yet
So he blew and he listened, blew listened blew listened
And the plant pushed out dark green
And began to twist and grow
A vine reaching for the breath
And stretching towards the song
(Because it was made from sun and rain, remember?)
So at the end of the vine that was the calabash
And the tree it was not a tree anymore
It was the neck and handles
That was when the man's partner Saba Kidane
Came out into the open (but that's another story)
And the breath and the music and the vine?
Well, there are 21 strings, what do you think?
And now you say what about the bridge and the cowhide
And the rings that tie the strings to the neck
So you can tune the kora
Hey, what about the thumbtacks that hold
The cowhide taut over the calabash
And the resonator hole
Well you go right on talking about all that
I'm playing kora now
Next time I'll tell you about the cow

On Changing the Past
for Abdel Aziz al-Maqaleh

Through the mandhara of your eyes,
                    dear Poet
I see each second of eternity pass, frame-
                        by-frame, over Sana'a
A Shadow constantly seeking its Object

Through the mandhara of your eyes,
                    dear Poet
I see the slow making of a City,
                    the slow making of a life

Here in the dust cloud
                we call Life
Figures call from corners
"Turn this way!
                Turn that way!"
Turning the ground
                into the dust
We sift for memories

Through the mandhara of your eyes,
                    dear Poet
The revolving figures freeze mid-
                dance, one leg off the ground

This is the Past
You are six years old
The name of the City is "Wonder"

You can return here if you wish,
                    dear Poet
You can start the dancers up again,
                join them,
Leave us to watch you

Through the mandhara of your eyes,
                    dear Poet
Through your six year-old's eyes,
                we see Sana'a rise

A City slowly lifting, rising

                      not to the sky
But to the word "sky"

Not beautiful but flashing
                   like desert lightning
The word "beautiful"

We see the Past through the mandhara
                 of your eyes, dear Poet

Its name was "Sana'a"
Its name is "Sana'a"
The name of the poem,
                   "Sana'a"

GRIOT

1
someone does something
someone else tells about it

2
someone has a purpose
someone else draws attention to it

3
someone preaches
someone else rousts the crowd

4
someone does
someone tells

5
someone leads
someone tells the leader
everyone else follows the leader

6
the teller does not lead
the teller does not follow the leader

7
I was very excited when my children started middle
school, their first assignment: trace their family tree
they had to talk to their relatives and get dates, chart
the families with dotted lines and symbols, arranging
history, adding footnotes and maps of farflung places

in The Gambia, the griot Sulea Susso (Elhaji Papa
Bunka Hassan) tells the genealogy of his tribe, his
audience, listening, back a thousand years' births
sung to the linking kora ears recording the words

8
in the USA, if you name a child
after yourself or your parent
they get to be "Jr" or "III"

in The Gambia, if you name a child
after yourself or your parent

other people can use that name
but you must call that child "papa" or "mama"
to show the respect due to the person
you named the child "after"

9
Mohammed always gave it all away
but he gave the griot the largest share
because if the griot did not gather the crowd
there would be no crowd
there would be nothing to give away

10
the only way to make a poem
is to tell what happened
what is happening now

11
the moment is the poem

12
the kora leads and the voice tells

13
the detail is the poem
he wears a gold bracelet every Thursday after he sleeps
with his second wife, gold bracelet that reflects
the empty spot where his eye-tooth was before his
first wife knocked it out

14
see the girl with the red dress on
I am in love with the woman next to her
that is my wife, my marriage, my life
mother of my children, she knows me better
than she knows herself, I know her better
than she does. And there is no competition
spent all those years looking at her looking
at me

15
the job of the griot is a job
no need to wait for/on the inspiring muse
right in front of you
red dress on

Issue #65

Katrine Marie Guldager

CRASH

It happens, of course, that you get a flat, that you will have to
get by with one that's too high: You cannot reach the pedals
and there are cars and crosswalks and rights of way: There's
asphalt and strange inklings in your hands, accidents hanging
in the wind, like seconds painted over with a total, total hush:
There's a scraping and asphalt, asphalt the bike rams against,
asphalt you plough your way through, small stones you hide
under your skin, and glass, and there's no way around it, or
getting down to it: There's only asphalt on top of asphalt,
there's a city on top of asphalt, and there's nothing underneath
it but earth: There's earth and asphalt and a city: There's a city
on top of the earth: There's a city on a city, there's asphalt on
top of asphalt, earth above earth, and there's no way getting
down to it, or around it, that's how it's always been: As when
you ride a bike, too high up, and you can't reach the pedals.

RED

That's what it's like to be born: You never get a day off, you never have one minute to yourself, not a second where you can look the other way, or one where you can turn your back: That's what it's like to be born, there's nothing you can do about it, the whole time you're just born, you can't quit, get off, be born again: There's nothing to be done about it, you are born, born in fluttering red, in a cry that remains in the body like an echo, and sleep, sleep doesn't make a difference, it can just be replaced by something else that fits right in where sleep was, there it is, it's there the whole time, the whole thing, yourself.

Issue #65

Traffic Accident

It's hard to tell if there *is* something outside the window, but a chronic curiosity forces you to draw in, wind, people. It's hard to tell how it happens, but you lean back in, into the shadow, and all senses are suddenly on DELETE: Suddenly you can't remember why you leaned out or in, or whatever you wanted, you feel most of all like 17 kitchen appliances not bought nor paid for, like a worn-out sack from Woolworth's you've put away and later forgotten: It's hard to tell how you do it, how you find your way back in, between everything you can't revive, yourself, the kitchen table, and a single traffic accident you hide under your chest.

EARTH

I don't know what I came here for, only that everything else was impossible, that the little No I'm now holding up in front of me is just a sorry shield against an abundance of milky stars, a slip of meaning: Only that my little cardboard sign is just a hint of what is unused and shiny and drawn through this morning completely untouched: I don't know what I came here for, only that a dream slowly moves into position and starts dreaming itself without any other aim than to let itself be repeated as a possibility: A dictionary that wants its pages torn out, blind earth that wants steps to vibrate below:

translations by Anna Mette Lundtofte

Nora Iuga

FROM CAPRICCIOS

13.

then the phone rang
a white horse appeared
and ate from my palm
my hand crossed the red sea
it reached the promised land
stone by stone my way is clear
stone by stone my flesh becomes thinner
there was a character who came out of nowhere
the very mouth of my beloved
today I crushed a hard black beetle
that looked so much
like Else Lasker-Schüler

Else Lasker-Schüler (1869-1945): German-Jewish poet, short story writer, playwright, and novelist of the early twentieth century. Her poems exploit a rich vein of fantasy and symbolism and alternate between pathos and ecstasy in their intensely personal evocation of her childhood and parents, romantic passion, art, religion, and other themes.

International

AU RELANTI

yes in a seductive jungle
I too would have liked to encounter the tiger
with a flower in its muzzle
yes I too would have liked
beneath the scourge of words
thoroughly confused and falsified
to find someone waving at me
from the crowd of skirts and soldiers

there are compressed spaces on maps
there are big houses with ominous windows like masks
there are old phonographs with horns that can swallow kilometers of silence
and I begin to detect violin bows cutting the way
for the minor failure that deliberately tries
                                        to die *au relanti*

hey you gellu naum shouted at me you buried woman
then he shoved a handful of leaves down my throat
what a green agony just imagine
                                what a green agony

—*translations by Adam J. Sorkin with Ioana Ieronim*

Issue #65

Eugen Jebeleanu

PATIENCE

No, the dead aren't getting bored.
Far away they are waiting for me to reach them.
And waiting, they leaf through a book
with wet pages—and they smile at me.

Eugen Jebeleanu

VENUS XX

Her teeth had all fallen out. She was still beautiful.
She had hips made of gulfs, and she swayed bluely.
She was entirely guiltless. She was walking straight ahead.
And she told me that she still had one more tooth.
She was so hot to the touch, so ardent.
I said, "At last a goddess who won't tell me lies!"

DON'T

No, don't enjoy
this life too much, this tumult
which makes you imagine
it's not the same thing as sand.
Don't imagine ...
because it's like this.
From flames she makes ash.
From ash, wind.
And from what's made from wind
she makes a room without walls,
without words.

—translations by Matthew Zapruder and Radu Ioanid

International

Yang Lian

Notes of a Blissful Ghost

1

leaking from the eye-socket   dog dragging half-stripped dog skin
     running   vision competes with stove-stuffed sparrow
flying

snow's touch always half-rotted
tumbledown ruins mask yesterday
painted   a colour less than white
horizon sprints back against the wind toward a drop of water

a teardrop has a pear-stalk   to lead a great hue and cry

bliss bliss

2

winter is home ground   bright shining cat
with one jump   squats on a child's face
claws sky-blue as a place-name
every plum flower hanging in mid-air, stepping on the place-name of coldness

screws tight the child's lungs
an ancient tree twisted into an afternoon's reality
a large jade in the mouth
voice   says nothing
and secretes the worst of all news for mothers
we are only reborn when sunlight is soiled

3

the road to the village wakes under rubble   adobe wall
delicate and lovely   as a girl observed

tongue-tip tastes of salt
is the ice her?   her back still to the window

both hands shield the centre   a ghost story gone in one gulp
     exposing growth   in wind-written confessions

the now endlessly collapses   an interior in the western hills

Issue #65

a piece of jasper hovering round zero
turn salt to fragrance   out blow wisps of the last life she never had
scarlet finger still familiar with crossing the boundary below the ice

crossing over   a millennium fabricated by hurting
who is too shy to be the detail of her fantasies?

4

the world is not afraid to go back to the past it knows so well
there crows scrape at the earth   the dead rinse out
a necessary face on an old photograph
last night tied in the doorway   rubbing worn brick
the fox just leaving a swathe of grass
suddenly called to a halt by a voice from the bed
aspens are not afraid to go back   to tower over rooftops reflecting light
the expandable well filled with twenty years of age that never stop
still not enough to invent an untried kiss
four knees colliding   inside the empty shell of love
the stars have just got here a lifetime late
the owl giggles at human laughter
loan out the moonlight   to miss this moment is bliss

5

ruins deny murder

the past has nothing to do with time

blood asks no questions

insomnia is not parallel to the sky

non-existent public geography

living with no strength to live

light years have never gushed from a blind spot

avalanches cannot move away

perfect non-direction

6

a taxi floats up like a fire-red submarine
collage in a forgotten margin

Issue #65

confronting alone a khaki storm

we have forgotten   the terrifying depth of waters inside us
a tone that speaks of the past
as if we had never crossed those seas

7
I have accepted any place
in a corner of this village   there is snow
the snow has small crystal balconies
and towers   twilight sniffs the station
a daughter studding the glass with stars
tree monsters posting up night outside   water
locking the door tight   destination infinite black
enchanting as the womb mother once used

that gives birth to a big bird in a down coat
flapping   space destroyed by the sound of melting snow
soaking an ear   hearing the sinking

8
a street slides slanting down toward a pear tree in full blossom

the past   gives the fire hose a hard squeeze

spitting   the white of flesh and skeletons

spring is a foreign language
grammar of perfume   carved and polished with precision
light   stirring the little pale black eddies behind every petal

call elapsed emptiness   the now
immature craftsmanship inlaying the blue
time's jeweller bows down   filing
february   so sweet to the ear, the sound made by cutting metal
reflecting the crowd soaking the beach with ink marks

street hanging inverted in the eyeball
is buried under its own foundation

greeting
spat out   sweet   sludge

9

two adobe walls sum up time differences in all the world

eyes can't slip away   even though looking is a sin

tumbledown ruins unhurriedly decaying
from a cemetery made of clouds
plum blossom   from a thought about disappearing

the pen's old cap that was lost   and our beautiful sex
recognizing that here happiness has walked out of the frame
taken as focus   summing up the light that all the world can't see
in the still life of death there is no yesterday
just like   there is no today

10

only when it disdains to endorse any truth
does happiness accumulate lies

11

there are no homeless ghosts.

home is what is homeless: a few steps away from where I stand, and I will have been separated. ditches criss-crossed. unlatched dry grass, man-high in summer, now concealing pitfalls. concrete blocks, reinforcing bars, old electric cables, indistinctly bare teeth. bricks, heaps here and there, smoke-blackened, revealing themselves as dismantled brick beds and stoves. a small animal has left tracks on the slush. wind blowing as always, paper window no longer trembling, no longer crackling. newspaper-pasted ceiling rustles, the rat with its little black shining eyes staring down, never expecting to be remembered by someone, is rolled up and gone, along with the house, the village and yesterday. a few steps away, and no-one can reach the world whose existence no one has ever proved.

huge adobe walls, filled-in ponds, the suddenly-recognised shape of a willow, has invented someone's pictography. yellow earth, to expose is to cover up, covering up with exposure. disappearance piles up, layer on layer. illusion of home, emptier than emptiness. I stand here, fewer than nobody. frontier of breath, the line of a broken fence resisting nothing, only showing how the living ruins of the past flood out to rush on me and then push past me. What is homeless, is what endlessly falls into the eye socket: a stretch of solidly-real, formed, destructive, nothingness.

inflamed red moon of mid-autumn festival, stuck between kissing lips, will we still be watching when a *blissful ghost's handbook* vomits us out everywhere?

International

12

in the tower is river too   flowing pitch-black upwards
sky   a stock of freezing fate
forcing two fish to answer a constellation
to look is to be hooked   a silver hook piercing flesh

like useless beauty   on the body's riverbank
is a faint path   and China's landscapes waiting in the woods

old bridge half its arch left
leaps into lies   fish pulling in yet more far-off water

to live is to be fated   simulating the madness of building the tower
secret pitch-black torrential force
flinging convicts   swimming all fish-scaled in
locked-up origin

13

three is the number of doom
three years   borrow someone's image to dissolve
her   those hers who far away walked over the ditch

shimmering and changing   light closes in on curses
lifelike white shadow fills in the walking silhouette
three summers' winds paint the room again
when so many tons of green are scrapped

in water those organs are empty
still not in time to practise lechery

and are no more   blood group's combination lock has been changed
three times   string music never again able to tear away pain
so far and no further   three counting infinity
kidnaps this poem   a whisper flying over the world in search of a far-off ear

take aim   at the next stupid cycle

14

detested place   help me imagine
a dotted line of life   stars come in one by one
assigning degrees of latitude to the window
for old age   punctually performing the darkness after the lamp is out
the aurora flickers   on the screen patterning beauties

Issue #65

spreading wings   exhibiting tightly nailed iron bars
unable to leave the place I hate
til I have bitten the bitter almond of fate

15
smelling
in the scarves of the dead is a smell not taken away
smell   suddenly remember days that were lived

the material in the smell is greasier and blacker
this is your air
tonight   the dead present you with flowers

floating all through the room two hands that can embrace
nose buried in buds woven by the grave
lungs like another blood-congested womb

warm knife-edge carves into your throat
distance deeply breathing   the fatally lingering fragrance of coma
let cheating chemistry go on cheating for a while

16
smelling
the only two words in the past   pain   or forgetting
when the dead escape from a scarf

the world disperses more easily than a smell
dream like a piece of silverware   feminine black rose curling
but without smell   you are kept outside of dreams

this tiny corner   by the rank stink of patterned wool
pushed   if you smell pain you still haven't forgotten
the dead go on climbing the stairs   watching the clock   playing the flute

half wanting you half arranging the next dying
smell gouges into cracks in bone   like rheumatism violently coming to
this is a now too strange for anyone

17
concrete's chords have filled up march
march seen from winter   ghost
components prefabricated elsewhere

International

Issue #65

arrive after a thousand-year shipping
swallows search for secrets at the village end
zero   violently scans the world

among broken walls some element is agitating   pouring
changeable landforms rehearse a password
turn to collective grey again   spring trims heartbeats
cubic moonlight glues the chorus together

in march's elegies   swallows drag lethal weapon-like phosphorescence

field mice endlessly digging a tunnel
inquiring about a season sealed in a flagstone
family photos decided   shifted to the negatives

18

poem which blindly takes what's passed as the theme
blankly climbing a concrete ladder
her toenail growing upwards a half oyster-shell
his anklebone   like a fish leaping in flashback
dragging the legs of an old slow-running film
sex projects a blaze on to the boulevard
she meekly sharpens her two-edged knife
he tastes the sweetness of cutting the corn
when the waist is tangled cloud penetrates cloud
night brimming with radio waves   whistles up the spine
between silvery aerials thunders the clink of glasses
caress a fabulous crashing   heart jumps in halfway through the incident
portrait at twenty smaller as it shrinks
earlobe exquisite   and nibbled for fun
ecstasy reveals pointed snake-tongues in tips of hair
overlooking   she has all along led a dog's barking
his cat holds its own innate wildness in its mouth
leaping down from the wall of history
a poem has no theme
because   no-one has passed by

19

your pillow is up against a cornfield
your dreams   burgeon in the sky
eyes closed sleepwalking snow   loses its way once
lost on the parquet floor of the concrete mansion

campfire   from memory's cave mouth
scatters the sky with ten million glittering keys

wild child's laughter swoops in the window
twine of time tying up your tinnitus
swinging back   empty space is never empty
just as a whistle   beyond a concrete wall
wakes you with a start too   in moonlight a sharpened sickle
is scything the roots of your sleep

20

crushed by the unending internal dialogue
ghosts understood
the park is where the dead can post-mortem wander

babies   use black boughs to burst out wailing
birds slowly hurl grenades toward you

flowers falling all around like wild pigeons
purples and whites all torn off their feathers
dried parasol-tree fruit hangs sexily in last year
old dogs pant slower and slower
green   hides at the horizon like a terrorist
talking to himself   controlling a huge timed detonation

no-one can destroy life   unless you yourself
destroyed   and joined the cold of the park   at springtime

21

thinking there is a past in past tense   just like
a madman is convinced there is a world in the eye
herds of cows through the snow-bright crystal lens
watch our sphere   grasslands   war   neighbours
a night just dispersed   pumps wetness from puddles
thinking butchery can still be restored as a style

thinking a stripped cow skin is still a cow
boots grinding the essence golden and soft
we put them on   convinced we've invented blood once again
verbs change and the sound of flowing begins
flowing into   the crystal dice behind the tongue spinning nothingness
madness begins from the instant we use substitutes to speak

Issue #65

22

bliss in the ruins   comes from old age
broken teeth left in the dark behind you
hearing the wind free-associating more rampantly still
the more day is dismantled   the more night gives you the chance
to bind a richer lie

23

flesh extends to the remotest corner of the village
spring incinerated   ulcerated   caved-in   is fixed up all new

doomsday like a geography lesson
the landscape everyone opens   only yourself can see

snow drifts commemoratively   rubble quietly incubating
a tourist map   leaves open blind eyes wide to search

in ghost reality rows of bouquets light firecrackers along the street
the living remember   magnolias raising their goblets toward the sky

skin the plastic bag used for all time to hold blood
wears out   dances in air   drapes the bushes

snick-snack of scissors   ungrudged footsteps
peel with great care
a teardrop is never short of dead birds' origins

24

the handbook has deleted the hand   names of the dead
leave behind a code for the red phone book
outside the window   the hardworking horizon has been decoding all along
to conjecture an ending is too extravagant
water is a room   the poet's shining metamorphosed waves
don't flow   enduring a colour less than the white of a line of poetry
to change an urn on the table is too extravagant
light   carves and polishes with precision in the sky each month
blood from inside a girl's foxy waist
shoots out   flowers are all like witches
the ghost settles down in place names oblivious to the world coming and going
on everyone's map everyone is the rainy season
wall is too extravagant   knowledge that corrodes
makes the bones in the bath eternally swelter

comb of syllables   has combed across the golden pubic hair of the lawn
    three hundred and sixty degrees of ruin on the dial
    affirm   death has no different language
    the poet has nowhere to return
    wild old beauty is the only beauty we know
time is spent   but the smell of blood in a line of poetry is far from enough
    deepening a storm that cannot pass
    reiterate this night   *ghost's first night of bliss*

translation by Brian Holton

IN THE TIMELESS AIR:
CHINESE LANGUAGE, POUND AND *THE CANTOS*

The Chinese version of "in the timeless air," from "Canto LXXVI"—"in everlasting time and space"—deviates from the original meaning of the poem: here the timeless air refers to a space separated from time (an artificial thought). The world exists timelessly. What "everlasting time and space" emphasizes is the permanent unity of time and space. Because of this misunderstanding, what should be a Tang Dynasty landscape full of Zen realizations of time and life has turned into medieval theological dogma. For me, Pound intended this line to pinpoint the emptiness and absurdity of recorded history. At the same time, set against the never-ending air, he demonstrated a transcendent synchronic dimension to people living in the diachronic. In a certain sense, this captures the fundamental theme of the entire *Cantos*.

In praising Pound, T.S. Eliot claimed that the poet "invented" Chinese poetry. What Pound invented was his unique understanding of Chinese written characters and some elements of classical Chinese poetry. In fact, a new perspective or mode of experience also updates what is observed. I once called Pound's English translations of some Chinese poems a "great misunderstanding": "great" because of his originality. Never had anyone (including Chinese poets) prior to Pound recognized the distinctive structural features of Chinese characters, the special functionality of Chinese grammar, the philosophy and aesthetics as exhibited by classical Chinese poetry and these features' importance for literary creation in the modern world. His misunderstanding resulted first from the fact that he was a poet writing in English. All his reflections on Chinese language and Chinese poetry served his poetic writings in English. A man rooted in Western culture, he tried to acquire revelations from Chinese and absorb all that he could: the word-forming approach of Chinese, the juxtaposition of images in classical Chinese poetry, Confucian thinking and the like. He had never (nor ever could have) recognized other essential elements of Chinese poetry, such as tonal patterns, rhyme schemes, poetic forms, etc. The "great misunderstanding" was actually a purposeful choice. He managed to find inspiration for his own poetic composition from his indirect understanding of the Chinese language. This was consistent throughout his career, from early Imagism that revolutionized the expression of English language and poetry to the late *Cantos*, which display a synchronic poetic sense and a unique perception of the Chinese language. I have to admit that all Chinese poets in the 20th century have been following Pound's path in taking an individualistic attitude towards language: what we have been doing is to transcend the unconscious use of language and reach conscious creativity.

In my opinion, Pound's study of "Chinese poetry" must have had a hidden core, that is, thinking about synchronicity. First, he grasped this revelation through a study of the structure of Chinese characters and poetry using his intuition as a poet. Then, he distilled his philosophical position and gave it full expression in *The Cantos*.

Chinese characters and poetry constitute a concentric circle of synchronicity: Pound paid close attention to the word-forming method of Chinese characters (cheng[1], meaning "sincerity," is a perfectly structured character) and thus grasped the spatial elements of Chinese characters right from the start. Characters are not only pictorial. The juxtaposition of different constituents of each character leads to visual, audio, denotative and associative combinations. A character itself is a poem, a multi-layered space.

Strictly speaking, Chinese has no "grammar" as defined in the West: describing a specific action or thing with meticulously defined person, tense, part of speech and number. One of the salient features of Chinese is that the form of the verb remains unchanged no matter how the person and tense change. Here the Chinese language abandons particularity for abstractness. It implies that "now" does not exist and there is only language. Once written down, "this" person, "this" action and "this" moment become something universal. Writing is synthesis rather than analysis.

The juxtaposition of images in classical Chinese poetry is an extension of the spatiality of the Chinese characters and the abstractness of the Chinese language. The grammatical and logical rules are abandoned that govern the links between different strokes, different parts of each character, different characters, various images and sentences. As a result, discontinuity and blanks are found everywhere. Robert Bly once pointed out that when the imagination is employed to link these discontinuities, the abstract levels quietly pervade them. From this Pound derived Imagism. However, the key point here is not only images but also a space detached from (or containing) time. The form of a classical Chinese poem is in fact a microcosm. Take for example the typical *qilu* (regulated verse: eight-line poem with seven characters to a line). The opening couplet avoids antithesis to imply the sense of time; the middle two couplets are antithetical and thus expand the spatial distance horizontally; and the final couplet returns to non-antithesis as an echo of the beginning. The theme is rarely linear argument as in Western poetry. It is more like uncovering layer by layer at a single spot. It is a field of resonance that incorporates whoever reads it.

The tradition of classical Chinese poetry has had nothing to do with so-called "natural poetics." On the contrary, its formal design reflects an extreme artificiality—so artificial that it is usually mistaken for "naturalness." "Nature" as subject matter should not and cannot replace poetics. I often emphasize "written" rather than "spoken" Chinese because in Chinese history the written and spoken languages have long existed separately. This facilitated the formal evolution from Han dynasty *fu* [rhyme-prose] to *pianwen* [rhythmical prose], *jueju* [quatrains] and *lushi* [regulated verse] with the aim of constructing an increasingly perfect and organically enhanced poetic space while erasing time. A poetic form like the qilu has been used by Chinese poets for over a thousand years. At the same time, poets have been busy compiling collections of poems to the neglect of writing a book on the history of Chinese poetry. Not until the 20th century was the first history based on Western evolutionary theory completed. Is this comic or tragic?

What is synchronism in poetry? In short, in terms of time sense, synchronism contains diachrony; in terms of life experience, the situation contains events; in terms of language consciousness, abstractness contains particularity; and in terms of point of view, non-person contains person. In the final analysis, writing does not only deal

Issue #65

with existence but is existence on another level, and everything in history has become the materials and fragments for writing to paste together. Poetry does not merely draw the past into the present because there is neither past nor present. Only "air" is "timelessly" written on paper. It is poetry.

For me, the fundamental theme of *The Cantos* lies between its synchronic poetic sense and its diachronic poetic language. This means that the poem integrates changing human history. Here, the dazzling inserts and juxtapositions of large-scale images (understanding "images" in a broad sense) are more historical imagination—the unchanging behind all changes—than history. Each person, including Pound himself, is only a part of humankind. The Greek myths, Confucian preaching, and the daily routine in the POW camp in Pisa all happen all the time. This is just like the verbs in the Chinese language that never change their forms. However, Pound faced a problem—he had to write in English. His pursuit of synchrony and attempt to break through the diachrony of English—transcending diachrony in diachrony—leads him into conflict with his native language, the Western mode of logical think-ing and the "historical narrative" that has existed throughout western cultural tradi-tion. I am deeply shocked by such "impossibility" as seen in every part of *The Cantos*. While synchrony in Chinese is something inherent, the elimination of diachrony in *The Cantos* represents a human wrestling in the true sense. Pound did not merely "expound" this theme but demonstrated a way of getting rid of diachrony. This determines the structure and language of *The Cantos*: discontinuity between differ-ent parts, ubiquitous fragments, unexpected blanks and transformations in which lie secret chains of cause and effect concerning destiny. Complicated times, locations, characters and multiple foreign languages represent a required effort rather than a trick of showing off his profound learning. The only prominent feature is that no dis-tinctions exist. What remains is nothing but *The Cantos* and the transcendent words: "in the timeless air," a synchrony containing diachrony.

The synchronic poetic sense is not merely a metaphysical game. What it touch-es on is exactly the absolute predicament of human existence. Synchronic fate adds weight to diachronic experiences. The synchronic has nowhere to go, which has been verified by the *samsara* of historical evolution. To sum up, the two dimensions act together to define a person. This accounts for a mysterious parallel between Pound and contemporary Chinese poetry: Imagism/*Menglong* poetry (in the early 1980s); the initial translation of the Chinese History Cantos/ "Roots-Seeking" poet-ry that reflected on Chinese traditions and language (in the mid- and late 1980s); and publication of the Chinese version of the *Pisan Cantos*/*Liuwang* (Exile) poetry and its international experience (in the 1990s). Chinese poets' experience of the realities, especially China's mixed "realities" of yesterday and today, provide the motives for poetic innovation. This can be seen in the following: the self-con-sciousness in "rewriting" traditions and language in order to explore the possibility of deepening the Chinese language. Contemporary Chinese poetry's leaping images, free sentence patterns, swift movements of poetic thought, rich layers of meaning and especially its creation of a spatial structure to take the place of linear description result not only from the influence of one or more modern literary trends from the West but also from the spatial-synchronic essence of the Chinese language. The best contemporary Chinese poets can directly confront the human condition of having no place to hide.

The publication of the Chinese version of the *Pisan Cantos* in the 1990s was a major event for Chinese poets and for Pound. Chinese readers at last had the opportunity to read this relatively complete part of that grand literary construct. Pound would be pleased (would that he *was* still alive!) to see that the gap between the synchronic poetic sense in *The Cantos* and the diachronic sense of English has been bridged. Owing to the square-shaped Chinese characters, those linguistic fetters tightly bound around him have been suddenly thrown off. The world returns to its original "timeless" state. Disjunction, intersection and convergence are fragmentary and integrated at once. There are no such fragments or whole. There is also no beginning or end to poetry—just as he should have originally written in Chinese. Here, *The Cantos* have reached their true completion.

April 12, 2000

—*translated by Yang Liping with Jeffrey Twitchell-Waas*

International

²This Chinese reads as the following: .

Gregory Pardlo

Translating Niels Lyngsø's "Constellation" Poems

True to the term "constellations," which is what Danish poet Niels Lyngsø calls the numbered poems in his book Force Majeure (Borgens Forlag, 1999), spacing and placement of the phrases and words on the page suggest their relative gravitational pull—the amount of contextual influence the poet intends the cluster to have upon its textual neighbors. Lyngsø challenges the physical limitations of the page, compelling the poems to bear a more prescient logic than those conceived of in a more linear manner. The dimensionality achieved alludes to the metaphysics of acrostic forms: that congruencies of texts and themes in proximity and/or crux evidence some divine intention. Lyngsø is far more empirical, however: While the narrative streams often intersect, not only maintaining grammatical sense but meaning as well, the poet is most concerned with the physical, rather than spiritual, implications of the coincidence. Mud and membranes, insects and flesh stand for the inscrutable energies of the universe.

Danish is syntactically similar to Middle English, and I found myself mistakenly keeping that syntax in translation. My early drafts of translations didn't read exactly like Chaucer, but my impulse was to keep inverted subjects and verbs in such cases as there were. The result was more Elizabethan than the original. Wherever possible, then, I tried to keep the language conversational. The difficulty arising from this is that Lyngsø has a decidedly musical ear. He toys with assonance and alliteration at times as thick and explosive as that of Hopkins. I've had to work this characteristic in wherever the English allowed me to. There were few fortunate occurrences where the sound work was immediately translatable.

Issue #65

Niels Lyngsø

I

I have seen a tunnel before
of ashes that opens itself
seen its abyss
of golden-gold light
heart throbbing I
have taken the first
step into the tunnel
then the light enclosed me
and I cowered
a beachcomber   in the pale yellow tread wheel   under-furrowed
filled with flowing wounds   that hung like fog   sateless sorrow
the knocking revolved
in on itself and away
then the pattern in my eyelid's
ardent blood left me
but with a step in
there is always a way
back and I went back
adorned with the rest
of the light in my hair
pus   now I will go on
howl   through the tunnel
and no further
simply consider the
still sulking
pattern but down
in the black figures and in
all there is found   paths in the fine woven fabric   Everything is found
in the current of half sleep that now turns so the blocks protrude like weights and dream
in all directions I drift   and I pass again
through the diagram's corridor   a child that sings itself to sleep
man
bicycle house
tree swan ship
car tent house bicycle I
can no more
before I vanish
I will come to see
that there is darkness
at the end of the tunnel
now there is no way back   I may go backwards back over-
now I may search the dark if I   buoyed by my heavy tongue
will be found again   and see it all

XLI

Sleepless a cloud of mosquitoes   Pieces of man stem
lifts from the lake's mirror polished floor   with filtered branch work
rises among black branches   is fallen and now lies
crosses out through the forest   out over the earth with roots
hunts through the land   hovering high in the air
in shifting formations   yet stuck into thick stinking mud
collects itself this way until a little   yet stuck tight in continuous decay
bent body in a temple of meat   I cannot   There is flesh beneath bark
            wrest me free   which in large flakes
for   The apple falls   but perhaps new seeds   fall from the branches and lie plainly
      sour and green   throbbing bluish-purple film
        and hard as heaven   with a mold of white
          thickens not far
            from the ancestor
             loose in the bark
Your stomach is a temple   white worms
    we worship the creature that lives there   under the skin
     even though we cannot see it   fumble forth while
      but merely suspect it in ultra-   it forms itself blind
        sound scanner's soundless
       pictures sent from that outer space
   a creature on the way in its blood capsule
we know approximately when it lands

XXXV

One after one all
the grinding voices fall silent
finally I am
master of my own house here where
no one is home

And I think of my old life
the life before the era of us
it seems so foreign and
familiar so close and remote
like the house across the street
empty and disordered

III

I scratch the ground
a swarm of ants
dart off   and
toward all the world's
corners
only there where
I scratched
Are there none

My mind is a thousand
grinding voices that
loudly discuss
thoughts I thought
were private

What is found
what as light here
through the branches
what now seethes
over moss and mould
are the elementary
memories dissolved into an alphabet that
now gathers as a swarm of insects
that ascend along the branches up and
out through leaves over the forest
up through the purl of double light and away

Issue #65

XXVI

you are red   I am blue
                              It is an electro-
                        magnetic field
                  one cannot see it
            but one can feel it   There are zones of
      invisible foam rubber balls   stand-offishness and zones of
unmanageable elastics   inevitable attraction   I get dizzy
      the doctor's nail is jaundiced   as now a neck a knee   place and time
                                          a dampness   disappear
                                                between pant-waist and shirt

            Vowels are red boys are blue
                  noise in the airstream vectoring
            the girls sing   The girls can't come along
      but then the boys come   to gym today
the boys disconnect inhibit close off   they sit on the bench and stare
      oooh say the girls   the boys fall down
            the boys say of for spore more store stool   noises resound
                  cast snowball of doubt into
                        the girl's blood
but

XLI

Sleepless a cloud of mosquitoes
lifts from the lake's mirror polished floor
rises among black branches
crosses out through the forest
hunts through the land
in shifting formations
collects itself this way until a little
bent body in a temple of meat   I cannot
wrest me free
for   The apple falls   but perhaps new seeds
sour and green
and hard as heaven
thickens not far
from the ancestor
loose in the bark
Your stomach is a temple
we worship the creature that lives there
even though we cannot see it
but merely suspect it in ultra-
sound scanner's soundless
pictures sent from that outer space
a creature on the way in its blood capsule
we know approximately when it lands

Pieces of man stem
with filtered branch work
is fallen and now lies
out over the earth with roots
hovering high in the air
yet stuck into thick stinking mud
yet stuck tight in continuous decay
There is flesh beneath bark
which in large flakes
fall from the branches and lie plainly
throbbing bluish-purple film
with a mold of white
white worms
under the skin
fumble forth while
it forms itself blind

Issue #65

Rainer Maria Rilke

LEDA
from Rilke's "Leda"

When his need forced the god to enter
the swan, he was startled by its beauty
and he let himself be confused and slid
into it and the swan carried him forward

before he had a chance to discover
how it felt to be swan. The undone girl
recognized who was coming in the swan
and understood he wanted one thing,

which, even as she resisted, she could
not withhold. It came down low, its neck
pushed past her vague hands, and the god

loosed himself into her, and for the first
time then he took joy in his feathers
and became a real swan inside her.

International

Rainer Maria Rilke

BUDDHA IN GLORY
from Rilke's "Buddha in der Glorie"

Center of centers, kernel of kernels,
almond which folds in on itself and grows
sweet—everything that exists, right out
to the last star, is your flesh, your fruit.

Look—it's as if nothing more depends
on you; your rind is infinite,
and the strong juice stands and presses
against it, and an outside brightness calls to it—

high above you, glittering
suns will circle—
yet inside you something has begun
that will outlast those suns.

Issue #65

ARCHAIC TORSO OF APOLLO
from Rilke's "Archäischer Torso Apollos"

We can't know the amazing head
with the apple-huge eyes. But
the torso still glows like a flame
as his inner gaze concentrates
itself and flares. Without that light,
the breast's curve wouldn't blind you,
and in the delicate turn of the thighs
you wouldn't see a smile aim for

conception. Without that light, the stone
would be misshapen below the shoulders,
would not glisten like an animal's pelt,

nor break free from all its edges like
a star. There is no part of it that does
not see you. You must change your life.

International

Rainer Maria Rilke

WASHING THE CORPSE
from Rilke's "Leichen-Wäsche"

They had become used to him, but when
the kitchen lamp quivered in the draft,
the unknown man was again wholly
unknown. They washed the neck,

and as they knew nothing of his life,
they made one up, together, while
they washed him. When one of them
coughed, she let the heavy sponge of vinegar

sit on his face. The other woman paused
too, and drops pattered down from
her hard brush while the grisly convulsed
hand insisted to the entire house
that this man no longer thirsted.

And he proved it. Embarrassed,
they began again, with a short cough,
more hurriedly now so that, until
they finished the washing, their bent

shadows whirled and writhed on the silent
wallpapered walls as if caught in a net.
Night in the curtainless window
was merciless. And a nameless man lay
there, bare and clean, and laid down laws.

—translations by Annie Boutelle

Issue #65

Jacques Roubaud

FROM "SIX LITTLE LOGICAL PIECES"

I.

It is raining

—I believe that it is raining, but it is not.
—You believe that it is raining and assert that it is not?
—Yes.
I believe that it is raining but I know that I am mistaken.
—How do you know?
—That is not the issue. The issue is: I believe that
it is raining
But I am wrong.
—Who says that you are wrong?
—I do.
—But if you are wrong to believe that it is raining,
If you know that you are wrong to believe that it is raining
How can you believe that it is raining?
I need a straight answer.
—Is it raining?
—No.
—You see!
—I see that it is not raining. But I do not see how you can
Say that you believe that it is raining
    And how you can
    At the same time say that this belief is mistaken. I
cannot
    Believe it.

—I believe that I believe it is raining and that I know
it is not.
—Fine.
—If I believe that I believe what I believe, I believe it.
—Fine.
—No one believes that and at the same time that not.
—That what? That what not?
—Whatever: that it is raining, for example.
—Go on.

—If I believe that I believe wrongly that it is raining,

In other words if I believe that it is raining even though it
is not the case that it is raining,
  It follows that I believe that I believe it is raining
  And at the same time that it is not the case that it is raining.
  And it thus follows that I simultaneously believe that it is raining
  And that it is
  Not.   But given that no one has ever at the same time
believed that it was raining and that it was not, it is
impossible that I believe that I believe that it is raining
  Knowing full well that it is not.
—To be sure.
—And yet I believe it.

—You believe what?

In any event, it is raining.

II.

The past

She said to him: "It is very nice out."
Therefore
It was nice out.
If it is nice out, it is not necessarily very nice out.
If she had said "it is nice out"
could he have understood that she had, as it were,
potentially
said
"it is nice out, but it is not very nice out"?
No.
"It is nice out" would not have signaled any reservations on her part.
But neither would he have heard in her
"it is nice out"
(if she had said "it is nice out")
"it is nice out, it is even very nice out."
"It is nice out"
would not have signaled
any insistence
on her part.

All the same if, having said "it is nice out"

Issue #65

(which had not been the case)
she had added "it is even very nice out"
would this have meant that she thought
that by simply saying
"it is nice out" she had not been precise enough,
that she had not sufficiently asserted
how nice the weather was?
Without doubt.
But could she have said
"it is very nice out, it is even very nice out"?
No.
Why?
It is simply not said. If she had said
"it is even very nice out" after having said
"it is very nice out"
she would have applied the qualifier "even" to the utterance
"it is very nice out." But when one says
"it is very nice out" in no case does one say
it is nice out but not very nice,
which added on to the utterance "it is nice out"
would be as unlikely as "it is even very nice out"
and it follows that this "even" cannot apply
to the utterance
"it is nice out".

—Really?

—And was it nice out?

—It was.

—*translated by Richard Sieburth and Françoise Gramet*

International

Issue # 6 6

Autumn 2001

Robin Mookerjee

A Note From All of Us at *PBQ*

At the time of publication, events in Washington, New York, and Pennsylvania have left us with a world that feels "all changed, changed utterly." Looking over this collection, we cannot help but notice how many of the pieces, assembled before September 11, speak to the tragedy. This confirms for us that the best writing, even as it focuses on aesthetic values, retains its connection to unfolding events in a troubled world.

Elena Karina Byrne

VANQUISH MASK: 9TH CENTURY JAPAN

okashi, a smile suddenly expressed and quickly gone.
—Bradley Smith, *Japan: A History in Art*

"You cannot break my breath," she says, "being at last
breath." Concealed
by cloud, cursive dissolve, her face
is made of gofun, the crushed aged oyster shell, white
powder pigment and perfection.
      Light sent adrift
on the wish to be like air, winter will come
composed of the breadash she carries in her sleeves.

There are no burdens of joy.
What might be invented is as
disconsolate and unrehearsed as devotion.

She sees him
from the inside of the mask. She's accurate
lament, daughter of animal glue and sawdust, daughter
of paper & grass doll sent adrift on the river.

"You cannot see past this," she accuses
in one gesture over her head
toward the windows.

She likes all talcum sounds before words.
She likes to whisper at night
because you can see the face better.

Haunts to keep still: *respiration, respiration...*

Colin A. Clarke

I Lost Half of My House This Morning

I lost half of my house this morning.
The two halves of what was to be
my home were hurtling down I-83.
The man driving my shower,
my living room, my tiled kitchen counter,
my southern exposure, fell asleep,
charged over the rumble strip, and ran
head-first down a steep, wooded slope
that served as median.
There was no fire, no explosion, just
a trail of wood and wall and pink fiberglass
insulation and the driver's body
in his cab in my bedroom.
A replacement will be driven to me tomorrow,
but they say the siding will be a different color.
Today the gaping hole
of my foundation is but half-covered,
damp with a persistent drizzle that streaks
down the plastic sheet of my open doll-house.
It gathers in puddles and weighs down
branches and stretches out the hours of the day.
Night will fall and a home will still be
hours away, and by mid-day carpenters
will be busy binding my patch-work house
together. Despite the siding the seams will
be hard to find. But I'll know they're there.
Early morning I'll feel along
the wall for them, my fingernails
will catch in them, scattering plaster,
winter frost will wedge into my walls
and slowly drive them apart, sending
splinters of light across the floor
and air currents whirling throughout
the rooms. I will catch cold.
My house lies in pieces still.
This is not the beginning I'd hoped for.

Issue #66

Alison H. Deming

THE BLACKWATER
after Elizabeth Bishop

Traveling past deadfall hickory
and cypress knees, past the
pearly eggs of apple snails
beaded onto pickerelweed, the
metallic lace golden orb spiders
had strung between us and the sky,
we paddled where the river
took us, easy bending
passage through a wilderness
that gave way only enough
for us to keep moving, unsure
where we'd come ashore
or turn back to pull upstream
and home.   Oh, but it was
peaceful, riding like flotsam
on the current, silently
scaring off the gator,
buzzard and hawk that
knew us even in
our gentleness as danger.
One glistening anhinga
noticed us so late it
stood frozen on a snag,
our plastic hulls nosing up
so close we felt at last harmless.

Cool amber dark moving element,
musk of peat, silt and root gnarl
suspended in its tannin tea —
why should I feel at home
in its tireless flowing, as if I'd
never left the amnion where
spirit first meets flesh, as if
I could remember what
lies ahead when the
molecules disperse to seed
the sea.   On the river
not knowing what's ahead

is what moves us forward —
one more oxbow, we think,
stroking our blades into
resinous riffle and pool, all
the while knowing
we'll never be more
complete than this, never
appetite more quiet than
gliding through the
sword-shadow of sabal
palm and saw palmetto.

William E. Dudley

DUST

blossoms into what
looks like wrens

that sleep minutes
with a woman who
paints them

living on the side of a hill
much closer than you realize

with a nose so straight
the point of perfection is silent

next to a garden that clings
to Martin Van Buren

Issue #66

Sascha Feinstein

CROPS

Some seasons the family remembers:
that spring when Po Sen's mother
gave birth to her in a field that yielded
nothing and forced the women
to buy rice near a river village.
They hunched and pressed their foreheads
into cloth straps—Like this, she seems to say,
and places my hand on her thigh
so I can feel it turn to stone as she lifts
water jugs filled from the stream.
Some had carried their babies
in sling bags across their bellies
as they climbed for seven hours,
sacks of rice fusing to their spines.

The next dry season, three daughters left
for the city American soldiers call
Paradise. No one here speaks of AIDS
or possible futures, and this year the first crop
failed, but Po Sen points to her father
handling their largest water buffalo's yoke,
and then to the wet sky. She's painted her face
with a lotion made of crushed bark
to make her skin delicate as the transient
rain, or this heavy mist. She peers beyond
the protective thatch as her mother plants
seedlings, palms open to the wind
and moving more quickly than the grain.

Issue #66

Daniel Kane

Absenteeism in the Work Place (Fat Song)

I'm cleaning like mad "Who did it and ran" is what they'll be thinking if they show up to find my house this pigsty as if I were never here

"Who did it and ran" I hope you're having a wonderful time this Labor Day weekend I can't come into work I'm making cheesecake for next weekend that's why no come into work tomorrow making cheesecake things like that

no LIKE THAT and I'm cleaning like mad "Who did it and ran" are you coming into work tomorrow I can't work not even next weekend can I might not be in tomorrow I might not be in for the rest of the week

and I'm making cheesecake and marinating beef for next weekend BEEF, things like that, making cheesecake and marinating BEEF things like that and I'm cleaning like mad "Who did it and ran"   I said "Who did it and ran"

they might say and "Catch as catch can" they might say and I hope you're having a wonderful time I'm making cheesecake next weekend making cheesecake and marinating BEEF

BEEF things like that so I might not be in for the rest of my life like a ball of yarn next weekend I am yes like a ball of yarn and it is beautiful isn't it and it is beautiful isn't

it and marinating beef and making cheesecake is there it is delicious isn't it it is beautiful isn't it

Issue #66

Ada Limón

AFTER THE STORM

Morning is too much
after the hurricane,
umbrella bones scattered,
sun baking wet sidewalk,
my mouth sour with alcohol,
feeling a little sorry for myself.
I put, *take a shower*
on my list of things to do.
Brush my teeth.
Get over big love.
My body is shaking.
I want to make a sound,
something that might travel
three thousand miles,
hit canyons and echo.
Boom. I think I want to boom.

From the gated park
there comes a rumbling.
Something rising, pulling
chords out of the earth.
I stop. Listen.
Maybe this is me.
Then, cracking in a violent
pounding of sound,
a tree falls. Limbs shaking,
in the echo of the aftermath.
Shh, I quiet my heart.
Sound still bouncing
in my belly, in my shoes.
Did you hear that? I say,
I made that big sound.

Carley Moore

ON BEING LOW

How are we the underside of snow?
Both on the street and in the trees?
I saw your shadow.   I saw you go.

You are underneath the car.   You are now
one in a series of larger keys.
How are you the underside of snow?

You are the hat and the pilot.   Low replaces low.
You are the lint and the dusting.   Here now stand above me.
I still see your shadow.   I see you go.

We should have rested end to end.   We know
the night, the push to see.
How are we the underside of snow?

The light is waiting or is it the waiting that glows?
I bend your neck.   You say we have our knees.
There's the shadow.   I see it go.

You give me the hat.   Here's to not knowing
what lives on top of us.   We
are the underside of snow.
We lose our shadows.   We watch them go.

Issue #66

Kate Northrop

BRIDES: 1

They must vanish of course
         who must go early to the arms
of grooms.   They must

take weight, who were momentarily
brilliant,
crepuscular even, shining—

Through a meadow, a window, a promise.

When the sun sets over the empty beach
the brides follow each other,

one by one, into the slow drift of the ocean. They slide
out of their gowns, escape

questions. They go down. So when the wind picks up,
it billows the loose fabric, billows
their perfect veils.

And the surface? The surface is sweet,
it remembers them, it slowly closes

over their delicate motions.

Issue #66

Simon Perchik

*

Falling where the sun refills, its light
from somewhere in this darkness
someplace near the floor, your footsteps

eaten as shadows have always known
—ceilings are ice and stone and hunger
and valleys swallowing lush streams and songs.

Your shadow is thinner now
and still I can't loosen it, not even at night
gnawing this rug, your heels and scent

—say something! feed this floor
as if it were a ditch
left open for my knees and listening.

*

Closer, my shadow
smells from broken apples, the closer
—it takes years.

Eventually I'm alone
—who needs the sun
always burning my footsteps
as if they come from a distance
brooding, afraid, helplessly
sifting for each other.

The night too stopped looking
scared off, ransacked
—my shadow can't hold on.

Always in autumn, in footsteps
drinking cold water.
Standing is impossible: my shadow

closer, then closer
needs more and more darkness
to forget and the sun

who comes so far to die
hears this blackening frost
and blacker water.

Issue #66

Jessy Randall

THREE MARTIANS LEARN TO MAKE MARSHMALLOWS

"I have been reading too much science fiction,"
he sighed. Giant feelers
grew out of his penis.
"I hate it when there is no dialogue," she quipped.
Her perky alabaster breasts stood at attention.
Her bionic alabaster breasts made zim-zim noises.
He sighed. The Martians
were approaching. They had
space suits. They had
a space ship. They
sighed. "I only like it when it takes place in the future,"
he screeched. His skin-tight skin
rustled in the outer-planet wind. She
removed her removable alabaster breasts. They
sighed.

T. B. Rudy

BRIDGES

For every bridge that's marked with paint, scribbled
messages proving love with algebraic signs

and aerosol devotions of *forever*, there's a boy
who's waited up all night to sneak out, alone,

cargo pockets rattling with pressure,
a navy jogging hood pulled over eyes

that never glance at headlights flying below,
his teenage bicep flexing, arm hooked

around the railing, the only thing
that keeps his body from floating away.

There is no danger more than love, no fear
for boys who think all night of morning,

how she'll pass and lift her face to his creation,
his monument to not believing anything can end.

Issue #66

Charles Harper Webb

Us and Them

The same old story: We're the grass,
and they're the feet. We're hors d'oeuvres,
and they are teeth. We stand

in a worshipful line outside the Hall
as they file past in yellow rain-
slickers, giggling like naughty kids.

We know our place by how many
of them speak to us, how long.
We find our rank by dividing

their conversation time with us
by ours with everyone who thinks
we're part of them. We lean close

to catch the spray their words make
as they crash against the Great Ideas:
"tulle . . . restrooms." "limpid . . . tapioca."

"The great Toucan . . . composer
Johann Sebastian . . . Beak." Wheee!
They're the divers; we're the boards.

God gave them wings; us, pseudopods.
Gee, they are Porsches; we are streets.
They're the lovers; we're the sheets.

Ellen Wehle

HERODIAS WITH THE HEAD OF ST. JOHN THE BAPTIST
painting by Francesco del Cairo, 1625

I
When no one is looking, she whispers in his ear. Sir, you have spoken
against me.

It's beautiful, such precision, such an exact measure of penalty to offense.

Her needles piercing the soft meat of his tongue.

II
Always the artist controls the path our eye will follow.

The swooning queen; the hand, upraised in mid-stitch; unboxed, the severed
head
    before her.

Light blossoms on her face, the line of her throat. Bright and unnaturally
glowing.

III
Intimate, the tip of John's tongue pinched so close between her fingers.

Water leaking from the wounds, from the lakes beneath his tongue that in
life wet
    every kiss.

The tip. Of that troublesome. Tongue.

IV
And each time we discover last—that is no table he rests on. Eyes,
follow.

Herodias, hand poised like a swan diving. Dissolving into darkness against
her black
    dress the needle, itself, invisible.

The saint's head in her lap.

V
Will you then, sirrah. Will you keep quiet.

Issue #66

Max Zimmer

NEWLY WED

When you pick her up at the hospital after work,
  in the light blue Volkswagen that still shows the phantoms
  of the wedding graffiti when it rains,
  you can smell the day's disinfectant in her green uniform.
When you take her head and put your mouth on the skin behind her ear,
  you can smell the disinfectant deep in her blond hair
  and feel the wet heat rise off the back of her neck.
  When she rests her hand on the thigh of your Levis you can feel the heat again.
She doesn't talk when you slip a right through the red light at South Temple
  and glance across at her to see points of sweat on the flares of her nostrils.
  You have nothing to say when she reaches down below the dash
  to untie her hospital shoes and her hair cascades across her flushed face.
When you get her home and her clothes come off
  you can see the welt the elastic band of her pantyhose has left
  like the scar of a thin bloodsucking worm around her waist,
  the way her pubic hair has been smashed as flat as winter grass
  against the field it makes below her belly,
  the way her breasts look molded and her nipples crushed
  by the cups of her bra when she shakes the straps off her arms.
When you drop your Levis you can see the way your t-shirt goes
  from gray to white at the line where your belt rode.
  When you pull its neck off your face
  you can smell, on your slick raw fingers, the metal and grease
  from the cutters and rivet gun you've used that day
  to nail sheets of quivering tin to the rafters of four more mobile homes.
You think, right then, that maybe you should take a shower first.
  Or wash your hands. Or wait for the welt to fade. Or the smell to leave her hair.
  Or her nipples and pubic hair to recover
  from the rigging of her underwear.
  Check the mail. Play with the kitten. Let the day fall back
  to where the two of you won't feel like you're doing this
  on the living room linoleum of a half built trailer house
  or on the tile floor of a hospital closet.
  Open this gift you both got married for
  with the reverence your wedding guests would hope to see you exercise.
But here you are. Here where the engine of your Volkswagen
  still ticks and pings with heat out in the parking lot.
  Here where she can see that your feet are welted with the stitches left in them

Issue #66

by the laces and the eyelets of your workboots.
Here where the tunafish sandwich you ate out of your lunchbox
has left the feel of old newspaper on your unbrushed teeth.
Here where she can feel how your knees are crabbed from kneeling on the scaffold
to get the rivets into the tin up under the overhang of the roof.
Here where her sweat takes the afternoon sun from the room's one window
and makes her waiting body gleam
where she's thrown herself across the crocheted bedspread
neither of you can take the time to tear away.
Here you are. Pitiless as jackals among your wedding gifts.
Ruthless as crows for what was always there. Here in this bedroom
among the Early American chest and dresser and matching nightstands
you sold your Firebird for a month ago,
her sweat is your sweat.
On the Beautyrest mattress and box spring with the headboard still on layaway,
her eyes are your eyes. Her arms your arms.
Your Levis and t-shirt her uniform. You've done your time.
Sent thank you notes to the friends and relatives
who hoped you could keep this decent. Take each other
here, now, in this instant where the evidence of what you are
is new enough to make you sob.
On the tile floor of the janitor's closet,
while the rubber wheels of a gurney roll past outside the door,
her surgical assistant's hands reach deep enough into your back
to drive their claws into your stomach.
On the linoleum floor of the half-built trailer house,
while rivets are punched through the tin
and workboots idle back and forth along the scaffold out the window,
your roofer's fangs reach deep enough into her throat
to draw new blood from her lungs. Here you are.
In the afterwork rush hour heat
in the airless bedroom of this rented second floor apartment.
Unclean and savage and stinking among your gifts.
The beasts that your wedding has finally let you make of one another.
Her cry your cry. Your flesh her flesh. A priest gave you this right.
A priest gave you this right.

SOMETIMES A CIGAR IS JUST A CIGAR

Frank and I were running a little short on money so we had to cancel our trip to Italy. Instead, we decided to spend a few days in NYC, not exactly an exotic place to go considering Frank is from Brooklyn, and I'm a transplanted New Yorker who worked for years in Manhattan until I met Frank and we moved upstate.

The change in plans was a pretty big disappointment, especially for Frank who has never been abroad. I was kind of neutral about the trip, having done my share of traveling in enough exotic places during my days as an unattached woman, sometimes work involved, sometimes not. My eyes were always open for the right man, Italian, French, Spanish. I fucked my way through Europe; that's kind of the way I think of it although I would never be so crass as to say that to Frank, the man I have lived with for five years now. I did find a couple of foreign men I thought I could tolerate for a few months or so but that, and the lack of a common language, did not seem to bode well for a future together. Not that Frank is much of a talker himself, but I like that about him even if I have to put up with the occasional moodiness. I come from a family of chatterers, and Frank's quiet periods are quite refreshing.

None of the relatives Frank likes still live in New York, his parents are in Boca Raton, so we got a fairly cheap hotel right near Penn Station, off 7th Ave., in the middle of a string of Korean restaurants. Okay, so the place had no room service, no mini-bar, no heat until a guy came up and fixed it, and the two of us couldn't stand in the bathroom at the same time. And the toilet didn't flush the second day but we got that fixed, too. Still, there was one of those little coffeepots, and after I left the maid a note to leave extra packets of caffeinated coffee, Frank and I had breakfast in bed each morning along with the bagels we bought each day.

The plan was to do cheap things. No Broadway shows, not even off-Broadway. Both of us are walkers so we decided we would walk all through Manhattan and use Metro Passes for the subway when we got really tired. We've done this before but would stop off for lunch at our favorite restaurant in Greenwich Village, Il Mulino, spending a hefty $150, or walk over the Brooklyn Bridge for lunch at The River Café. Frank had checked out all the $25 and under places Eric Asimov wrote about in the *Times*. We would not go hungry.

The weather was fairly decent for mid-March. We sat in Washington Square, watched a few drug deals, the free entertainment in the fountain, shared a soda and pretzel. We went to the Rose Center for Earth and Science, Frank ignoring the new name, still calling it the Hayden Planetarium, telling me about how he went there for every school trip, all the way through high school, and how he loved to stand on the scales to find out how much he would weigh if he were on other planets. The scales were gone, the show in the planetarium looked like a bad imitation of the current crop of computer produced sci-fi movies, with Tom Hanks as narrator. Frank was disgusted. He hates Tom Hanks.

The Butterfly Conservatory in the American Museum of Natural History was a real knockout, though. We entered the small, incredibly humid vivarium and just stood still as Blue Morphos, Monarchs, Malachite, Stinky Leafwing, and dozens of other butterflies feasted on fruit and sugar water. One landed on Frank's hand, a spectacular Orange-barred Sulphur. Frank didn't move for ten minutes, he was that thrilled. So I walked over to the young woman who was giving out information and making sure certain kids didn't chase the butterflies, a homely girl with a bad case of acne, unfortunate to have to stand there in the midst of all that beauty, and asked her how long they live. One to two weeks, she told me. And when they die, she pointed to a case that contained eggs and pupa in different stages of metamorphosis, the staff just throws away the bodies and replaces them.

This was not information to impart to Frank who would only get depressed. When we were ready to leave, a guard checked us to make certain there were no butterflies attached to us. We both laughed at this, but only I knew the sad truth that they were already under a death sentence.

I wanted to go to the Frick Collection but Frank didn't because the last time we were there, he stretched his arms out, which is what he does automatically when he yawns, and a guard came running over and told him that if he did that again he would have to leave. So Frank says he will never go back because he just might yawn again.

I wanted to go to the Morgan Library but Frank didn't want to look at medieval manuscripts in dimly lit glass cases because he said it would give him a migraine. Frank really does get migraines, bad ones. We always travel with his medication. He was really getting into a bad mood so I decided not to argue with him.

We ate at the 2nd Ave. Deli, sampled hamantaschen at Moishe's Bakery served to us by a girl with short blue hair, multiple facial piercings and a heavy Hebrew accent, ate at a Korean noodle shop across from the hotel, ate Persian food on 8th Ave., ate shish kebob from a vendor on Columbus Circle and topped it off with steaming hot honey almonds from another vendor.

By late Thursday afternoon the mild weather changed to rain. We had left our umbrellas back at the hotel so we quickly dashed into the first movie theater we saw, found a movie that was just starting, the new Julia Roberts movie, even though Frank doesn't like her teeth, and within five minutes we were seated in the packed balcony just as the previews began.

As we walked back I noticed that police were blocking off parts of 5th Ave., and that bleachers had been set up. We couldn't figure it out until a bunch of people, dressed entirely in green, singing drunkenly, passed us. Friday was the St. Patrick's Day parade down 5th Ave.

I'm not crazy about parades and Frank hates them. "I hate a parade," he sang to more drunken people who passed who had no idea that he was singing the Frank version of Judy Garland singing, "I love a parade." Sometimes Frank is just a little too subtle for the general population.

By the time we got back to the hotel Frank was really low. He lay down on our double bed in our tiny room and pointed out that the frame around the door of the bathroom was not at right angles to the ceiling. Then he said that we could have been in Venice now and I told him that Venice really stinks, as in smells awful. He said we could have been seeing Tintorettos right now and I reminded him that we just did at the Metropolitan Museum of Art and he didn't appear that thrilled.

I started to nibble at his neck. He ignored me. I unbuttoned his shirt. He stopped ignoring me. He really can't resist me, we both know that, which is one of the reasons this relationship is working out. I'm not the moody person that Frank is. And the way to get him out of one of his bad moods is simple. A blow job will do the trick every time.

When I was done and he very nicely reciprocated, Frank came up with a plan for Friday. He would show me his Brooklyn. We'd go to Coney Island, walk along the boardwalk to Brighton Beach, go to the Aquarium, eat hot dogs at Nathan's. "You haven't had a real hot dog until you've had one at the original Nathan's, not those shit chains." He was happy with his plan. When I said that the weather didn't look so good for tomorrow he said it didn't matter. If Frank was happy then I was happy. So we fucked again, cuddled up in each other's arms and went to sleep.

The next morning we looked out the window to see what the weather was like, but since we faced an alley and another huge building we couldn't even tell if the sun was shining. Frank put on the TV. Rain, turning to snow, said the announcer. "But, believe me, with the luck of the Irish, when the parade starts at 11:30, the sun will be out."

I looked at Frank, waiting for him to say forget it, put the pillow over his head and go back to sleep for a couple of hours. But he had a smile on his face.

"Fuck it! Coney Island is better in the rain."

That was fine with me. I wanted our last day to be a good one, leaving NY on a happy note. By Monday it would be back to work for both of us. I liked the idea of escaping to Brooklyn, getting away from the crowds. I told Frank and he gave me one of his bear squeezes. "You are not going to believe this aquarium."

I had my doubts but I didn't say anything. After all, I have been to aquariums all over. Fish, lots of fish. Seals, and maybe if you were lucky, an electric eel. Theme aquariums like the one in Monterey. Big ones like the waterfront one in Boston, my home town. Too many to count.

We were out of the hotel by 8:00 a.m., dressed in layers of sweaters, umbrellas in hand. It was freezing out, a thin drizzle that I knew would turn into sleet, and then snow. We decided to splurge and get coffee and hot muffins at a deli right around the corner from the hotel. I could have sat there all day, it was so nice and warm, the coffee was so good, but Frank was anxious to get to Brooklyn.

In the subway station we got our Metro Passes, slid them through the device on the turnstile that made me feel I was back home at Wegmans, shopping for groceries and paying with my credit card, and stood on the platform waiting for the D train that would take us to Coney Island.

It was a long ride which grew progressively more interesting as we got out of Manhattan. The subway riders themselves changed, the ones early on walked on as though they had a purpose, carrying books, newspapers, dressed for the weather. Later, the car we were in cleared out except for a man who plopped down, seemingly asleep except for every 30 seconds or so when he would open up bloodshot eyes, stare directly in front of him, realign his untied sneakers and close his eyes again, and a man with long unkempt hair who chewed gum in time to the clanging of the wheels on the track. Soon the subway became the el and Frank excitedly pointed out streets to me, through the dirty, scratched windows, where a certain uncle had lived, where he and a favorite cousin had gotten thrown out of a candy store for looking at dirty magazines except the candy store was no longer there, replaced by Nails For You.

It was too early to begin feasting at Nathan's although it was open so we decided to start out at the Aquarium. Frank said he had to take a wicked piss, but when we got there we discovered the Aquarium wouldn't be open for another hour. So we walked down the empty, wide boardwalk, the ocean strangely calm, the Cyclone in the distance, the concession stands all boarded up.

A few joggers passed us. Frank looked happy, the wind blowing his black hair off his forehead. It had begun to sleet which made him laugh. He told me about the man who operated the Cyclone when he was a kid, who lived in a little room that was attached to the roller coaster. He grabbed my hand and started running, pulling me with him, the hood of my sweatshirt flopping off my head. He kissed my nose which he informed me was bright red, and I licked the sleet off his cheeks.

We walked to Brighton Beach and got off the boardwalk at 8th, walked five blocks under the el where all the shops were, where Frank said his family used to live.

I felt like we had gone abroad after all. All the store signs were in Russian, the people walking on the street had purpose, carrying shopping bags, pausing at outdoor stands to select foods that looked foreign to me. Frank insisted on walking into several stores, huge places where everyone spoke Russian, noisily, yelling across the aisles, pointing out to me this and that delicacy, telling me a story from his childhood about each item he saw, the stuffed cabbage, the enormous loaves of bread, the loose bins of kasha that his mother would buy and make into kasha varnishkas.

We headed back to the boardwalk. The sleet had now turned to a light snow. Frank spotted a public men's room but when we got closer I noticed that below the sign, someone had written in, "Blow Jobs This Way" with an arrow pointing to the door. The door was locked so we continued our run back to the Aquarium, Frank complaining all the way that his bladder was up to his neck.

I have to admit that the Aquarium, which looked tiny from the outside, was filled with interesting exhibits. Maybe I was just happy that Frank was happy. I had never known him to be so talkative. I held a horseshoe crab at the Touch Me! Exhibit, offered to me by a very young girl who told me this one doesn't bite, only the ones at the beach do. I dropped it back into the water and picked up the starfish.

We saw the blue lobster. The otters performed just for us. We studied marine life in the Hudson. We saw the baby Beluga. After a while I lost Frank and went back inside to view some of the underwater tanks.

That's when the most amazing thing happened. I was standing alone in front of the tank of Pacific walruses when the male, twice the size of the two females, came speeding toward me, crashing his whiskered head into the thick glass, making audible moaning noises, his brown eyes staring directly into my face. Then he pulled back and out of his lower belly, from some kind of enormous sized navel came a three foot penis, at least that was my estimate. Still looking at me, even though the female walruses swam right by him, he backed up again, and then rubbed his appendage with his huge back flippers for about ten seconds. When he was done, he swam away and came right back, staring at me even though several other people were now standing in front of the tank, repeated the entire thing, crashing into the glass, moaning and then masturbating.

Mothers pulled their children away. A couple of people laughed. Some took pictures. A crowd gathered, including Frank who arrived just in time to see the walrus' cock emerge from that navel. Frank stared at the walrus as the walrus stared at me, backing up to rub himself with those flippers. He had eyes for no other woman, I told Frank, jokingly. But Frank wasn't smiling.

Frank finally grabbed my arm to pull me away when I started to put my head against the glass to gaze back into the walrus' eyes. I wanted to stay longer, to see how long I could hold his attention but Frank had had enough.

While Frank got the food at Nathan's, I listened to two homeless people, absolutely filthy, sharing a bowl of clam chowder, while they discussed Mahler. Shoving the best, juiciest hot dogs and French fries I had ever eaten in my mouth I said to Frank, "Wanna get a pair of flippers and masturbate under water for me when we get back to the hotel?"

"Wally really turned you on, huh?"

"Who's Wally?" I asked, wiping a fried onion off Frank's chin.

"Wally, the walrus."

"Oh, please, Frank. His name is definitely not Wally. That's the stupidest thing I ever heard. He is just a Pacific walrus at the Coney Island Aquarium who had the biggest dick I've ever seen."

"Who wanted to fuck you." I told him to stop being so ridiculous but secretly I was pleased. How many women can get a walrus sexually aroused?

We finished up, continued on to the Brooklyn Museum of Art. Frank seemed tired but I felt oddly exhilarated. Later that night we took the subway into the East Village to go to a cheap Thai restaurant Frank had read about. The food was terrific and plentiful. Since it was our last night we splurged on a bottle of overpriced wine.

The streets were packed with kids. Frank stopped in front of a store that had a display of dildos, lubricants for the "anally challenged," devices whose purpose I couldn't even begin to imagine, bins of phallic-shaped pasta. He wanted to go in but I felt squeamish.

"Looking for flippers? We could go into a sporting goods store for that."

He got annoyed and we walked on. Eventually we got back on the subway to the hotel.

As I was getting undressed I told Frank what an incredible day it had been. I was packing up the extra sweaters and the dirty laundry into our suitcase because we had a 7:15 train to catch in the morning, and I am somewhat compulsive. As I was bending down a nude Frank wrapped his arms around me, and from behind pulled my sweater over my head, unzipped my pants, pulled off my panties, threw me down on the bed and fucked me so quickly that I didn't have time to come.

When he was done, he lay on his back, sweat sliding off his forehead. He turned on his side and smiled at me. "Good, huh?"

I didn't know what to say. I have never lied to Frank about orgasms, never even had to fake one because he is such a good lover that I always come. I was just about to tell him the truth when I sensed that he would stop smiling and turn back into moody Frank.

So I lied.

When we got home and made love again, everything started to change. A few times Frank asked me, trying very hard to make it seem like a joke, "Still thinking about Wally?"

Indignantly I said, "What is your problem, Frank? Are you jealous of a walrus?" But the truth was that sometimes when we made love, I did think about him, the way he moaned, his desperate masturbation, his beautiful brown eyes staring into mine. But of course it wasn't sexual attraction for a walrus; it was fascination with animal sexual behavior. And that is precisely what I told Frank, getting tired of the whole flipper incident. Really. Enough was enough.

Frank became even more demanding. One Saturday night we went to the X-rated room of the video store, something we had never done before. I was to be the lookout person, warning Frank who would select the videos, if someone we knew was nearby.

Saturday night is a very stupid time to do something like this. Each time Frank approached the room, we would run into someone we knew. He finally got in. Just as he disappeared, a colleague from work, holding the hands of her two little girls, gave me a big hello. "It's so hard finding nice family movies that we can all watch together." I agreed with her, grabbing a few videos off the shelf, praying that Frank was taking his time.

We ended up with the videos I had grabbed, *Mary Poppins*, and *The Sound of Music*, and the ones Frank had gotten, *Busy Little Beavers*, *Jane on Dick*, and *Pussy*

Does the Dog.

We were both kind of nervous as Frank popped in *Busy Little Beavers*. We had both seen porn before but the ones he chosen made me feel uncomfortable. But *Busy Little Beavers* was not about men fucking animals; it just had the usual inane plot of a group of silicone enhanced women, one of whom, who looked like she was wearing a wig for pubic hair said, "I have a great idea, girls! Let's use our luscious bodies and put on a show!" Frank fast-forwarded most of it and then popped in *Pussy Does the Dog*, which despite the title had to do with fucking doggy-style, Pussy being the generic name for each actress in a three minute segment of groaning. This one did not have any plot, thank God.

The best one, as far as being interesting, was a "documentary," kind of an educational film, like when I was in school and one night was set aside for all mothers to take their daughters back to the school auditorium to watch a film on menstruation. Dick and Jane were just two people with really bad bodies, Dick was bald and Jane had breasts that looked as though a couple of kids had nibbled at them for a few years, who did all kinds of sexual stuff. The movie had talking heads—from the Anal Expert known as the Avatar of Ass, to Johnny Seconds, who explained the delights of butt-fucking, to Millie Masters, PhD (in what? I asked Frank) who narrated the segment on erotic massage.

When it was over, Frank and I agreed that we didn't need a movie to teach us about sex, although that night in bed I got, thanks to Millie Masters, PhD, the best massage of my life.

Everything was back to normal. Wally's name hadn't come up for two weeks. The incident was over. I have to admit that I still did think of him every once in a while but only in a detached way, fascination giving way to curiosity, always meaning to consult with a marine biologist, or get a book out of the library to find out if what Wally had done was what all male Pacific walruses do. But I never did.

Mainly I was just happy that Frank and I would not have to go for counseling. What would we say? We had been living together for five years, five terrific years of great sex. Then one day, my lover gets obsessed with the idea that I am sexually attracted to a walrus because he has a three-foot-long cock, and Frank feels sexually inadequate because he is merely a human male with a cock the proper number of inches it should be.

Sitting in my office at work one day, I received an e-mail from Frank, working at his computer in his office across town. We often send each other little messages, a little bit of gossip, a suggestion for plans for the evening, a joke someone had passed along. The subject of this one was Ha-Ha, our term for a joke, followed by Penis Tax Time.

> The only thing the IRS has not yet taxed is the penis.
> This is due to the fact that:
>> 40% of the time it is hanging unemployed.
>> 30% of the time it is hard up.
>> 20% of the time it is pissed off.

Issue #66

10% of the time it's in the hole.
It has two dependents, but they're nuts.

Effective January 1, 2000, penises will be taxed according to size…

The brackets are as follows;
10"-12" Luxury Tax
8"-10" Pole Tax
5"-8" Privilege Tax
4"-5" Nuisance Tax
Males exceeding 12" must file under capital gains.
Anyone under 4" is eligible for a refund.
PLEASE DO NOT ASK FOR AN EXTENSION!

Issues still under consideration are as follows:
Are there penalties for early withdrawal?
Do multiple partners count as a corporation?
Are condoms deductible as work clothes?

I hate getting e-mail jokes. Some go on forever and then I automatically delete them.

This was an unusually long one for Frank; his are two lines at the most, kind of like the way he talks. But this one made me laugh. Also, knowing Frank and his black moods, it was a clear indication that the Wally incident was now to be viewed as a joke, to be allocated to the archives of our relationship.

On impulse I stopped in at a sporting goods store on my way home from work and bought Frank a pair of flippers. If he could joke, so could I.

I got home first and shoved the bag in my closet. The next time we took a bath together, something we did fairly often, candles, bath oils, wine, the whole thing, I would give Frank the flippers.

That Saturday was the first really warm spring day we had had so far. On the front page of the *Post-Standard* last week was a picture of Susu, the baby elephant who had been born only six weeks before. She was the third baby elephant to be born at our zoo. Frank and I have seen each baby. Such goofy kids! Stomping in the mud, running to nurse from mom, seeking shelter with one of the "aunties," generally finding delight in anything noticed, a stick, a ball, the straw on the ground. The article said that the first day the temperature was over 65 degrees, Susu would be on display outside.

Frank and I stood in the crowd of screaming toddlers, adults like us, laughing uproariously at all of Susu's antics. A 300-pound adorable kid. One father holding a baby no older than six months kept up a steady stream of scientific information to his baby who did not appear at all interested in the elephant but was fascinated by the people around him, and gave gummy grins to everyone.

Frank, knowing I would watch Susu for quite a while, wandered off to see the new bat exhibit. Bats give me the creeps, and my having lived in Austin, Texas, bat capital of the country, for a few years only increased my phobia.

The zoo had enlarged the elephant exhibit. Recently added was another spacious holding area. The last time I was at the zoo it was empty, but out of the corner of my eye I spotted something moving.

I eased my way out of the crowd and wandered over to the pen. A zoo volunteer in high rubber boots was cleaning up some debris outside the pen but no one else was there.

There stood the most magnificent elephant I had ever seen. His body was facing the pen where the females were and he was making a low frequency, muted sound, as if calling to them.

And then he spotted me. He walked in an aggressive stance, head held high, chin tucked in, ears waving, toward me, stopped only by the moat of water. Out of a sheath, his penis emerged, dropping down so low it was just inches from the ground. He bellowed at me.

"Tony's in musth, you know. Ready and willing to..." and the volunteer mouthed fuck, smiling at me. "He's looking for a female in estrous, poor guy. His testosterone level is surging. See how swollen the sides of his head are, that area that is wet? Those are his temporal glands. He'll be nuts like this for a few months."

As he stood there bellowing at me, waving his ears, a liquid dribbled out of his cock. Then it would stop, he would move to a new position, brown eyes still on me, and dribble some more. Sometimes it just gushed out, his inner legs black with wetness. At the same time, his temporal glands were secreting a copious, viscous fluid.

As I watched him, a small crowd had gathered. Some people were taking pictures. A bunch of teenage boys were in hysterics at the size of the drippy penis. An elderly woman turned to me and said, "I think Tony likes you." Mothers rushed by covering their children's eyes.

Frank appeared at my side. I didn't know how long he had been standing there, so fascinated was I by the spectacle in front of me. In his hand he had a small bag. His face was neutral, revealing nothing, as he stared at the elephant. "His name is Tony," I said to Frank. He looked at me, his dark brown eyes intense, nodded, and looked back at the elephant.

We left the elephant exhibit and wandered aimlessly for another 20 minutes, not talking. In the car he handed me the bag. Inside was a stuffed animal, a baby elephant.

"What a sweet thing to give me, Frank!" I have an enormous stuffed animal collection. Someone had handwritten "Susu" on the label.

We went out to our favorite Chinese restaurant. We made small talk. Frank and I are not small talkers.

At home I put my little elephant next to my much bigger gorilla, thinking automatically that gorillas have such teeny cocks. Not that I have ever seen one, but I read that somewhere. I told Frank that a long time ago, and we both laughed about it.

Frank came out of the shower and I jumped, wondering if he could read my thoughts. But he didn't look at me. I showered. We both read for a while, then simultaneously turned off our reading lights, and said good night, each turning away from the other.

The following Monday I came home from work, carrying my briefcase in one hand, in the other the take-out fish fry from Doug's that would be my dinner. Frank had e-mailed me earlier in the day to remind me that he had a staff meeting and would be home later in the evening.

Dumping everything down on the kitchen counter, I went into the bedroom. I took off my work clothes and went to the closet to hang them up, unhooking my bra and stepping out of my panties at the same time. There was the bag with the flippers. I took them out and put them on, and stared at myself in the mirror. And then I went to take a bath.

Denise Duhamel

Letters to Wendy's

Letters to Wendy's
Joe Wenderoth
Verse Press
Paper, $14

Letters to Wendy's is simply one of the funniest, most irreverent books I've ever read. I've been a fan of Joe Wenderoth's work over the past two years, ever since Ross Martin, an editor at *Nerve*, told me, "You have to see these Wendy poems we just published..." I am very intrigued by the notion of a poem-a-day, which is how these gems were written, over the span of two years (1996-1997), and if you can believe the author, they were actually first composed on Wendy's "TELL US ABOUT YOUR VISIT" cards. The titles of the poems are dates, as in David Lehman's *The Daily Mirror*. But unlike *The Daily Mirror*, which is populated with friends and civil lunches and parties, the narrator of *Letters to Wendy's* is a cheese-burger-chomping voyeuristic lowlife who visits Wendy's each day, alone.

But maybe I am mistaken (not about the voyeuristic lowlife part, but)—maybe *Nerve*'s Ross Martin said, "You have to see these Wendy short-shorts we just published," for when I finished *Letters to Wendy's*, I was surprised to see "Fiction" slapped on the upper-right-hand corner of the back cover. I immediately thought of Nin Andrew's *Book of Orgasms*, also first published as "fiction" by Asylum Press, and reprinted by Cleveland State University Poetry Center last year.

from "December 31, 1996 (NEW YEAR'S EVE)"
> Eschewing everything, I've assumed it best to break my lines like prose. I've
> assumed a visit a full thing—a thing demanding as many words as possible....

Although I think prose poems and microfiction are basically kissin' cousins, Joe Wenderoth's work does feel more like poetry to me—like a modern (or rather post-modern) Baudelaire, full of sardonic social commentary. In any case, Wenderoth certainly is pushing the boundaries of genre-blurring. Are these pages simply prose in chapters? Prose in poetry's drag? They also seem to be straddling some wide-open space between poetry and pornography. Are these pages full of porn? Kiddie porn? Wendy porn? (Would this account for the austere navy blue stock and the rather delicate gold lettering on the cover?)

Another wonderful surprise is a CD of the work, spoken by actor James Urbaniak (who played Simon Grim, the bus driver/poet in Hal Hartley's *Henry Fool* and Harry in *Sweet and Lowdown*). Urbaniak delivers the poems in slow deliberate deadpan, reminiscent, actually, of a Hal Sirowitz reading, if Hal Sirowitz were rated X. Don't be misled by the work reprinted in the March 2001 *Harper's* (which explains Wenderoth's form as a novel in prose poems)—*Harper's* printed the tamer entries—many of the entries are much more depraved. Urbaniak reads the poems/chapters one after the other, without dates, like so many greasy but delicious bitefuls.

from "July 17, 1996"
> ...I imagined Wendy was in my car with me. She said, "I'd like you to take your fat tongue and run it from my asshole to my clit and over again." I said, "I'd like you to punch me in the face."

At first, you can't believe what you're hearing or what you're reading, but there it is. And it's very funny, once you get over the shock. Wenderoth in "January 29, 1997" writes, "Could it be that everything that is is just a funny after-taste? That brings us to the terrible question of what is funny..." Wenderoth perhaps knows that his poems aren't for everyone and delights in being the outsider. The "writer" of these letters imagines the Wendy's employees as porn stars, watches porn during breakfast at home, and writes in September 24, 1996, "I love to watch a dick slamming in and out of a cunt or an asshole. The only way t.v. could enhance Wendy's is if it was confined to showing non-stop hardcore pornography without sound...."

George P. Elliot once defined pornography as "the representation of directly or indirectly erotic acts with an intrusive vividness which offends decency without aesthetic justification." Elliot's definition is slippery, since who can say for sure when a poet is justified aesthetically?

But I think his definition can be used as a window into *Letters to Wendy's*. Wenderoth does write with "intrusive vividness," like one chewing with his mouth open, but I think Wenderoth's aim is social satire. Elliot goes on to write, "Even the breast of a healthy woman is revolting when inspected too closely, as Swift knew when he had tiny Gulliver revolted by every blemish on the breast of the Brobdingnagian wet nurse suckling the baby." So is there a bit of Jonathan Swift in Joe Wenderoth? I think so.

from "August 5, 1996"
> ...I like to eat the flesh of certain animals three times each day and to lick the flesh of my own animal. It seems careless to say, but then saying in itself is a kind of sudden ignorance of where everything is coming...

from "August 18, 1996"
> We've become a throw-away society! they gasp. Well, could this be because we've discovered, finally, that we're a throw-away organism...living in a throw-away land? ...I'm happy to every day get a brand new ornate yellow cup, drink half my coke, then abandon the thing altogether and forever.

from "August 22, 1996"
> There used to be a little Ma-and-Pa restaurant across the road, but it couldn't keep up...Build Wendy's everywhere and all alike—and do not fear: you cannot, you CAN NOT ever step into the same Wendy's twice.

from "December 24, 1996 (CHRISTMAS EVE)"
> If we must put people to death, why not at Wendy's ....The refreshments allow the audience to take in their own hands the tamed substance and to feel themselves securely on this side of the blender.

from "January 17, 1997"

> I'm comforted to think of Wendy's as a miraculous heap of meals, and to come to it every day like a vulture to a battlefield it could not have seen coming.

from "February 5, 1997"

> I never see deliveries being made. I'm glad....

and from "April 18, 1997"

> Nowadays a corporation needs to support a cause now and then... Wendy's could launch a "Catheters For the Birds" campaign. The goal would be to capture, catheterize, and rehabilitate all natural birds...

Wenderoth is so tongue-in-cheek, so gristle-in-teeth, that *Letters to Wendy's* can be read as a fast food send-up, as an animal rights manifesto, as critical of environmental waste. What about all those slaughtered cows? What are those Frosties made of exactly? Is corporate greed so despicable that Wendy's own father Dave is pimping his daughter to sell burgers? Should *Letters to Wendy's* be mandatory reading for members of the Green Party? To keep didacticism in check, Wenderoth has created an often unreliable, sometimes hallucinatory narrator who gets five free refills of Coke while high on whiskey and sudafed ("July 6, 1996") or visits Wendy's still reeling from marijuana brownies ("August 26, 1996" and "August 27, 1996") or forgets to shower when he gets good pills ("April 29, 1997"). He even writes "I believe I'm actually going to have to be strapped down..." ("February 18, 1997"). In this way, some letters to Wendy's are not unlike the fourth book of *Gulliver's Travels*, which is supposedly the commentary of a madman.

And what about the letter writer's lust for little Wendy herself? The narrator sees Wendy as a billboard Lolita. What attracts him is "...something about her face and the shape of her hair, the muffled red coherence of a head and torso, and perhaps too her lack of arms and legs..." ("September 21, 1996"). I'm reminded of the title poem of Rick Peabody's book *I'm in Love with the Morton Salt Girl*, but while his poem is a tender and nostalgic look at pop culture imagery of little girls, Wenderoth's letter writer employs a lust that is dark and more than a little creepy:

from "July 4, 1996 (Independence Day)"

> I'd like to spank Wendy's white ass and fuck her hard....

from "September 14, 1996"

> Last night I dreamt that I pissed on Wendy's head....

from "September 21, 1996"

> If I had to say what Wendy really was...I think I'd have to say she was a penis....

from "February 7, 1997"

> Wendy, soon I will kiss you passionately in the cunt and hold on tight to nothing.....

The absurdity of abusing Wendy who is basically a sign, a billboard, an image on a yellow cup takes a leap to show the absurdity of abuse in general. For some, these poems may be a little harder to laugh at. I attempted to introduce some of Wenderoth's poems from *Nerve* last year in a graduate poetry class, and many students were genuinely upset by their graphic nature.

One woman said, "Child abuse is never funny..." which, needless to say, is true, but again if we think in terms of satire, these poems border on both the funny (ha ha) and the funny (extremely strange). I am reminded of the Todd Solondz films *Welcome to the Dollhouse* and *Happiness*, dark comedies that both use child abuse as a plot device.

What makes this book quintessentially postmodern and avant garde is the mix of high art with low art. The same letter writer, who watches porno, is also a reader of Foucault.

from "August 18, 1996"

> Foucault says knowledge wasn't made for understanding but for cutting. For the Wendy's worker, that's especially true. The Wendy's worker knows—he does not understand—and his knowledge is alive with results....

from "August 26, 1996"

> It's hard to get served when one understands the signifier as a process....

from "February 11, 1997"

> My desire causes an order and then I wait as it gets carried over into the real. This carrying over produces a delicious fact, which the order cannot have signified...

He is also full of classical literary allusions and philosophy.

from "November 11, 1996"

> Can you not feel Wendy's blindness, her exile, as she looks down at you from the sign? What terrible thing has she done to deserve exile in such a barren place? She, like Oedipus, was a child. Surviving infancy is the true Oedipal crime....

from "November 26, 1996"

> Artaud prefigures the experience of being on speed while standing under a Wendy's menu when he writes: "In it we feel a grinding of sluices, a kind of horrible volcanic shock from which the light of day has been dissociated...."

from "December 30, 1996"

> ...Marx wanted to take a sledge hammer to all registers. He hoped we'd recover our senses in the long lines that ensued...

In fact, Wenderoth envisions Wendy's as a place of knowledge.

from "April 8, 1997"

> Sometimes I think of a Wendy's as a library without books. Without records, magazines, maps, or videos. Without a rare books room, and without an information desk. As such, it is the most pleasant library I've ever visited...

Wenderoth takes a great idea—a poem a day on a "TELL US ABOUT YOUR VISIT-CARD"—and pushes it further than most poets/prose writers would dare. *Letters to Wendy's*, be it poetry or porn, prose or propaganda, is one of the most innovative books I've ever come across, which ups the ante for the literature of the next couple of decades—at least.

Issue # 6 7

Winter 2001

F i l m

SHAPESHIFTERS: AN EDITOR'S INTRODUCTION

I.

In the days after the tragedies of 9/11, some of us sought refuge in movie theaters. In fact, one theater in the frozen section of lower Manhattan opened its doors to shell-shocked patrons and offered free soda and popcorn and movies. God bless a film like *Rat Race* in days like these.

But as we know, films offer us much more than escape, especially when we look at film texts (and their popular reception) as cultural artifacts that refract the age in which we live.

The call for submissions for this issue was as big and vague as we could manage without sounding like dolts. We cast our net as wide as possible, lest we stunt, shut down, or otherwise alienate "good writing on or about film." We wanted to see how film suffuses other arts, other media. We wanted to see how one medium might be refracted through another, and how creative writers, among other artists, make that happen.

What we didn't expect was the subtheme of labor within the culture industry. You can watch this theme unfold in Daniel Nester's interview with Paul Thompson of NYU film— an actor turned playwright turned director turned teacher—and in Greg Pardlo's interview with Dylan Tichenor, film editor for *Unbreakable*, *Boogie Nights* and *Magnolia*. You can trace it across MJ Robinson's essay on *The Blair Witch Project* as an allegory for the popularity of film schools, and in James Polchin's essay on celebrity—of the Hollywood and the academic varieties. You can even follow it in CAConrad's Elvis sequence and in Daniel Nester's "Leslie Nielsen Signs Autographs, Comments on His Disaster Movie, *The Poseidon Adventure*." These pieces seem to be grappling with shared questions: Put simply, what does it mean to be a working actor, director, or screenwriter at the end of the twentieth century? What are the conceptions and consequences of celebrity?

In this issue you will see screenwriters writing poems, film editors and directors talking about their craft with poets, scholars and academics using film to trace larger cultural shifts regarding celebrity, and more. Storytellers in one medium here convey a preoccupation with other media. Writers in one form or medium hold up a mirror, a lamp, a sonnet (see Kevin DiNovis's *Jaws* poem) to another.

II. Shapeshifters

> *The hybrid or the meeting of two media is a moment of truth and revelation from which new form is born* —Marshall McLuhan

If you've cast even a fleeting glance at our previous online issues, you can guess at an obsession. In what ways does one medium or technology of storytelling affect another? How might one inflect the features, style, content, craft of another? *PBQ*'s reflexive concern with the relation between online magazines and traditional print forms is demonstrated by our editors' participation in a number of academic panels and workshops, and by the numerous essays they have penned on the subject.

Working out this theme has been like getting gum out of my hair. With our move online, we have lingered over questions of Web publishing versus print publishing, and we've noticed the way our readers and contributors have reacted to the changes we've made. Though many are enthusiastic, a good many remain suspicious, distrusting our Web issues' status as a "real" publication.

Thus this intro is the third in a series of pieces about the anxieties PBQ has tapped with our move online. The Web has provided us with a way to resurrect/preserve/grow an offbeat high-quality 30-something venue for new writing. But some writers balk at Web publication.

With this film issue (the third of its kind in *PBQ* history) we expand the circumference of the debate between the book and the Web and locate a new terrain on which to map emerging ideas and concerns about writers and writing: film. Popular film reflects (and affects) the social imaginary. Consider the ways in which films have spoken to a cultural preoccupation with new technologies of communication.

One of the late twentieth century's most interesting films about writing and writers is *Shakespeare in Love* (1998). Its surprise box office success evidenced a cultural preoccupation with the role of the writer. Academy award-winning, wildly popular, the film was produced and released in a time marked by the "new economy" and e-commerce. In an era of soaring new technologies, when, barring a few Luddite holdouts, most writers were composing with computers instead of pen and paper, the most popular romantic comedy of the year featured a playwright scribbling with a quill.

This preoccupation reveals a deeper anxiety. Recall *Sneakers* (1992)? *The Net* (1995)? *Johnny Mnemonic* (1995)? Or more recent films like *The Matrix* (1999), this summer's *Swordfish*, even, arguably (or, rather, aargh) last summer's *The Cell*. These films are driven by plots that contain characters who crack the code, speak the new language, access and deliver information (so, OK, J-Lo as a virtual psychiatrist intervening in her patients' alternative universes to get them to rewrite their traumatic narratives is a bit of a stretch).

That these films fit in the generic categories of crime and sci-fi suggests that what fascinates us also gives us the creeps. Note, for example, the peculiar absence of writers as characters in the films above. Not that writers are central to sci-fi or noire crime drama, but it's worth noting that they are not visible in the recent spate of popular films that deal with the digital, the virtual, with computers.

Such films reveal that our preoccupation with writers exists on a continuum with anxieties about their perceived disappearance in the twentieth century. It is as if film, video, and digital technologies threaten to erase the art and practice of writing, and this anxiety gets articulated through high-tech movies.

But perhaps the best example of a film that takes writing as metaphor of agency and control has nothing to do with computers. Director Christopher Nolan's *Memento* (2001) is marked by narrative innovation and structural pyrotechnics; the film makes your heart race with uncertainties—everything in the plot is destabilized, glimmering into narrative focus before disappearing. Suffering from severe short-term-memory loss, Leonard Shelby (Guy Pearce) takes to writing on his body. His short-term memory has literally crashed, and the only way for him to know "truth" is to indelibly mark it on his body. But even that text can have multiple meanings and thus the narrative unfolds, and unfolds again, in dizzying concentric circles. The film is a near parable of the risks and rewards of (dis)embodying memory: Truth is contained in memory, and memory can be lost. Or worse, the "truth" you carve out and save can be appropriated by someone else who would tell a different story.

Storytellers are haunted by new technologies of communication. Our dependence on machine memory holds us in thrall—we delight in its expanse, dread its collapse, and promise ourselves we'll always "backup." But new technologies are haunted by storytellers. The absence of the traditional figure of the writer as a character in these films belies a spoil of riches for writers in our age. McLuhan argued that when a technology becomes most popular it has already begun to wane. If we tease that claim out, then the invisibility of writers and writing in popular film speaks to a renaissance of the art and practice of writing. The imaginative writer — regardless of genre—tries to open up the smooth surface of things with each keystroke. And this issue of *PBQ* is my proof.

Perhaps more than ever the writer is part seer, part maker, part shapeshifter. Lewis Hyde writes that "trickster is the mythic embodiment of ambiguity and ambivalence, doubleness and duplicity, contradiction and paradox." Anxieties about the role of the writer and the effect digital technologies have on writing express the trickster myth.

"That trickster is boundary-crosser is the standard line," writes Hyde, who complicates that idea "in one important way, for there are also cases in which trickster creates a boundary, or brings to surface a distinction previously hidden from sight." Boundary-maker and -crosser, trickster opens up space for surprise. Watch how the writers in this issue play across genres, conduct border raids and borrow/thieve characters, content, and form from other media. What's more, they do so in a venue (*PBQ* online) that blurs technological boundaries. We are a book, and not.

The trickster, god of the threshold and the crossroad, is an archetype that offers us a way to understand the writer's work within the shifting technologies of communication. And in times like these, when things threaten to fly apart, it is the writer who calls up the world in beautiful, shimmering, truthful lies before it disappears.

Lisa Beskin

ESCAPE FROM THE PLANET OF THE APES

Dr. Zaius, I love you.
Come back to me.   My thumbs,
my beard, my cold human feet.

Film

Regie Cabico

FROM THE TWILIGHT STORIES

Judge Judy

I am taking my mom to court because she never lets me go on field trips. The judge rules in my favor. The child is always right, she says. My mom throws a lollipop at Judge Judy's face. The sheriff peels the sucker to reveal that Judge Judy is really Judy Garland.

Virgin Megastore

Susan Sarandon bumps into me at the cafe. She is with her two sons, a basket and a cow. I only come here to kill the time, I tell her. I'm here to find a slice of life, she whispers. I am going to play Mother Goose. Her eyes get large as eggs, Don't tell anyone I'm here and don't take my kids.

Chocolate Martinis

I am on a gondola, staring at the sunset. When I open my mouth a lady's operatic voice comes out. I yawn and a note of doom fills the streets. A disastrous quake hits Rome. I reach for my chocolate martinis but they're gone. I think the diva drank them.

Angelika Film Center

I break through the long lines and beg the usher to let me in. What show are you watching? It's the film of my life, I cry out. And I think the wrong person is playing me. When I get to the theater, the audience does not recognize me. I find a fresh cup of popcorn and save it for dinner.

Tooth Fairy

The tooth fairy is wearing a bomber jacket & jeans. Are you gay, I ask him. No, he says. I'm a fairy. I offer to buy some teeth from him. For a dollar I get a grab bag. Those are my baby teeth, I tell him. Then you can just have them, he says and disappears.

Issue #67

C.A. Conrad

Four Poems from ADVANCEDELVIScourse

Elvis didn't know why His foot wore a black veil to be away from the world. People asked Him, "Whose foot is that with the veil?" Embarrassed, He'd say "I don't know I don't know!" One day a passing truck blew the veil away. Startled, they stared at one another. "It is good my foot," He said, "You will have a new life." Next morning His foot was wearing a pink and yellow suit with gold and silver buttons.

Dear Elvis, I work in a gay and lesbian bookstore in Philadelphia. There's a 6 and a half foot lesbian who shops here who looks like a cross between You and Golda Meir. She was flattered on hearing this comparison. She's invited me to play golf with her, she LIVES for golf! I think I'll go, just to see the old men react when she screams and bellows while swinging her club.

That's all for now.

P.S. Did you know there are no lesbian romance titles that begin with the letter R? Sometimes it makes me sad as a round dog caught in a tidal flush (as my Gramma would say). But sometimes I'm elated for the possibilities of R in the realm of women who love women. If You were a woman Elvis, You'd be a lesbian no doubt, and no doubt understand. Wish You had lived to do a duet with K. D. Lang.

Yours,
CAConrad

The quavering, sensual voice of Elvis Presley is coming from the juke-box in lonesome, sad, sustained, orgasmic moans...."
     —from *City of Night*, by John Rechy

While catching a breath between "Jailhouse Rock" and "Don't Be Cruel" in His famous 1968 Comeback Concert, Elvis picks up the mike stand like a harpoon and shouts "MOBY DICK!"

Why would Elvis reference Melville between "Jailhouse Rock" and "Don't Be Cruel" ?????? I'm sitting on the bank of the Mississippi, Arkansas is on the other side. I'm staring at the colors of the setting sun on the passing river like I'm running out of time, like I need to find the cure, "Moby Dick?   MobyDickMobyDickMobyDick. Hm." You can stare at the passing Mississippi all you want but Melville won't come any clearer.

"Consider, once more, the universal cannibalism of the sea; all whose creatures prey upon each other, carrying on eternal war since the world began."
     —Herman Melville

Film

The truth of the matter is if Elvis and Priscilla ever had a yard sale on the long lawns of Graceland they would have sold everything in three minutes, customers screaming, crushing one another to buy the King's used socket wrenches and ashtrays. It used to take me hours to sell only half the things my mother wanted to get rid of. We had a set of Sonny & Cher napkin rings that always wound up back in the attic 'til next summer's yard sale. For five years I put on my finest Capricorn salesmanship, "And over here, ma'am, we have a lovely set of Sonny & Cher napkin rings." None of our yard sale customers ever had dinner events fancy enough to employ the likes of Sonny & Cher napkin rings. Of course neither did we, that's why we wanted someone else to get stuck never using them. A set of Sonny & Cher napkin rings at Elvis' yard sale would have been swiped up by some shrieking, weeping yard sale customer. If Elvis had dropped by my own yard sale and just touched my Sonny & Cher napkin rings they would have been transformed into the Sonny & Cher Touched By Elvis Napkin Rings. Every one of my shrieking, weeping yard sale customers (it was very uncommon for me to ever have shrieking, weeping yard sale customers) would have wanted one of the eight Sonny & Cher Touched By Elvis Napkin Rings. No one would have had a complete set! Yeah, Elvis would have been a big help back then. But He had His own successful three-minute yard sale to worry about. Only a few other Americans could have had yard sales as successful as Elvis'—the president for instance—as long as he was still in office; no one wants to buy used rollerskates from an ex-president. I wonder if Jackie O was ever given a complimentary set of Sonny & Cher napkin rings? When she smiled for a photograph with them in her hands they would have become the Sonny & Cher Touched By Jackie O While Being Photographed Napkin Rings. Is it true there were also Elvis & Priscilla napkin rings? Did Sonny & Cher have a set?

"The President lives in Washington, D.C., but the King is from Memphis!"
—graffiti on the Graceland Wall

Book 3: A Loose Lamb in a Jungle

[From "Phoebe 2002: An Essay," a collaboration in progress. "Phoebe 2002" is a mock-epic based on the 1950 movie *All About Eve*, starring Bette Davis as Broadway star Margo Channing. Margo's lover, director Bill Sampson, is about to fly to Hollywood to work on a film. "Starstruck" fan Eve Harrington, who Margo has just befriended, accompanies them to the airport. Birdie is Margo's maid and companion.]

After Bill gets on his airplane,
Margo grants Eve ingress.
Outside her idol's dressing room,
Eve grasps the Bo Peep dress.

Mankiewicz's plotting is urgently dramatic: like stations of the cross, each locale is freighted with passionate signs:

Eve accompanies Margo and Bill to the airport,
effectively amplifying the train station as film's conventional crossroad

(cf. Minnelli's *The Clock*; Kubrick's [version of the same film] *A Killer's Kiss*;
  Hitchcock's
Strangers on a Train)

as planes are faster, more dangerous (Carole Lombard criss-crossed with
Eve's cunning).

Bill's departure quickens Margo's ardour and terror, that he will die or
  never return,
10   Hollywood a brute signifier of her mortality,

where some "glamourpuss" or another is always younger than she; where her
  artistry
has no currency.

Eve makes herself useful, insinuating herself here best as Margo is missing
one diamond

(never mentioned again in the film, though reconstituted in the image of the
  stars that line
Eve's dreams)

pendant: her life as a woman and artist (a crucial dichotomy in the film)

is suspended,
imperiled.

Bill and Margo embrace and Eve comes between them, nominally a "lost lamb,"
20   a classical image of Christ that Bill subverts, naming Margo this.

It is futile to read Margo as Christ, better to situate her within the deluge of
    images
attendant this figure:

within the stations of the cross.

Yet if "the Theatuh" is "all the religions of the world rolled into one"
& those at the top (per Margo) are Gods & Goddesses

(You've got to climb Mt. Olympus to reach the Valley of the Dolls),

then Margo's jealousy aligns her with Hera—
Goddess of marriage, wife of Zeus, Queen of the Olympians.

Her intense fear of the aforementioned "glamourpuss," of "some gorgeous
    wide-eyed young babe,"
30   makes her "meek" (submissive) & "mild" (malleable), "a little child":

"As of this moment you're six years old . . ."
Eve materializes: "All ready."

Margo is rendered defenseless ("NO SMOKING [guns] BEYOND GATE"),
"a loose lamb in a jungle."

Tyger-fire burns in Eve's eyes:

   "On what wings dare [she] aspire?"

Arm in arm, bride & groom (Margo & Eve) walk down the aisle (airport
    corridor):
"the honeymoon was on . . ."

Eve becomes the Personal Assistant from Hell.
40   Birdie, temporarily displaced, is hurt/disgusted,

sees the (embroidered with sequin pine cones) wool (sweater) pulled over
    Margo's eyes.
In no time, Eve ("Giver of Life") rejuvenates the dressing room:

Issue #67

a junk yard made gay with blossoms & tufts, pillows & frills;
homemade curtains; fresh paint where, once, wallpaper peeled:

"earth now / Seemed like to Heav'n, a seat where gods might dwell"

Margo curtsies to a worshipful audience, unaware Eve waits
in the WINGS clutching the curtain, vicariously lapping up her praise.

[Sissy Spacek stands on the stage in her tiara, dazed by surreal applause,
clueless to evil Chris's grip on the rope and her teetering bucket of blood]

50   "What—again?" says Margo, snapping Eve out of her teary performance,
then steps out of the Little Bo Peep hoop; Eve goes for her back,

removing the sash, undoing Margo's Southern Belle gown made tight
by a few extra "Mr. Sampson's been gone a month" pounds.

["Young" Charlotte (57-year-old B.D. forced into a white ball gown, her face
shadowed) screeches "I could kill you!" and storms out of the summer house.

Minutes later, Charlotte (now the young Alida Aldrich—Bette's understudy?)
enters the party in the white blood-splattered dress: but for tinkling wind chimes,
  all is hushed . . . hushed]

Sweeping into her dressing room, Junior in tow, Margo barks at Birdie:
"You bought the new girdles a size smaller—I can feel it."

60   "Somethin' maybe grew a size larger." (Birdie's acumen in rib matters)
"You're going to get into one of those girdles and act for two and a half hours."

Birdie rejoins, "I couldn't get into the girdle in two and half hours!" Margo
lets out a hearty laugh. Eve, sensing the genuineness of true friendship,

chimes in, "You haven't noticed my latest bit of interior decorating,"
and proudly calls attention to her chintz curtains: "I made them myself."

Pleased with her successful killing of their moment, Eve checks her reflection
in the vanity mirror, primps like a cat, her pointy breasts aimed at Margo's back.

"Adorable," mocks Birdie.

Eve takes the coveted costume for pressing; Birdie reminds Margo
70   of her own "slave labor" status, but that the wardrobe mistress has a union.

  "Eve . . . trembling aside, / Looked where the red fruit hung
  like coals of fire, / Overhead the reddest.

Film

She lifted her long arms and tried /
To pull down the bough . . . ."

Margo dashes out the door looking like a Civil War victim
with bandaged (wig tape) head and discovers Eve

holding the gown up, "pressing her supple body into [its] cool dark leaves—
Her breasts uplifted in endeavor—" in front of a full-length mirror.

Sans false eyelashes, but with makeup still intact, Margo is framed
80   beside the harp case ("HANDLE WITH CARE") as the camera pauses to read

her face. She's amused by what she perceives as childish adulation.
"Eve, we'd better let Mrs. Brown pick up the wardrobe."

Startled and culpable, Eve clings to the dress, pressing her breasts flat,
then walks toward Margo with the flounced gown cradled in her arms.

[After Jodie Foster confides her story of the slaughtering of the lambs,
the camera pans Dr. Hannibal Lecter's "cage," revealing a tape player,

a copy of *Poetry* magazine, and a charcoal sketch of Clarice holding lamb]
["Miss Charlotte, Miss Charlotte, there's blood all over your dress!"]

Notes

7. Actress Carole Lombard was killed in a plane crash in January 1942 while returning to
California from a US-Bond-selling tour of the Midwest.
26. Jacqueline Susann, *Valley of the Dolls* (New York: Bernard Geis Associates, 1966), p. 3:
"You've got to climb to the top of Mount Everest / to reach the Valley of the Dolls."
30. "meek", "mild", "a little child": William Blake, "The Lamb," lines 15-16.
36. William Blake, "The Tyger," line 7.
43. "made gay", "blossoms", "tufts": John Milton, *Paradise Lost*, Book VII, lines 318-327.
45. Ibid., lines 328-329.
48-49. *Carrie* (movie), 1976.
54-57. *Hush . . . Hush, Sweet Charlotte* (movie), 1965.
71-74. D.H. Lawrence, "Eve," lines 13-16.
77-78. Ibid., lines 17-18.
85-87. *The Silence of the Lambs* (movie), 1991.

Issue #67

Kevin DiNovis

Baiting Leviathan; or, Watching Jaws Again

we often cast the lunartide your nude
to lure what primal scream writhes sternum-driven
from beneath-
                serrated teeth occlude
each femur rend your sinews hewn like riven
timber-
          swimmer don't you know by now
what swells below-
                   the undertow-
                              you've breached
this self-
        same sheen and swum at least a thou-
sand times at our command-
                      they found your beached
remains tomorrow every time-
             and yet
not once do you prevent the reel its draw
and stay-
        the spinal surging and descent
of mythic megalodon's seining maw

eternally denied deliverance
your thrash becomes relent-
                      less present-
                          tense.

Film

Time Delay : Twenty-One Stills

[Still 21]

Me getting out of the truck. I think I was telling him we had to get out of there, which he knew. Nothing felt right but we at least had some money now and we could pay for the gas.

[Still 20]

Joey getting us some gas. You should send this one to him he'd like it.

[Still 19]

The gun in my left hand.

[Still 18]

I didn't see any of this but I've made it up in my head and it didn't look that different. You know how people do that when they can't figure shit out? He's collapsed and the people I guess don't realize he's hit. He's a carcass already but he doesn't look dead. Wait he's not dead here. I didn't — I can't believe — that fucking bullet hit him.

[Still 17]

How is there a shot of that fucking bullet floating on air like a big boat? Doesn't look like it'll hit anyone right because you see my left hand aiming up? You see me aiming my left hand above their heads. My hand's blurry and it felt blurry. I remember that so well. Look. Nobody's anywhere near there, no guy in the yellow shirt.

[Still 16]

That's him. A yellow shirt and I think my eyes went to him in the crowd because of that. Like a bee. It was hot and I couldn't really see well from the drugs. I'm righty but I switched the gun to my left hand because my right froze up. What the hell was I doing. It's like it's not even me. Why this one guy in the yellow shirt and all these other guys started running towards the truck I have no idea so I got freaked out and I yelled—

[Still 15]

—get the fuck away from me motherfuckers! but they kept coming like they didn't care. I mean, we hadn't done shit at this point but take a little from the register. These people were crazy. You see me in this one looking like a lunatic cause I had a mob of people chasing me down. I still don't understand where all those people came from.

[Still 14]

The man in the yellow shirt, there he is. Didn't know him or anybody else. It was like all these men came from nowhere. They started chasing us so we jumped in the truck. He looks older than he really is, he was only 35 I think.

[Still 13]

The truck.

[Still 12]

Okay, not sure why there's a close up of fish n' chips in here but okay, whatever! See how nasty that is? That's why I would never put that in my body. Who would put this shit in their body?

[Still 11]

They stayed on the ground, huh. I didn't know that because I couldn't see them at that point and I didn't turn around. I was halfway out the door by this point. I should have just stayed in there because we were fucked anyway already.

[Still 10]

Me and Joey leaving Long John Silvers. First Joey.

[Still 9]

Joey realizing there's time delay on the safe. No way we could wait that out. We got what the register had that's it. We had to get the fuck out.

[Still 8]

This is exactly what I saw too. It's almost like I shot it from this angle myself. All these people outside looking in the window staring at me and Joey. Where the hell did these people come from? What were they doing?

[Still 7]

This fucking video. Everyone saw us so it's not like it matters but still I didn't see cameras so where'd you get this? They're from all angles like everybody's eyes were filming on their tongues. When I started waving the gun like I am in this one nobody was screaming like I thought they might, thank God. It's like they knew

Film

what to do. That's when the silent alarm got hit I think. They just got down quickly but were all looking up at me like this guy's going to do whatever he's going to do now. I kicked a few of them in the ribs similar to how the report says I did. I couldn't see what Joey was doing. One guy I kicked in the face because I was freaking out, why was he trying to memorize a guy with a fucking gun's face? Even if he's a decent guy he's going to kick your eyes in.

[Still 6]

Joe looking at me like what the hell are you inside for? I thought you were going to stay out there.

[Still 5]

I don't know how you got this shot of me — where was the camera? I don't even remember pulling the gun out outside (I thought I pulled it inside) but I guess I did when the kid started coming at me cause I didn't expect him to be out there. He was like eighteen and really skinny but I wasn't taking chances and we didn't have a lot of time besides. My finger is on the trigger and I'm about to tell him he needs to go back inside. Everything sounded like it was coming towards me and I just needed to get my ass inside with Joey too.

[Still 4]

I think that's the manager's son coming toward me. Yeah, it is. She saw me out there, I guess I looked suspicious and they didn't know me so she sent him out to see what I was standing there for. I don't remember what the kid said because I was thinking about what I was going to do too much. I shouldn't of looked like that standing there so obvious.

[Still 3]

Me outside Long John Silvers. Joe's already inside. I never ate there before since I don't like fish and chips or whatever else they have. Joey used to work at the one down the road but quit because the hours sucked and they didn't pay well. His idea for us to get this one and the one he used to work at, instead of like a bank which obviously has more money but we couldn't have pulled off anyway. In this photo I didn't realize there was a time delay on the safe inside.

[Still 2]

Joey.

[Still 1]

Me.

Issue #67

LAWRENCE WELK DIES

And men in Craftmatic adjustable beds recline,
their hearts on momentary pause—my father
one of them; all our fathers one of them, those
fathers who made us turn the show on to light
up evenings otherwise irreducibly devoted
to the one long task, shoveling the snow back
from the driveway—six inches accumulation
each hour, and the plows steady on the roads,
plowmen grinning, filled with Citgo Cappuccinos
and old mail-order mints. Pine-smelling fathers
in from the woods and that hack day of work
felling Christmas trees with manual saws back
and forth and axe-arcs generated by shoulders,
let loose into air. That man in the great suit
and those twin conducting arms long enough
for two trombones is dead. And liquor is still
being sold to minors trolling in on snowmobiles—
machines that serve as proof of age—and men
are losing limbs. The old high school is down;
all that architecture dusted, and the future is on
skis cross-countrying towards this house tonight.
That future has a thirty-ought strapped to its back,
bolt-action digging in below the scapula and xyphoid
process. Kids in school are still afraid to perform
mouth-to-mouth on that nasty dummy, in spite
of all the antiseptic sprays and what-if-it-was-your-
dying-sisters? Who among us will be the one to press
our lips to it, to breathe that cord of wood
back to life, to take up the old and greased
garage sale trombone, lead the band, stun
a life right out of Branson and the Lennon
Sisters and listen to that Jo Ann Castle play.

Film

Daniel Nester

Pay-Per-View Étude

When we see old actors play roles past their prime,
why do we not swell with the sunrise of pity?
Perhaps we pick out terrible infants hidden
beneath their vivid fitted suits. Time's gracious wooden stakes
could straighten them, like tomato branches

stretching for the sun. Or think of Monet, his
late-life flowers. Fingering our own crow's feet,
it's assumed we meet them halfway, add import
to dry and score-bright words. We might even think
of our own lives—their obvious, profiled arcs.

LESLIE NIELSEN SIGNS AUTOGRAPHS, COMMENTS ON HIS DISASTER MOVIE, *THE POSEIDON ADVENTURE*

Splintered, with metallic plastic shards,
    the ray gun a Leslie Nielsen fan brandishes
        is the genuine article

    from Forbidden Planet.
    "Just point it at me!" he shouts, squinting,
chunky girlfriend standing ready

with the Polaroid. He refused to hold it,
    but posed nonetheless, ever the trooper.
        I walk up to him. Too cheap to buy

    his new how-to golf tape, I offer him
a promotional flat of the cover. Pushed-in
by the line but still determined,

I spoke. "I just wanted to say
    that I agreed with you—that if you
        had taken up more ballast, you could've

    withstood that wave." Still looking down,
    signing, Leslie Neilsen paused, as if the burden
of an upside-down Shelley Winters

had been lifted, the chandeliers untousled
    right here in a suburban B. Dalton.
      "You think so, huh?"

    Smiling ear-to-ear, Leslie
shakes my hand. "But then we
wouldn't have had the disaster

—and all that conflict."

Elizabeth Scanlon

WILDLIFE DOCUMENTARY

Livid with this life, she is awake,
two years old and too much to be
contained in bed and dreams.
Quick text of change, the psych book says
she won't remember any of it—
no matter how idyllic, it's too traumatic:
the maturation process is utter.
Her fierce cognition mercifully lost,
it is said, to save her from herself.

The public broadcast at two a.m.
is a bleak nature program on oysters.
They, silently kvetching, pried for pearls,
are engineered for profit and pleasure.
They don't have much personality, these mollusks.
It is hard to feel compassion for them.
They have no keen look
in the eye, or a howl of any kind.
They seem intelligent as cabbages only less
green and faceted. But look:
such small moons of perfect irritation.

No one has ever solved colic.
It's odd there's a word for it—
a null valve, a goose egg.
In infants we see pain and say gas,
to say something,
as if we could know rapid-fire synapses,
screaming for its own sake, their minds
at all, much less, in our grown guts.

Trailing off over a vista of glistening South Sea,
the filmmaker lets us believe that somehow,
they don't mind much, it's their calling.
She dozes in the undulant light of the credits.
Sacked out mouth agape,
a sliver of molar winks in the deep
and I peer in with ravenous attention,
a sponge on the serene reef of her sleep,
relieved, hushed, bewildered.

OF MIDDLE, MIDDLE, AND MIDDLE, AND MAKING LIES BELIEVABLE: A CONVERSATION WITH PAUL THOMPSON:

For a few years after graduate school, I worked at NYU's Department of Film and Television as a lowly administrative aide. Pulling double duty as the editor of the department's internal newsletter, I had the opportunity in 1997 to interview Paul Thompson, a screenwriting and directing professor fresh from the Australian Film, Television and Radio School. The "new faculty profile" discussion ran the gamut of topics, from Muhammad Ali to Aristotle to the Elizabethans. This was not your everyday internal newsletter article.

Five years on, Thompson is preaching his idiosyncratic, no-nonsense pedagogy, to the delight of NYU screenwriting students. And though it's a golden rule in movies that sequels never equal the quality of the original, this second conversation, which took place in Thompson's office at NYU, left me with ideas echoing in my head. It's not every day you meet a former resident dramatist for the Royal Shakespeare Company who also is a fan of *South Park* and can articulate the different storytelling techniques from three continents. And so, with the early evening streets below us filled with moviegoers running to catch the opening of the *Planet of the Apes* remake, I got to do some re-shoots and questioned Thompson.

DN: I'm curious about your evolution from actor and theater person, to dramaturge and director, to your present incarnation as a film professor.

PT: The way I describe it to myself— and of course my life always makes much more sense in the telling than the living—is that I am a completely uneducated person. I mean, I was actually educated at Speaker's Corner, which is this sort of marvelous thing in London, Hyde Park, where you've got people up on soapboxes. I used to go there every Sunday to listen to a Marxist, an Anarchist, and a Methodist. And I felt that that was a perfectly rounded education. And then as extension of that I became an actor, and for ten years I worked as an actor, mainly in television—sitcoms, costume dramas, cop shows, that kind of stuff.

So that was ten years as an actor, followed by ten years as a writer and director. And that was in theater, film, and television. And then basically ten years as a teacher, dramaturge, all those things.

DN: I remember signing away my life for the newsletter—for that BBC photo of you playing a heavy, with big, lamb chop sideburns. It was my only brush with copyright law. I laid down my life for you!

PT: Really? You would have been OK, because I know for a fact that their records are not that good!

Film

DN: I remember asking you to repeat some notable lines you had as a heavy, but you recited something else, and I don't quite remember it. . .

PT: Well, yeah, there's that one line, and I know it's the line, because it's the only line I ever remember. In *The Man in The Iron Mask*, I had just one line, and of course you're always scared when you're doing one line, it was a particularly dodgy line, and anyway, I learned it so well I could probably repeat it now. The line goes like this— "Monsieur de Saint Angon, Monsieur le Barron du Vallon de Brassieux de Pierre Fond is waiting to be received."

[Laughter all around]

DN: Thank you. That was it!

PT: Not a line you're likely to forget.

DN: I think I just needed to hear it again. It was a real pain to transcribe last time. Was this a production in London?

PT: Yes. I started off as an actor, training—I say I was uneducated person, but I did train as an actor, actually, in London. And then I went to Perth, and Pitlochry in Scotland, where I worked for two seasons of rep, which is a wonderful thing, region-al theater, and then I came back to base myself in London, and worked mainly in television, mainly for the BBC, and that was really in London the whole time, except for the odd excursion to Ipswich, where I played Mr. Sloane [in *Entertaining Mr. Sloane*], and also location shoots.

DN: You've described your roles as mainly working-class guys, heavies. How did you get typecast as that?

PT: It's really interesting as an actor when you realize you have your appearance, and you know exactly who you are, and for a brief period, I could see myself clearly as a kind of Villain of the Week, and I did tend to do that, and a lot of cop shows, and I suppose it was because I did come from a working-class background myself, and I looked the role. It was the right kind of look at the right kind of time when all those things were being made. And then I graduated to playing students, and then I graduated to . . . being less in demand, I think.

DN: How did you end up in Australia?

PT: After working in England for about twenty years, ten years as an actor and ten years as a writer-director, and doing a lot of work for places like the Royal Shakespeare Company, the National Theatre, the BBC, you got to a point where . . . it's not that you've exhausted the possibilities in England, because they are inex-haustible. It's just that you had worked in all of the best places, and you had no

Issue #67

money. I mean, it was just so hard to make a living. And with a resume that looked quite strong, I just let it float out there to see who would respond. And the response came from Australia. I was offered the job as the head of directing at their National Institute. I had never been to Australia before, I went there on a one-year contract and stayed for thirteen years.

DN: Now that you've taught in England, Australia, and couple years on in the States, could you describe to me, if any, the differences in the students' scripts?

PT: Well, there's a number of generalities in which there resides some truth. For example, you know that the general American movie will end happily. There's only one narrative, and that is that good triumphs over evil, and the hero triumphs and succeeds. In Australia this is not exactly true. In Australia, the hero loses in the narrative sense, but morally wins. So in *Strictly Ballroom*, for example, you will obviously lose the ballroom competition, but you have some higher moral victory. In Europe, of course, the hero will, very simply, lose. So there's the three generalities.

But the other thing I've noticed with screenwriters is that the British tradition is one that is very skeptical of teaching, because it is one that is based upon a four-hundred-year history of dramatic writing and a great deal of confidence about writing drama. That is particularly true of theater and television, not quite so true about writing for film. In Australia, there's a sort of national inferiority complex, because they don't have that tradition. But what they do have in Australia is a recently aquired tradition of generous government subsidy. And this is a great thing for Aussie writers. Incidentally, one of the differences with Australian writers—compared to, say, America—is that whereas in America there's a strong cinematic tradition of there being a beginning, middle, and an end, in Australia there's more of a television tradition. So they're not so strong on beginning, middle, and end; they're actually better at middle, middle, and middle.

DN: One thing that has always struck me with Australian films—and I'm thinking about this because I just saw *Muriel's Wedding* again—and there are so many examples of what I appreciate, as an American weaned on middlebrow tastes, is an almost obsession with the quotidian. Say, Abba records or banal set designs.

PT: It's a very very interesting observation, because it took me a little while to understand that. In Australia there is a very suburban culture and very strong working class traditions and trade union traditions where to be ordinary is a virtue. And that is a really good thing about Australian people. It is reflected very interestingly in movies like *The Castle* and *Muriel's Wedding*. There's respect for the ordinary person and ordinary values.

DN: There's no stunt casting in Australian movies.

PT: Hardly. You just don't have the good-versus-evil, simplistic narrative of American films in Australia. Of course you do have the Mad Max films. But there are remarkably few films of that kind or any kind made in Australia.

DN: Seems that there should be more, considering how good the ones are that make it here.

PT: Well it goes in cycles, in waves. There was a barren time after the *Muriel's Wedding* period, but then recently there's been some really interesting films out of Australia, particularly *Chopper* [directed by Andrew Dominik]. It's a really tough movie about a highly celebrated criminal in Australia, and it's not an easy night out.

DN: How about comparing Australian students with those in New York? Is there a difference in what stories they want to tell?

PT: There are differences. It's very hard to compare the three countries—England, Australia, and America. It's hard to compare them because their traditions, their politics, their sociology, the economics of these countries are so very different. For example, at NYU, we have almost a thousand students in the undergraduate area studying film. Now that's an enormous number of students. I think with that vast number of students you really would expect there to be some success stories, and of course there are. The top one hundred students at NYU are really impressive. At Australia, at the national school, there were one hundred students in total studying film and television. And of those students there would be fifteen or so that were specializing in screenwriting. It's such a different environment for them, because first of all, they hardly pay any fees. Essentially what used to happen is that the Australian government would fully subsidize their education, and in fact we used to pay them a small living grant to attend school. Obviously, it was very competitive and very hard to get into that particular school, and all applicants were expected to have a track record of achievement. But once they were accepted, they would then be responsible for virtually no fees, and get an office, a computer, a production subsidy, a living allowance.

It's a very interesting situation in Australia, because at one point or another in the seventies, the government decided that film was important and set out to artificially create a film industry that would have never existed in such a small country. As a consequence, the government expects—and I think this is right in some respects—that you are going to deliver. They expect those students to be successful. Just to give you one example, a couple of years ago, there was a survey of all the students who had been through that school—twenty-five years of the school, one hundred students per year, all trackable and traceable. And it was found that the number of students who are still earning a living or making their primary income from the film and television industry was ninety-six percent.

DN: Wow.

PT: It's a very different culture. And in England, I suppose you'd get a mix of those two. It's a culture that used to have that sort of Australian identity but is now moving towards a more American model, which is making it quite tough to attend film and drama schools. So it's a thing that Australia needs to be proud of, they need to celebrate, they need to defend, because those things are always under threat. There are good things in all of these cultures in terms of education. Somewhere, somebody, someday, someone will make the ideal film and television school from the combination of these three experiences. But exactly where it will be, I don't know.

DN: It was Coppola who said something to the effect that "Until we can get a girl from Ohio to carry her own DV camera and make a movie with no other hindrances, film hasn't accomplished its mission," that the logistics hold it back from being a "pure" art form.

PT: Well, I like Coppola's idea about girls, and this leads me to another observation about Australia. When you think about Australian film, you often think of women. You think of Jane Campion, you think of Gillian Armstrong [My Brilliant Career] and Shirley Barrett [Love Serenade], and that is a result of a political and social decision about equal access. The people of Australia, the government thought it was right that women should have equal opportunity in film and television, we therefore set up structures to make sure that that happened. And as a consequence, it's not uncommon to see women cinematographers in Australian films, and women are well-represented as writers and directors. Our success simply demonstrates that once you level the playing field, if you decide that you want a level playing field, the result will be that women are equally represented in film.

DN: That's one thing I love about the NYU film program—is that, you know, it fights those stereotypes, that shtick of "boys with toys," women not being so attuned to a equipment-obsessed mentality and somehow not being suited for film. NYU fights that on a lot of fronts.

PT: I think we do, but of course it's easier to effect real change in places like Australia, where the state can intervene. When you're expecting the market to deliver equity and social justice through a system of trickle-down or whatever, then you need to be an exceedingly patient human being. Because it ain't gonna happen for ages. I don't know when America will get a woman president, but it will one day, years after Norway, England, New Zealand, Sri Lanka, India. I think it's time that America addressed these kinds of issues. But a country has to decide if they want it to happen. If they want it to happen, then of course the resources are there to make it happen. The knowledge is there, the money is there, the technology is there. It's like universal health coverage—until America decides that this is what it wants, it actually will never happen. And until America decides that it wants gender equity in the film industry, it will never actually happen.

DN: So I have some questions now for our core audience of fiction writers and poets. A couple summers ago, I went to a lecture by the fictionwriter Lee K. Abbot, who is a fiction maven and renowned teacher, a kind of McGhee-type of guy, and he says that "Dialogue is a distraction," that the real "stuff" is description, exposition, narration. And so as a writer, I'm wondering if you think the same goes for film. Or as a Shakespearean, perhaps I should ask you: What is the place of dialogue in film?

PT: Well, it's interesting, because up until about fifteen years ago, that was the kind of received wisdom in the film industry. We went through a period where dialogue was not important, when it was all about structure. Until Quentin Tarantino started to remind us that, actually, language is also exceedingly important. And amongst the many things for which we should be grateful to Quentin Tarantino, I think one of them is his sheer enjoyment of language. And it was a liberating thing. Quentin Tarantino, I believe, is actually a Jacobean dramatist. He's somebody who loves the marriage of violence and language, he's in love with both of these things, as were many Jacobean dramatists and Jacobean audiences. And I think he was a breath of fresh air.

DN: I don't think I'll ever think of a foot massage the same again after watching *Pulp Fiction*. And what was interesting about Tarantino, even that scene where John Travolta and Samuel L. Jackson are talking about foot massages, is the stagy-ness of the dialogue. They're uttering these statements at each other, the best things they could say to each other. Right now, I'm stammering, trying to get this idea across, but in film, it's the best things you can say . . .

PT: . . . It can be. But the one thing about dialogue is that we went through a period where it had to be low-key, functional and realistic. Well, it doesn't. It can be at times, and there are some films where that is of course appropriate. There are some films, of course silent movies and Jacques Tati films, where dialogue is of no consequence, but what is wonderful about, for instance, the Coen brothers, is just how much they love language, and you look at the, say, artificiality of their language and that is a joy in itself. They endow their characters with vocabularies and speech patterns that are totally outside the realm of realistic possibility. These brave decisions. All Coen brothers pictures are rich in dialogue. In movies, we should respect the potential, the great potential of dialogue.

DN: Tell me about your appreciation of Shakespeare. Is it the stories or is it the dialogue for you?

PT: Well for me, I suppose I think that Shakespeare is such an important influence on film writers because he is the most produced screenwriter. If you were his agent you'd be doing quite well out of it, because you know when it comes to getting gigs, Shakespeare gets more than most. And then they remake his films and remake them and remake them, one generation after the next. So there must be something about this man and his work that lends it . . . that attracts filmmakers to them. And I think it's to do with, amongst many other things, it's to do with the scope of his vision, the scale of his imagination, the epic nature of many of the narratives. I don't actually think it's to do with language; actually I think it's to do with the demands that an epic narrative makes upon the imagination of the people who are telling the story as well as those watching. Whereas I think for example that Dickens is a television writer because of the kind of episodic nature of his narratives and how marvelous the characters are. Television is great for the close-up, the focus on character. I think that if you can tell an episodic story the way Dickens did—he was paid that way and he wrote that way—you would see how unsurprising it is that so many of his works should lend themselves to good television.

DN: I think episodic shows such as *The Sopranos* offer some of the best stuff I've seen, period, film or TV.

PT: I am a great believer in television. I love television, mainly for what it could be rather than what it is. But I think it is really silly of people to dismiss television, even though when you look at American television now, ninety-five percent of it is junk. But ninety-five percent of movies are junk. Ninety-five percent of novels are junk. It's amazing.

DN: For the record, ninety-nine percent of poetry is junk.

PT: [Laughs] I defer to you on that one. But you see, even within that terribly demanding, corrupt corporate culture that television represents, out of that can emerge something so magnificent as *The Sopranos*, or *South Park*, for example.

DN: You're a fan of *South Park*?

PT: Absolutely. I think it is so much more imaginative and provocative than ninety-five percent of the theater that you're likely to see in New York. But while we're on the S's, we might as well say that *Seinfeld* too was wonderful. So was Gary Shandling. I mean, you could stay on the S's for quite a while. And you'd say you'd have to conclude that from that letter alone. [Thompson calls later that night to add *The Simpsons* on to the S list, and months later to add *Six Feet Under*.]

Seinfeld was so interesting. In many ways, it was kind of a endorsement of single people who are living outside of the family structure. Which is a very New York thing: four idiosyncratic characters who in a sense belong in the same movie, but somehow their differences and their isolation make them four separate islands. It was delightfully written and delightfully played, and played in four totally different styles. It was a very very interesting piece of work.

DN: And a lot of the dialogue and most of the characters, if you even want to call them characters, was kind of a Becketian exercise.

PT: Oh wonderful, minimalism, and sort of . . . I think a marvelous piece of work. I'm a great fan of Gary Shandling's work, particularly *The Larry Sanders Show*. Very subversive and very funny.

DN: Do you think that staged dialogue can go too far? I mean, do you think there are examples of, I wouldn't force you to say it, where sometimes that's the case? Maybe it's a matter of taste, but I think it maybe goes too far with, say, Hal Hartley movies, where they quote Kierkegaard to each other and they're not really interacting.

PT: I think that's really interesting.

DN: Maybe it's the absence of wit in the Hal Hartley films, but . . .

PT: Well that's really interesting about those movies—and I'm not a great Hal Hartley fan, and I don't like all of Jim Jarmusch's films, for example—but what I find is interesting about those kind of writers and those kind of directors is that there's something a little bit reported about everything. The dialogue is kind of quoted. The performances are kind of reported. I think that's a stylistic choice which wouldn't necessarily appeal to everybody, but it's a very interesting addition to the repertoire of cinema. What does that mean? What does that mean in terms of demands it makes on actors? It's a very Brechtian. It appeals to the intellect more than the emotion. Those are things I actually like about those kind of films, although in the end I have to say that there are not that many Hal Hartley films or Jim Jarmusch films that I actually enjoyed.

DN: You've said that, besides the Elizabethan period, there was maybe a hiccup of Brecht's influence on drama somewhere in there, and I wanted to have you maybe explain that a little bit more.

PT: For me, Brecht has always been a really influential writer. I like to see traces of his work, in theories and practice, reflected in cinema. And I think that some of these people like [Finnish director] Kaurismäki or Hartley do try to do that in some ways, by delivering restrained reported performances. Of course, the political nature of Brecht's work is something that is often absent from American cinema, with the notable exception of someone like John Singleton, who I think is one of the most thoughtful filmmakers. I mean, *Higher Learning* is one of the most underrated films, not a totally successful film, but just in terms of the analysis of society. I'm really looking forward to seeing the new film. So there is a Brechtian, Brecht is more noticeable in the films of somebody say like Jean Luc Godard, where you really use commentary, he uses titles and a lot of voiceover, and this gives you that sense of distancing, of commentary, a reminder of the artificiality of the medium.

DN: A tragedy in wide shot, like in Godard's *Contempt*.

PT: Yes, all those things that draw attention to themselves.

DN: It seems as if that all of these advances or diversions in the storytelling tradi-

Issue #67

tion in cinema—French New Wave for one, maybe an American auteur such as Orson Welles or Cassavetes—add up to an influence that hasn't been completely understood or appreciated or implemented. This is a break in a tradition, a young tradition, but you could lump it in with a long storytelling tradition back to drawing on caves.

PT: Absolutely. I mean, there are a couple things you've said right there that I think are interesting, and one is the reference to the cave. This was really brought home in Australia, which has the Aboriginal tradition of the tribal storyteller. You realize there is this wonderful connection between the storyteller as an essential member of the tribe—as necessary as the cook, as necessary as the hunter. It is not a person who is peripheral or an optional extra. It is the person who has a meaningful and necessary role to play. And then you see the tribe gather around the storyteller for a purpose, which is to explain the inexplicable, to help them overcome their fears, to help them with their lives. I think modern storytellers are aware of that role. I think a number of them have an insight into that. They realize that when you go to a multiplex, lots of teenagers gravitate toward that one particular cave, where anxieties will be addressed by that particular storyteller, and families go to that cave, and they all gather around this flickering light, the same way we'd gather around the fire, and this ritual somehow addresses your concerns. That, for me, is so important about storytelling—Who is it for? Whether it's a bedtime story or a movie, it has a function, it has a purpose, and a story has a power. What is amazing is that children, when they're frightened, they ask for a story. Children know that a story has power. And I think that we sometimes, as storytellers, we forget who we're telling the story to and why.

I'll say something here too about Brecht. Even in situation comedies, in a very early Gary Shandling situation comedy, he did some very interesting things—I used to watch these late at night at two o'clock in the morning in Australia. And sometimes the shows were not funny. They didn't always succeed in that very fundamental test of a comedy. It certainly succeeded in some extraordinarily adventurous thing he was doing, like walking out of a scene in the middle, sitting amongst the audience, commenting upon the action that was happening in front of them. I mean, truly Brechtian, truly experimental, much more adventurous than a lot of student films. And here we're talking about that much denigrated, much despised medium of television. I mean I just find the gems of television are worth all the dross you have to struggle through.

DN: So you have eighteen-year-old film students who say, "Television, Shmelevision"?

PT: Yes I do. I find it weird and bizarre that in all the film schools in the world, television is so neglected to the point of being almost invisible, that the students will rarely admit to watching it. Well, of course they do watch it, it's just that they perhaps don't realize they are! There's such an unconscious fog.

I'm not trying to defend the continual barrage of commercials. I would ban the

Film

commercials. I wouldn't ban the sex, the violence—I don't think there's anywhere near than enough sex and violence. But there are too many commercials. They're loud, they're aggressive, they appeal to the basest elements of human beings, and if a mind is ever going to be corrupted by television, it would be the commercials. It's not the violence—the thing to point out here is that the whole world is watching the same movies. The Germans are watching them, the Japanese are watching them, the Swedes are watching them, the entire world is watching the same show. It's only the Americans who are acting on them. So I don't think you can draw a single connection between gun-related deaths and television violence.

The only use of commercials is to sell products that you don't want or don't need. And it's such a diminution of the possibilities of television. When you think what it could be, this wonderful medium for informing, educating and enlightening human beings, at its best it does do that. I actually think, controversial as it is, I think *South Park* is a force of great good. I think it's more truthful than Fox News.

Teaching screenwriting, I begin all of my classes with a quote from Picasso: "Art is a lie that enables us to see the truth more clearly. Our task as artists is to convince others of the truthfulness of our lies." And when I first heard this idea of Picasso's, I was offended by it, affronted by it, and upset by it, but I've since completely adopted it. And it's not completely uncommon for people to see the screenwriter as a professional liar. I think that if you have this wonderful ability to seduce people, to entrance people, to enchant people with your storytelling, then what you're doing is you're making your lies believable. You create a fictional narrative, and I think that's a great thing to do, when the only things that you've got are your experience, your observations, and your imagination, and you're using those to make your lies believable. And that's where I begin my screenwriting classes, with Picasso. Who, as I think of it, was not very well-known as a screenwriter. [Laughter all around.]

DN: He had a couple optioned, I think.

PT: Yes, but none greenlit.

Steve Fellner

INSPIRATION

No movie biography has disturbed me more than Ed Harris's *Pollock*. My dislike for the movie centers around one key scene: the moment Jackson Pollock finds his Inspiration. It's the scene that attempts to show Pollock's discovery of his Action paintings. The Big Moment of Discovery.

This is the Moment: Pollock is doing one of his more typical paintings. He drops his brush. Paint splatters all over the floor. Frustrated, he takes a step back. He recognizes Genius. This is the beginning of his Abstract Expressionism.

Could there be anything more reductive than representing Pollock's Inspiration as the accidental dropping of a paint brush?

I confess that I avoided seeing the movie when it first came to theaters, even after Marcia Gay Harden won the Best Supporting Actress Oscar for playing the role of Pollock's sassy, long-suffering wife. Movie biographies always bother me. They almost always try to cover way too much time, advancing to the Major Dramatic Scenes with shameful excitement. They're also often dull and earnest.

Before I saw *Pollock*, I read numerous interviews with Ed Harris about the making of film. His attraction to the material. (Should we assume that Harris tripped over a book about Pollock and then had his Epiphany: Pollock must be made into a movie!) The painstaking research. The usual production problems. It sounded like good news copy. Only an unkind person like myself could fail to be touched.

I can still remember the fateful night several other English teachers and I ended up in Blockbuster Video, desperately trying to find a movie to rent. It was the first time we all went out together and everyone wanted to look respectable.

"Has anyone seen the latest Stephen Segal movie?" I said.

"Who's he?" someone said.

"I don't know," I lied. "The cover looked interesting." I put the movie back on the shelf and decided that I wouldn't offer any recommendations.

"How about *Pollock*?" someone else said.

Everyone agreed and we walked out of the video store, victorious.

When it came to the Moment of Inspiration, I burst into laughter. Someone thought I was choking on popcorn, so they grabbed the remote control and asked me if I was OK.

"I was laughing," I said.

"At what?"

"That scene," I said. "It's ridiculous. To think that the birth of Abstract Expressionism is predicated on Pollock's accidental dropping of a paint brush is insane."

Everyone looked at me like I was crazy.

"Do you think you're being fair?" someone else said.

"Fair?"

Film

"Yes, fair," the person said. "Inspiration is a very difficult thing to represent on film."

I couldn't disagree with my colleague. Inspiration is a very difficult thing to represent on film. Or for that matter explain in any way. But I couldn't drop the subject. I pushed it further: "Hubris."

"Hubris," someone repeated.

"Hubris," I said. "That's what this movie is guilty of. That's the sin I attach to Ed Harris. He's an artist. A really good actor. How dare he think that he can explain a fellow artist's inspiration in one quick, glib scene."

Someone excused themself to go to the bathroom. Someone else went to get more popcorn. Two others marched outside and shared a cigarette. There was one other person in the room. He was in the philosophy department and he never engaged in conversation. He hoarded all his thoughts. His name was Phil.

"So," Phil said. "What else do you think of the movie?"

"I didn't know much about Jackson Pollock going into the movie," I said. "And having watched the movie for about an hour now, I don't think I know anything much more."

He looked at me with the blankest of expressions. This made me want to rant more. But I had nothing else to say. I was tired.

"So," he said, "The movie hasn't offered you any insight into the character of Jackson Pollock." He spoke slowly and deliberately. I could imagine him paraphrasing his students' comments in class, and his students cringing, wondering how their words were going to inevitably make them look stupid.

"Yes," I said.

"Is that a good thing or a bad thing?"

"When I see a biography, I want to know something new about the person. Isn't that why we rented this film?"

"Is it?" Phil said. "Or is it an odd success of the film that Ed Harris chooses not to offer any dazzling, new psychological insights into Jackson Pollock? Harris allows the superficial myths surrounding Pollock to remain untouched, unexamined. Like the fighting. Like the drinking. Like the depression. His refusal to delve deeply is an act of kindness. Harris doesn't pursue what makes Pollock tick, because he knows he can't do it. And to pretend to do so is ultimately unethical. So he uses the myths as a way of showing off his own acting talents. While leaving the more human aspects behind those very myths alone."

"But what about the scene I was talking about?"

"Comedy," Phil said. "Pure comedy."

At the time I didn't know what to say, so I said nothing except the obvious: "Inspiration is a funny thing." It's not like I could offer any effective solutions to Harris's dilemma: representing Inspiration in a convincing, edifying way. You couldn't show Pollock summoning the Devil, engaging in some sort of Faustian bargain, offering his full mortality for Artistic Genius. Nor you could ask Julia Roberts to contribute a cameo as a Muse, offering sassy, cogent advice whenever Harris's Pollock grows tired, inert.

All I knew was I wanted Something More.

"Don't we all," Phil said.

"Is that bad?" I said.

"No," Phil said. "But you're forgetting something."

"What?"

"There's the paintings," he said. "There is always the paintings."

Film

James Polchin

THE ACTOR AND THE ACADEMIC

Lecturing in his blindness, the aged Argentinean writer Jorge Luis Borges contemplated the nature of immortality, quoting Thomas Aquinas: "Intellectus naturaliter desiderat esse semper," the mind naturally desires to exist forever. To this Borges asked, "But in what ways does it desire it?"

Obscurity is a tragedy in our times for it denies the possibility of immortality. The fear of falling into obscurity feels like a struggle against our own death, a ceasing to exist not merely in the here and now but also, and more importantly, in the here and after. We deny ourselves such thoughts about the after, more content with the here. Yet we fear our mortality in ways much different than Aquinas's intellectual spiritualism, or even Borges's modernist contemplations. In a culture where celebrities hold power, where Warhol's dream that everyone will have their fifteen minutes of fame feels more likely, the fear of obscurity takes a particularly crucial form.

Academics are often fearful of obscurity. The demeaning metaphor of the "Ivory Tower" offers an easy dismissal of the academic as an isolated, aloof being, packed away with books and ideas, in laboratories and library reading rooms, determined and pursuant of passions that are ultimately insignificant to the larger world. The Ivory Tower rests on the obscure and inconsequential where immortality rests on hopeful threads of notoriety within the academy. Fame, however, is a different matter.

The "star system" of academics, like that of Hollywood, rests on the cult of personality. Academic celebrities command attention, lecture fees, adoring graduate students and comfortable offices with large windows. They are figures we want to see as much as hear. "I wonder what so and so looks like?" is a common question in graduate school in reference to some well-known and oft-quoted working academic. For those academics who put their photographs on their book jackets, celebrity status becomes more tangible. Like head shots, these iconic images tell us nothing about the academic worth of the book, the ideas inside, but only what the writer looks like: a fashionable attribute to a carefully constructed idea. "I'm thinking of including a photograph of myself with my curriculum vitae," a graduate student colleague recently said to me. Of course, one of the more famous academic book photographs would be that of Camille Paglia. Paglia, refusing the obscurity of the back cover, instead preferred the front for her second book, *Vamps and Tramps*. She commands big lecture fees these days. A star is born.

I live in New York City, specifically in the neighborhood long-known as Hell's Kitchen. It is a changing, gentrifying neighborhood just west of the theater district and Times Square. To live here is to live in two worlds: one of old brick tenements, warehouses and theaters, recent immigrants from Latin America and elsewhere; the other, more trendy side, with chic restaurants and bars, tourists flowing over from their matinees and evening concerts, and the growing population of younger residents moving into fairly cheap housing with expectations of acting and modeling

Issue #67

careers. I live in this neighborhood, a graduate student among performers and audiences, among the working-class and celebrity hopefuls, all within the horizon of mid-town Manhattan skyscrapers and on the fringes of Broadway. In the shadows of such giants, we live in hope.

I belong to a gym near my apartment. It happens to be next door to Studio 54, which now hosts the successful revival of *Cabaret*. I often maneuver my way through the matinee crowds on my way to the gym. Most of the people who go to this gym are aspiring for performance work: actors, dancers, singers, models. Others find their livelihoods behind the cameras and curtains. On one Saturday afternoon, while riding the stationary bike, I overhear a conversation behind me. A tall, bulky man, tanned, dark hair wearing a white t-shirt is talking with a petite woman. She, thin and agile, smiling and laughing. "I can't continue doing this work," he says to her. "I'm 35 now and I'm tired of going to the calls, waiting for call backs that never come or that never materialize. I'm trying to figure out something new." The woman listens, encourages and supports "Maybe you just need to network more. Maybe you need a new agent. Have you called Tom?" I listen and watch one of the seven television screens playing VH1 "Before they were Stars" (or was it "Where are They Now?"). I pedal and pedal, and forget the conversation for awhile—wanting to forget it for it sounded so familiar to me. It sounded just like a number of conversations I have had with fellow graduate students over the past few years. Change a few words —campus interview for call back, conference presentation for network, faculty advisor for agent—and the conversation was the same. I kept pedaling, hoping that I would get away from these two. I didn't get that far.

The actor and the academic are, in many senses, hybrid forms in a culture obsessed with obscurity. I say obscurity here and not celebrity because they are mutually dependent experiences. The actor and the academic represent two halves of a culture where the burden of fame looms large, and the demands of obscurity even larger. It comforts us to think of the actor and the academic as distinct and different for we don't have to deal with the possibilities of our own obscurities, the struggles of being on the margins; and, ultimately, the realities of our own mortalities. Our culture's worship of fame reflects such insecurities. As the song from the eponymous movie tells us, "Fame. I want to live forever." The idea of fame holds our desires to be representable, known, remembered.

Increasingly we are attempting to find fame in our obscurities. We are resurrecting our lives on the margins through an immortality of obscurity, where the marginal and the outcast are figures we adore; where we can all set up a "stage" on the Internet; where we can all imagine our obscurities as precisely the stuff of fame. Gone are the celebrities of the past, glittery personas that seem unreal and distant. Their flaws, while human, were certainly not our flaws. Their image was grander than us, projected on wide movie screens in dark theaters, they were unimaginable. These days, fame seems less distant, much closer to our lives, much more imaginable. In cutting down those wide-screen images, we use them to cover our fears of obscurity. Obscurity and immortality feel not so far apart.

Film

* * *

In the 1999 Oscar-winning film *Good Will Hunting*, obscurity and fame play a particularly ironic game. Will Hunting (Matt Damon), the working-class South Boston janitor with innate skills in advanced mathematics, becomes the center of a struggle between sensitive psychologist and community college professor Sean (Robin Williams) and the distinguished and honored MIT math professor Jerry Lambeau (Stellan Skarsgård). In one scene Sean and Lambeau are having lunch in a South Boston pub, and Lambeau asks the waiter if he knows of Albert Einstein or Jonas Salk. He knows both, and Lambeau bemoans the fact that while he may have received academic accolades in his field, he has yet to achieve real notoriety — real fame. Will Hunting is Lambeau's path to such fame. Of course Sean, played by the ever-eccentric and always emotional Robin Williams, argues with his old college roommate and now Harvard professor. Lambeau engaged Sean to treat the troubled Will who was orphaned at a young age and had a history of criminal arrests. His therapy is of course two sided, for as much as Sean shows Will how to live beyond his past—his abuses in foster care, his inabilities to sustain meaningful commitments—Will shows Sean how to embrace the world after the death of his wife. The therapist and the patient teach each other a new way of living, both obscure figures in the larger social world: an orphaned working-class youth and a community college professor find a connection here precisely in their obscurity.

Lambeau's desires for fame cast a shadow over the frailties of the obscure. You know who is good and who is not so good. You know you'd rather be in Sean's small cluttered office instead of Lambeau's richly furnished salon. Yet the film plays with these desires of ours, for films do imagine for us our own fame. We are likely to identify with those aspects of characters that feel like us. The irony, however, is a deeper and less apparent distortion of this feeling.

In an early scene, Will and his friends are in a bar in Cambridge where a mixture of locals and university students hang out. Will approaches Skylar, a university student played by Minnie Driver. Her English accent seems perfect for the scene. A male graduate student, sporting the requisite ponytail, who comes to save Skylar from "townie" harassment, quickly interrupts their conversation. Will and the graduate student engage in an academic debate about commerce in the colonial era (it is Boston of course), with Will, who we later learn can also speed read, outsmarting the Harvard educated just as he will outsmart the mathematics faculty. Will shows he knows more of the theories of colonial mercantile trade than the history graduate student, and can even evaluate the merits of such theories, whereas the graduate student is left only to regurgitate the ideas he reads. In anger, the graduate student rests on all that he has left: his class status. "I'll have a degree. And you'll be serving my kids fries at a drive through on our way to a skiing trip," he says, as the last effort to hold on to his intellectual integrity and barroom pride. Will responds, "At least I won't be unoriginal."

Will's success is not simply that he can outwit or outsmart an academic. Rather, he can be original in a way that the academic can never be. The film imagines success as precisely this quality of originality: a success so keen to acting that the film

Issue #67

at times feels overly self-reflexive. Real success, the film seems to suggest, is achieved through originality, the kind of originality that we often associate with fame: the unique actor, the personality, the individual. These are the qualities that make us celebrities in a society so worshipful of fame. Fame trumps class status in such a way that we believe in its democratic power. The Ivory Tower, shadowing the day-to-day life of the working-class "townies" of Cambridge, holds a promise of wealth that, in the end, fails to live up to real social status, to real originality, to real fame.

As the film ends, Will drives west to California, leaving his South Boston world to be with Skylar, now a medical student at Stanford. He has come to a reckoning about his past and is ready for a relationship he initially rejected. Thus, Matt Damon as Will drives out of the landscape of the film and is launched into his own Hollywood fame with Oscar nominations and cover stories on all the glossy magazines. The meaning feels almost intended: Will the gifted working-class youth goes off to a new life in California; Damon the Harvard graduate goes off to California to achieve fame. His face, with its bright white smile, is ubiquitous. He becomes a star. He is Matt Damon, the Harvard graduate, the actor, the screenwriter, the personality. In this sense, the film allows us to both identify with Will's obscurity, an obscurity we desire for its originality, its talent, its feistiness, as much as we desire Damon's own fame. The film makes Damon immortal as both character and actor. The film allows us to imagine our own obscurities as fame itself.

*　　*　　*

Writing to his friend and fellow poet Yvor Winters in May of 1927, Hart Crane questioned the contours of work and writing through a critique of a recent poetry review by Edmund Wilson. "It is so damned easy," Crane bemoans,

> for such as he, born into easy means, graduated from a fashionable university into a critical chair overlooking Washington Square, etc. to sit tight and hatch little squibs of advice to poets not to be so 'professional' as he claims they are, as though all the names he had just mentioned have been as suavely nourished as he—as though 4 out of 5 of them hadn't been damned well forced the major parts of their lives to grub at any kind of work they could manage by hook or crook and the fear of hell to secure! Yes, why not step into the State Department and join the diplomatic corps for a change! indeed, or some other courtly occupation which would bring you into wide and active contact with world affairs! As a matter of fact I'm all too ready to concede that there are several other careers more engaging to follow than that of poetry. But the circumstances of one's birth, the conduct of one's parents, the current economic structure of society and a thousand other local factors have as much or more to say about successions to such occupations, the naïve volitions of the poet to the contrary.

Wilson's criticism is but an outgrowth of the Ivory Tower, yet its weight in the world held value at a time when literary critics said things about poets, and people beyond poets and academics read them. Crane, the poet writing to another poet

(Winters was himself preparing to enter graduate study at Stanford University), contemplates with anger the predicament of the artist, and, by implication, the obscurity that shrouds him from other more "courtly occupations." It is the nature of work that Crane inveighs against here, resisting the force of the "professional" that weighs on the realities of laboring at menial tasks—so romanticized in our concepts of the struggling artist. The artist labors for the love of the work itself, we say. They struggle, live on the margins, accept their fate. But what do they struggle for? Or rather, what do they struggle against? Crane was caught in between these struggles, fighting his own financial hardships that plagued him for most of his adult life, and courting desires of becoming an important, perhaps even famous, poet. Underneath his rage, Crane's words to Winters hold a reality even more felt today: how can we represent ourselves within a world so burdened by the fear of obscurity? Like the poet, the struggling actor, the contemporary academic, many of us confront this question—a question that bears on our own mortalities.

In his essay "Representation of the Intellectual," Columbia University professor Edward Said writes that "intellectuals are individuals with a vocation for the art of representing, whether that is talking, writing, teaching, appearing on television. And that vocation is important to the extent that it is publicly recognizable and involves both commitment and risk, boldness and vulnerability." For Said, the "art of representing" is a social performance that impresses upon the intellectual the need to question, critique, and challenge injustices and inequalities. The intellectual, now so often housed in the halls of the university, the Ivory Tower of inconsequentiality, functions in the domain of the representable, and needs to find a place in the iconic images that construct the public life of our nation. To recover the place of the academic, Said places the more traditional work of teaching and writing within the domain of celebrities: television.

Yet what if you can't perform in such public ways, in such celebrity-like contexts? What then? What may it mean to exist, to represent, precisely in between the domains of "Before they were Stars" and "Where are They Now"—a domain that holds many of our possibilities and our fears. As we labor at our daily lives, burdened by the expectations of fame, we may wonder how we attempt to represent ourselves within another realm of fame—the realm of obscurity itself that fame so desperately needs and demands. The distinctions we draw between the actor and the academic serve us well in blinding us to that place where our minds desire a fame so unlikely and struggle with existing in an obscurity so inevitable.

THE BLAIR WITCH PROJECT: AN ALLEGORY

The Blair Witch Project marks a watershed moment in cyber-hype. In the same way that *Jaws* revolutionized distribution by blasting into saturation bookings in 1975, this "little" film redefined "synergy" by synthesizing film, video and the Internet. Movie Web sites can no longer contain merely interviews with the cast and crew and hotlinks to Blockbuster. In a post–*Blair Witch* world, these sites must create interactive universes. According to *Time* magazine, the careful manipulation of cyberpublicity in the summer of 1999 made *The Blair Witch Project* "the must-attend social event for plugged-in America" (58). While the film itself has been relegated to the waiting room of cult cinema, its repercussions continue to echo throughout the Hollywood publicity machine.

It is a story that has attained legend status. *The Blair Witch Project* was made for $25,000, $30,000 or $35,000 (depending on which version of the legend one hears). Artisan Entertainment paid first-time filmmakers Daniel Myrick and Eduardo Sanchez $1 million for the distribution rights at the 1998 Sundance Film Festival (Corless 59). In its first week in nationwide release, it made $50 million on 1,101 screens (58). The film stands to be the most profitable movie ever made—in theory it earned back its production costs in the first hour of its release. The week of August 16, 1999 both *Time* and *Newsweek* ran cover stories on the film. *Newsweek* featured the three actors on its cover. *Time* placed Myrick and Sanchez within its red frame.

The Blair Witch Project is a horror story / mockumentary with a fairly facile plot. Three film students, Heather Donahue, Joshua Leonard, and Michael Williams, go into the Maryland woods to make a documentary about a local legend—the Blair Witch. The film is Heather's senior project and to be shot in black-and-white 16 mm. Heather, devoted to process and "her vision," has brought a video camera to make a record of the making of the documentary. (Will self-reflexivity never end?) The three proceed to film, videotape, and wander their way through the wilderness. Trudging through the eerily banal woodlands, Heather, Josh and Michael become increasingly lost, paranoid, and angry. They are terrorized by strange noises, a Karo syrup–like substance, bunches of twigs and stacks of rocks. The film climaxes in a series of motion sickness–inspiring sequences. By the end of *The Blair Witch Project*, the audience can safely assume that the witch "got them" and thus the ersatz "project" has become part of the legend it sought to chronicle.

What I would suggest is that the importance of *The Blair Witch Project* lies in its value as an allegory. The film can be read as a cautionary tale. It details, as clearly as the myth of Daedalus and Icarus, what happens when humans seek the knowledge of a power that is beyond them. Or, more specifically, when film students graduate with their BAs and go enthusiastically into the "dark night" of the film industry. Encouraged by success in an educational institution and the praise of their film professors, they forge ahead into the unknown. Happily, they include their classmates in their quest, proudly waving maps of random internship connections and phone numbers gleaned from *Variety*'s "In Production" column. Boisterously they announce: "I know exactly where we are, I know exactly where we're going, I can read the map." Then, in the midst of their voyage toward an Oscar for Best Direction, confusion sets in. Calls are not returned, people they thought were their friends disappear, the map becomes increasingly useless. Disoriented, they try to read the signs, but unfamiliar fetishes await them every morning and they fear the coming of night. Terrified, they stumble through an increasingly claustrophobic wilderness, their assertions of power transformed into a plaintive mantra of "What the fuck was that?" Ultimately they disappear, seemingly without a trace, destroyed by a power that existed long before they came along and that they never really understood in the first place.

In his chronicle of seven film school graduates' experiences in Hollywood, Billy Frolick writes, "Film school is commonly thought to be one of the better routes toward directing professionally. But if there is a more worthless college degree than Philosophy, it might just be film" (3). With all due respect to Plato, it does not require an investment of thousands of dollars to complete a philosophy thesis. Semi-professional bindery at Kinko's still comes in under $7.99. In 1996, Mary Schmidt Campbell, Dean of NYU's Tisch School of the Arts, estimated that "the average for student films, which are about twenty minutes long, is between $10,000 and $12,000. Except for a small film allowance provided by the school, students must raise the money for their own projects" (Hawkins 10). This is true of all of the "major" and "minor" American film schools. Still, film programs continue to be huge draws for American universities.

These are the same universities that boast about placement rates as they compete with each other for prospective students. Students are the all important Full-Time Equivalencies (FTEs) whose money pays the electric bills, waters the grass, maintains the buildings, and supports the tenured faculty. Universities sell themselves by highlighting the ways in which their educational programs provide students with "real-world" skills and contacts. Undergraduate programs remain competitive by becoming increasingly vocationalized and professionalized. Thus, higher education in America is perceived as the key to high-paying and prestigious jobs rather than an intellectual endeavor.

What is surprising is that film school has become a huge draw in the commodified educational environment. Interest in production programs has increased dramatically since the 1970s despite the lack of placement rates and the dearth of any clear post-graduation career trajectory. In 1992, Deyso Magyar, director of the American Film Institute's Center for Advanced Film and Television Studies, estimated that "only five to ten percent of the 26,000 students who graduate from film study programs each year actually find their way into the industry" (Buzzell 101). That same year, applications to such programs numbered in the tens of thousands nationwide.

Film production programs do not cite placement statistics in their admissions

Issue #67

materials. Instead, they sell a dream. On the base level, film schools advertise themselves by making the implicit promise that: the student + his or her parents' money + the school's program in film production = the name of your favorite wunderkind director. Ironically, the most popular fill-in-the-blank is Steven Spielberg—who never went to film school. Indiscriminately lumped together with USC's George Lucas, UCLA's Francis Ford Coppola and NYU's Martin Scorsese, Spielberg is perceived as one of the mid-1970s' "collegiate new wave" (Frolick 4). Spielberg wannabes are attracted by "his attitude—a fierce drive to break new aesthetic ground coupled with an encyclopedic knowledge of film history" (4). Frolick suggests, however, that it is more than mere hero-worship that brings students to production programs. As a group, Frolick characterizes "most film students" as "driven by arrogant, at times delusional, beliefs about themselves. They believe they have stories to tell, but that writing is too limiting; that they are not simply actors or dancers but can manipulate performance; that they understand visual composition but cannot find in still photography the third dimension they need" (3). While this is clearly observable in the ill-fated, tyrannical, and whiny Heather, it is overly simplistic to attribute the creative drives of a group of students to mere celebrity emulation or psychological aberration.

I would suggest that the rise in the popularity of film production programs indicates that youth are media savvy and understand the power of the image. The same images that tell them they must have NIKE and Tommy Hilfiger to belong, that they must lose weight or bulk up to fit in, also tell them that to have power, one must make images. Control over the image, its creation and distribution, is the highest form of fame and fortune in our postmodern capitalist culture. Why, then, wouldn't students seek out training in image production? Why wouldn't they voyage into the woods in search of such power?

Certainly Andy Warhol's prediction that "In the future, everyone will be world famous for fifteen minutes" seems to have come true. Warhol made Joe Dallesandro, Ultra Violet, Candy Darling and the other "Superstars" famous for at least twelve minutes each. Yet what we learn from "The Factory" over and over again, like so many silkscreened Elvises, is that the power, the fame, the glory, and the money go not to the image, but to its maker. Young people who have learned about their world through tabloid exposés and news magazine shows know that Rock Hudson was gay, Judy Garland was addicted to pills prescribed by an MGM doctor, and that actresses over 33 have trouble finding work. They've seen the "stars" through rehab, recovery, and relapse. For them, those in front of the camera are idle rather than idol images. The true power is behind the camera, calling the shots. The American promise of individual potential—that "anyone can grow up to be President"—has been rendered impotent (pun intended). The new aspiration, the new promise, is that "anyone can grow up to be Steven Spielberg." It is this promise that film schools sell to prospective students. It is this promise that keeps students flocking to the film schools.

And yet this flocking could be an optimistic sign for those of us who study and

Film

teach media and communication. It may indicate that our students recognize the influential power of the image in consumer society. Knowing that culture is created by those who produce and control these images, they seek to occupy those positions themselves. Some seek to replicate the images of the hegemonic powers, others to challenge the images that have shaped them. All of them wish to realize their "vision" and by so doing transform the representations that create meaning and identity in our culture.

Few ever achieve these goals. While the movement in other disciplines is toward increased vocationalization, film programs remain almost purposely naive to the realities of the marketplace. Students are not taught how to negotiate the industrial landscape of the image-makers—how to loosen the hold that an ever-decreasing number of CEOs have upon the creation and circulation of images. The challenge is for the film school faculty members. How can these educators, many of whom have themselves taken refuge from the wilderness of the industry in the universities, teach not only image creation but industrial negotiation? How can they demystify the witch—a force which is impervious to imagery and destroys those who try to capture it?

Works Cited/Consulted

Ansen, David and Corie Brown. "How 'Blair Witch' is Spooking Tinseltown." *Newsweek*. August 16, 1999. 50-55.

Block, Mitchell. "The Training of Directors: From School to Screen." *Journal of the University Film Association*. Fall 1980, V32(4) 35–44.

Buzzell, Linda. *How to Make It in Hollywood*. New York: HarperPerrenial, 1992.

Corliss, Roger. "Blair Witch Craft." *Time*. August 16, 1999. 58–64.

Frolick, Billy. *What I Really Want to Do Is Direct*. New York: Plume, 1996.

Graham, Amy and Robert Morse. "How U.S. News Ranks Colleges." *U.S. News and World Report*. August 30, 1999. 84–105.

Hawkins, Denise. "Flocking to Film School: Learning the Realities of Hollywood in the Classroom." *Black Issues in Higher Education*. January 11, 1996. V12(23) 8–15.

Kelly, Karin and Tom Edgar. *Film School Confidential*. New York: Perigree, 1997.

Leland, John. "The Stealth Blockbuster." *Newsweek*. August 16, 1999. 44–59.

Myrick, Daniel and Eduardo Sanchez. *The Blair Witch Project*. Haxxon Entertainment, Artisan. 1999.

———. *The Curse of the Blair Witch*. Haxxon Entertainment. The Sci-Fi Channel, 1999.

Issue #67

Vicki Weissman

Harry Potter – The Renaissance of Reading?

You can't, as they say, argue with success, and there's no doubt that J. K. Rowling's success has been phenomenal. She is now a very rich woman and that's before she has finished the series. Not only has her boy hero made her rich, he has also given her the chance to tell the BBC what to do—a rare and wonderful privilege. Rowling would only allow the Corporation to broadcast the boy wizard's adventures if the tale was uninterrupted. So Stephen Fry read *Harry Potter and The Sorcerer's Stone* from start to finish on Boxing Day and netted one and a half million young listeners. The *New York Times* Parent's Guide to the Best Books for Children ends its Harry Potter entry, "Read 'em all. In order." But the judges of the Whitbread Book Award, one of the foremost UK literary prizes, passed Harry Potter by. Despite having sold 833,000 hardback copies since July 2000, *Harry Potter and the Goblet of Fire* did not even make the short list and one judge was quoted as saying that it "wasn't up to it." No doubt J. K. Rowling was able to bear this with the equanimity colossal commercial success tends to impart, but it was certainly a sizeable put-down.

So if it is not literary merit that sells the books, then what is it that does? They are first and foremost extremely approachable. There is not a lot of difficult vocabulary. The most challenging words in the books tend to be those Rowling has invented—witches' charms, the names of the Houses at Hogwarts, the names of some of the characters—but for the most part the books' diction is easy and seldom polysyllabic. A child with a fairly low reading age would not find the pages a challenge. This is immediately attractive. The story is accessible without overmuch effort. But then so is *Alice in Wonderland*.

> Once more she found herself in the long hall, and close to the little glass table. "Now I'll manage better this time," she said to herself, and began by taking the little golden key, and unlocking the door that led into the garden. Then she set to work nibbling at the mushroom (she had kept a piece of it in her pocket) till she was about a foot high; then she walked down the little passage: and then—she found herself at last in the beautiful garden, among the bright flower-beds and the cool fountains.

So we can't take Rowling to task for not demanding more of her readers. As great writers before her have done, she makes it easy for them to enter her world.

This approachability extends to the characters. Harry himself is a nice straightforward boy and (leaving aside the ability to travel via chimneys and cook by magic) his best friend Ron Weasley's family is similarly perfectly ordinary, i.e., there are too many children for the budget, Dad is overworked, Mum keeps the show on the road and they are a happy lot. Hermione, third member of the central triumvirate, is a grind whose parents are dentists (and nonmagic Muggles), but she is also loyal and true. Of the staff at Hogwarts, Professor Dumbledore, the Headmaster, is a genial, wise father figure, Hagrid the giant game-keeper, a burly loveable chap with a heart of gold, and Professor McGonagall, though strict, is always fair-minded. Even the bad guys are standard issue. Draco Malfoy is the snobbish sneerer beloved of all writers of boarding school stories, and his lieutenants, Crabbe and Goyle, are the thickoes who always trail along behind such a fellow. So far, so straightforward. Harry is also obliged to spend time with the Dursleys, his uncle and aunt and revolting cousin Dudley, grotesques who could well have stepped fully-fledged from the pages of Roald Dahl. Over the course of the four volumes a large cast of characters emerges —elves, trolls, goblins, mad professors and the like—all of whom are easy to understand or recognize. Gilderoy Lockhart in *The Chamber of Secrets* is one more blowhard; Rita Skeeter, in *The Goblet of Fire*, a tabloid muckraker with an appalling prose style and ethics to match. There are a lot of those about. So it is not hard for the reader to catch hold of the players. Even the blackest of all—Lord Voldemort, or He-who-must-not-be-named, a.k.a. as You-Know-Who—is not someone it takes long to get to know. He is unspeakably evil, has orphaned Harry and, as his final revenge, is plotting a comeback to finish him off. Harry has a permanent souvenir of his childhood encounter with Voldemort: his forehead bears a lightening-flash scar, which throbs agonizingly when danger from the Dark Lord is close. Voldemort strikes terror into every heart.

So both language and character are easily absorbed. But there is more to success than this. It is not, I think, the magic that does it. Magic has been around for a long time. How about this?

> For a few moments, Diamond seemed to be borne up through the depths of an ocean of dazzling flame; the next, the winds were writhing round him like a storm of serpents. For they were in the midst of the clouds and the mists, and they of course took the shapes of the wind, eddying and wreathing and whirling and shooting and dashing about like grey and black water, so that it was as if the wind itself had taken shape, and he saw the grey and black wind tossing and raving about like grey and black water, so that it was as if the wind itself had taken shape, and he saw the grey and black wind tossing and raving most madly all about him. Now it blinded him by smiting him upon the eyes; now it deafened him by bellowing in his ears; for even when the thunder came he knew now that it was the billows of the great ocean of the air dashing against each other in their haste to fill the hollow scooped out by the lightning; now it took his breath quite away by sucking it from his body with the speed of its rush. But he did not mind It. He only gasped first and then laughed, for the arm of North Wind was about him and he was leaning against her bosom.

Issue #67

Magic, in 1871, from George Macdonald's *At the Back of the North Wind*. Magic is nothing new. Alice, *The Wizard of Oz, Peter Pan, Charlie & The Chocolate Factory, Cinderella, Snow White, The Phoenix and the Carpet*—the magic list is endless. And how about all those cartoon characters? Smashed to smithereens, splintered beyond repair, up they pop, bold as brass, in the next frame.

It is the word *cartoon* that holds the clue. Much has been made of the fact that the Harry Potter series has taken children back into the wonderful world of reading.

Countless tots now long for nothing more than to curl up in bed with a book. But what is reading? What is it for? As a child, out of sheer desperation I would read the back of the cereal packet, just to feel the print going into my eyes. I don't think it did much for my overall literacy. It wasn't really reading, just word gobble.

The same might be said of these four books. They are the direct result of television, comic books, and newspaper strips. The *Independent* on Sunday put it well: "Like Gameboys, Teletubbies and films by George Lucas, Harry Potter has permeated the national child consciousness." Event follows relentlessly upon event, as J. K. Rowling conjures up yet another Hippogrif, Grimm or Basilisk, another feast of "Blocks of ice-cream in every flavour you could think of, apple pies, treacle tarts, chocolate eclairs and jam doughnuts, trifle, strawberries, jelly, rice pudding . . .", another ghost or ghoul, another magic device, another game of Quidditch. Nothing happens as a result of character, many episodes are irrelevant to the basic plot. The books feel more and more like pieces of string, joined together with random knots, until, at the final chapter, there is enough to roll up into a ball.

What, for example, is the point of Gilderoy Lockhart, featured in *The Chamber of Secrets?* He in no way advances the plot and serves merely as a page-filler. That's not to say he isn't quite a good joke, but he is a superimposed joke, not an intrinsic and necessary part of the tale. The same could be said of the Knight Bus in *The Prisoner of Askaban*, or the camping episode in *The Goblet of Fire*. They are funny, but they don't move us along. Perhaps the most striking example of sacrificing character to plot requirements comes in *The Chamber of Secrets*. Here a sequence of nasty events—strangled roosters, a petrified cat, an attacking serpent, terrifying writing on the wall—all turn out to have been the work of Ginny Weasley, young sister of Harry's best friend Ron. But as she was enchanted at the time, she is not responsible and after a rest she feels "perfectly happy again." This is the Agatha Christie school of cheating—the murderer is always the person beyond suspicion. The reader, paying attention and trying to solve a mystery, has been shortchanged.

Some might argue that over the course of the four stories there is change. But it is cosmetic. Students develop crushes on each other, they use cooler slang, their magical abilities become more sophisticated. But they do not change. Even supercilious Draco Malfoy only manages to play slightly nastier practical jokes (that usually fail) and develop a more vicious tongue. Despite always being presented as a most unpleasant piece of work he never does anything of consequence. Hermione acquires a social conscience, but it only sends her back to the library for research. The plots themselves involve death, fraud and family betrayal. There is an attempt at class consciousness, Ron and Harry quarrel and, at one point, nobody will even speak to Harry. But it all passes. Nor does Harry himself change. At the end of the last book he is once again off to spend his summer holidays with his loathesome relations. Having managed to defy death at the hands of You-Know-Who several times by this stage, it would not be beyond him, surely, to decide he would rather go somewhere else.

But Harry must go back to Privet Drive, for what we have here is a formula. In

each book the gameplan is as clear-cut as are the rules of Quidditch. Trial and tribu-
lation, interspersed with jokes (some of them rather good), mistaken identity, further unravelling of the past, all lead to another triumph for Harry. Harry Potter four,
Voldemort nil. There is never a doubt in the reader's mind but that Harry will win
through. Harry may be apprehensive, but we are not. In *Aspects of the Novel* E. M.
Forster wrote of how "tell us a story" was whispered by cavemen at night around the
fire, asking "and then, and then, and then?" He goes on to make the point that the
great story makes us ask "why? why? why?" and that the transition from "what next"
to "why on earth?" is where art begins. In none of the Harry Potter books do we ever
ask "why?"

J. K. Rowling deserves her success. I had rather be tied to a wheel of fire than
have to sit down and push the saga of Harry through to its conclusion. More jokes
required, more ordeals, more spells, more words before Lord Voldemort can bite the
dust. More conversations with publisher, agent, and film producer, more marketing,
more product. For the Harry Potter series is a marketing triumph. Books are under
embargo, then released simultaneously country-wide, while children camp on pave-
ments to be sure to have the unattainable under their arms before it's sold out and
they are the odd one out in the classroom—from the publisher's point of view it is
almost as good as selling state-of-the-art trainers. But I do not think the end of the
story will be a dramatic change in children's reading habits. Libraries will not be
filled with kids weeping over the death of Little Nell, or wondering if Romeo and
Juliet are going to get it together. Harry Potter is a craze—who knows what the next
one will be?

There is perhaps a lesson to be learned here. When I read the first book, by far
the best, formulaic, humorous, and inconsequentially alarming, it reminded me of
the stories I used to tell my daughter, making them up in the dark before she went
to sleep. Eventually, peaceful breathing would mean enough coincidences and sur-
prises had been pulled out of the air until the next night. Maybe that's something
parents could be doing more?

CONTRIBUTOR NOTES
updated contributor notes available at pbq.rutgers.edu

RAPHAEL C. ALLISON (issues 64, 65) earned his Ph.D. at New York University in twentieth-century American poetry and American philosophy. His work has appeared in *Willow Springs* and *Northeast Corridor*.

SCOTT EDWARD ANDERSON (issue 63) received the Nebraska Review Award in Poetry in 1997 and won the 1998 Larry Aldrich Emerging Poets Competition. His reviews and essays have appeared in, among other publications, *The Philadelphia Inquirer*, the *Bloomsbury Review*, and *Painted Bride Quarterly*. Anderson is also the author of a book of natural history titled *Walks in Nature's Empire*.

PRISCILLA ATKINS (issue 64) has work appearing in *Poetry*, the *North American Review*, *Passages North*, and other publications. She currently serves as Arts Librarian at Hope College in Holland, Michigan.

JOHN BARGOWSKI (issue 64) received a New Jersey State Council on the Arts Grant and the 1999 Theodore Roethke Prize. He has new work scheduled to appear in *Poetry* and *Poetry Northwest*.

WENDY BARKER (issue 64) lives and writes in San Antonio, Texas.

HERMAN BEAVERS (issue 63) teaches literature at the University of Pennsylvania and lives in Burlington, New Jersey with his wife and son.

AMY BEEDER (issue 63) has served in Haiti as a human rights monitor with the United Nations and has worked in West Africa and South America. Her work has appeared in *Boulevard* and *Free Lunch* and has been nominated for a Pushcart Prize.

MOLLY BENDALL (issue 65) is the author of *After Estrangement* (1992) from Peregrine Smith Books and *Dark Summer* (1999) from Miami University Press.

LISA BESKIN's work (issue 67) has recently appeared or is forthcoming in the *Denver Quarterly*, *LIT*, *Conduit*, *Jubliat*, *Boston Review*, and other publications. She has taught creative writing at Mt. Holyoke College and Yale, and she is a contributing writer for DVD Advance.

ERIC BIRKHOLZ (issue 64) lives in Springfield, Virginia and was recently named Poetry Fellow (1998) by the Virginia Commission for the Arts. His poems have appeared in *Atom Mind* and the *Coe Review*.

BRUCE BOND's poetry (issue 64) has appeared in the *Paris Review*, the *Yale Review*, the *Ohio Review*, *Ploughshares*, and other publications. *Radiography* (BOA, 1997) won the Natalie Ornish Award from Texas Institute of Letters. He is presently the Director of Creative Writing at the University of North Texas and Poetry Editor of the *American Literary Review*.

RITA WELTY BOURKE's work (issue 63) has appeared in *Witness*, *Shenandoah*, the *Indiana Review*, *Mid-American Review*, *Chelsea*, and elsewhere. Two of her stories have been nominated for Pushcart Prizes.

Born and raised in Scotland, ANNIE BOUTELLE (issue 65) was educated at the University of St. Andrews and New York University. She is the author of *Thistle and Rose: A Study of Hugh MacDiarmid's Poetry* and many scholarly and popular essays. Her poems have been published in *Yankee*, *Poetry*, and the *Hudson Review*.

ELENA KARINA BYRNE (issue 66) is a teacher, fine artist, and full-time regional director of the Poetry Society of America. A five-time Pushcart Prize nominee, Elena's poems have appeared or are forthcoming in the *Paris Review*, *American Poetry Review*, *Poetry*,

Ploughshares, Prairie Schooner, Parnassus, and *The Anthology of Magazine Verse & Yearbook of American Poetry,* among many other publications.

REGIE CABICO (issue 67) is single, his e-mail is missbamboo@aol.com, and he accepts movie dates. His work appears in *Bum Rush the Page: Def Poetry Jam* and *The World in Us: Gay and Lesbian Poetry of Our Time.*

NATE CHINEN (issue 63) is a jazz musician and a contributing writer for the *Philadelphia City Paper.* His poems have appeared in *CrossConnect, Gulf Stream,* and various other journals.

COLIN A. CLARKE (issue 66) has taught composition and literature at George Washington University. He is an Assistant Professor of English at Louisiana Tech and is working on a critical study of mid-twentieth-century American poets.

GRANT CLAUSER (issue 64) is a former assistant editor for the recently dissolved poetry journal *Janus.* His work has appeared in the *Literary Review,* the *Seattle Review, Caliban,* the *Pittsburgh Quarterly,* and more. He works currently as a senior editor for *Dealerscope* and as a freelance writer.

CHRISTOPHER CONNELLY (issues 63, 64, 65) lives in New York City.

C. A. CONRAD (issue 67) lives in Philadelphia. He coedits *Frequency Magazine,* an annual audio journal, with the writer Magdalena Zurawski. His chapbooks include *Frank* (Insight to Riot), *Evaporate Again* (Mooncalf), and *The Leo Journals* (Mooncalf). His forthcoming books include *Completely Frank* (Jargon Society) and *advancedELVIScourse* (Buck Downs).

JEFFERY CONWAY's poems (issue 67) have appeared in journals such as *The World, The Portable Lower East Side,* and *No Roses Review.* His work also appears in many anthologies, including *Poetry Nation* and *The World in Us.* His chapbook *Blood Poisoning* was published in 1995. He lives in New York City.

LYNN CROSBIE (issue 67) is the author of two novels, *Dorothy L'Amour* and *Paul's Case,* as well as four collections of poetry: *Queen Rat: New and Selected Poems, Pearl, VillainElle,* and *Miss Pamela's Mercy.* She is also the editor of two acclaimed anthologies of feminist writing, *The Girl Wants To* and *Click.* She lives in Toronto, where she contributes regularly to the *National Post* and *Eye.*

ALISON H. DEMING (issue 66) is the author of *Science and Other Poems, The Monarchs: A Poem Sequence,* and three books of essays, most recently *Writing the Sacred into the Real.* She is director of the University of Arizona Poetry Center in Tucson.

An excerpt from KEVIN DINOVIS's (issue 67) screenplay *Surrender Dorothy* appeared in *PBQ* 59 in 1996, a full two years before the film took top honors at the Slamdance, New York Underground, and Chicago Underground Film Festivals. He is currently polishing *Marlowe,* a period adventure about Renaissance poet and spy Christopher Marlowe. (*Jaws* still scares the hell out of him.)

WILLIAM E. DUDLEY (issue 66) has had work published in *Whetstone,* the *Concho River Review,* the *Artword Quarterly* and the *Brownstone Review* as well as many small press journals in the United Kingdom. He works with the Teen Creative Writing program at Glendale Public Library in Glendale, Arizona, teaching workshops and publishing *Woodprints,* a teen arts journal.

DENISE DUHAMEL's (issue 63) most recent titles are *The Star Spangled Banner* (winner of Crab Orchard Poetry Prize, Southern Illinois UP, 1999) and *Oyl* (a collaborative chapbook with Maureen Seaton [Pearl, 2000]). Her other books and chapbooks of poetry include: *Exquisite Politics* (a collaborative work with Maureen Seaton), *Kinky, Girl Soldier,* and *How the Sky Fell.* She has been included in four editions of *The Best American Poetry* (2000, 1998, 1994, and 1993).

SAMUEL EXLER (issue 64) has published in *Poetry East*, the *Literary Review*, *New York Quarterly*, and elsewhere. He also has work in numerous anthologies, most recently *Beyond Lament* (Northwestern UP), a collection of poetry that deals with the Holocaust.

SASCHA FEINSTEIN (issue 66) won the 1999 Hayden Carruth Award for his poetry collection *Misterioso* (Copper Canyon, 2000). He is the author of two critical books, including *Jazz Poetry: From the 1920s to the Present*, and coeditor (with Yusef Komunyakaa) of *The Jazz Poetry Anthology* and its companion volume *The Second Set*. He is Associate Professor at Lycoming College in Williamsport, where he edits *Brilliant Corners: A Journal of Jazz & Literature*.

STEVE FELLNER (issue 67) is a PhD candidate in creative writing and literature at the University of Utah. Poems and essays of his have appeared or are forthcoming in *Doubletake*, the *Alaska Quarterly*, *Poet Lore*, and *Another Chicago Magazine*, among other publications.

NICK FLYNN's (issue 63) first two collection of poems, *Some Ether* (2000) and *Blind Huber* (2002) were published by Graywolf Press. He is the 1999 winner of The Nation / Discovery Award and the PEN / Joyce Osterweil Award for Poetry. He lives in Brooklyn.

JEFFREY FRANKLIN's poems (issue 64) have appeared in the *Asheville Poetry Review*, *Cumberland Poetry Review*, The *Hudson Review*, and other publications. He holds an MFA from the University of Florida and teaches in the English Department of East Carolina University.

MARTIN GALVIN's poems (issue 64) have appeared in *The Best American Poetry 1997*, *Atlantic Monthly*, *Onthebus*, *Red Rock Review*, and *Folio*, as well as other publications. This summer, Bogg, an American-British publisher, released his chapbook, *Appetites*.

MICHAEL GRABER (issue 64) works as an editor in his native Memphis, where he moonlights as a poetry reviewer for *Commercial Appeal* and as a vaudeville, old-time, country blues mandolin and guitar player. He has work forthcoming in *Spoon River Poetry Review*, *Crab Orchard Review*, and the *Habersham Review*.

JEFF HARDIN (issue 63) teaches at Columbia State Community College in Columbia, Tennessee. His poems appear in *Ascent*, *Amaranth*, *Crab Orchard Review*, *Hayden's Ferry Review*, and other publications. His manuscript, *A Large Land Where No One Dies*, several times a finalist, seeks a publisher.

MARY CROCKETT HILL (issue 63) is the director of a local history museum in southwestern Virginia. Her first book, *If You Return Home with Food*, won the 1998 Bluestem Poetry Award and is available from Bluestem Press.

SEAN HILL's poems (issue 65) have been published in *Figdust* and *Callaloo* and are forthcoming in the *Texas Review*. In 1999 and 2000 he attended Cave Canem on a fellowship, and he recently attended Breadloaf Writers' Conference on a Waiter Scholarship. He is currently pursuing an MFA in Creative Writing at the University of Houston.

BOB HOLMAN (issue 65) is the author of seven books of poetry and editor of two anthologies, including *Aloud: Voices from the Nuyorican Poets' Café*, winner of the 1994 National Book Critics Circle Award. In 1996, he cofounded Mouth Almighty / Mercury Records, the only poetry CD label to ever gain distribution by a major label. Between 1986–94 he produced more than 50 "Poetry Spots" for WNYC-TV, a period during which the series won three Emmys. Since 1991 he has worked with Josh Blum, the President and Executive Producer of Washington Square Films and Arts, to produce the breakthrough PBS poetry video programs *Words in Your Face* and *The United States of Poetry*. In 1998 he was appointed Visiting Professor in Writing at Bard

College, where he teaches the course Exploding Text: Poetry in Performance.

BRIAN HOLTON (issue 65) graduated in Chinese at Edinburgh University and has taught at the Universities of Edinburgh, Durham, Ningbo, and Newcastle upon Tyne. He is currently teaching translation in the Hong Kong Polytechnic University. He has published translations in English and Scots and is working on a new collection of poetry by Yang Lian.

KIM HORNER (issue 64) teaches composition and literature at local colleges in Missouri. Her work has appeared or is forthcoming in *Potpourri, Mid-America Poetry Review*, the *Midwest Quarterly, Georgetown Review*, and *Poem*.

MICHAEL HUDSON's (issue 64) work has appeared in *Columbia, Green Mountains Review, Poetry East, Sulfur, Passages North*, and elsewhere.

IOANA IERONIM (issue 65) is the author of seven volumes of poetry, as well as articles, reviews, and translations from English, French, German, and Swedish. Ieronim has served as Cultural Counselor in the Romanian Embassy in Washington and publicity director for the Soros Foundation in Bucharest; currently she is a Program Director for the Fulbright Commission in Romania. Ieronim is the translator of Andrei Codrescu's poetry into Romanian in *Alien Candor / Candoare straina* (Bucharest 1997).

RADU IOANID (issue 65) performed the literal translations of Eugen Jebeleanu's poems, and is a historian who lives in Washington, DC. He writes about Romanian fascism and the Holocaust in Romania, and he wrote the introduction to the recently published *Diaries of Mihail Sebastian*.

The poet NORA IUGA (issue 65) was born in Bucharest in 1931 and, after graduating from the German faculty of the University of Bucharest, began to publish books of poetry in 1968. Her most recent collections include *Night Typist* (1996), *Dangerous Capriccios* (1998), and *The Hospital of the Mannequins* (1998). She has also published a novel, *Leopold Bloom's Soap* (1993) and translations from Herta Müller, Günter Grass, Ernst Jünger, Strindberg, Hamsun, Nietzsche, and others. Iuga has been the winner of numerous literary prizes, including prizes for poetry, fiction, and translation from the Romanian Writers' Union.

MAJOR JACKSON (issue 63) is an Assistant Professor of English at the University of Vermont. *Leaving Saturn* (University of Georgia Press, 2000) won the Cave Canum Poetry Prize and has been nominated for The National Book Critics Circle Poetry Award.

EUGEN JEBELEANU is one of Romania's most important and challenging twentieth-century poets (issue 65), but is virtually unknown in the West. He published more than twelve collections of poems during his life, received numerous prestigious European literary awards (including the Italian Taormina Prize and the Austrian Herder Prize), and in the 1970s was nominated by the Romanian Academy for the Nobel Prize.

DANIEL KANE (issue 66) has poems published in *The Hat, Exquisite Corpse, TriQuarterly, Denver Quarterly*, and other magazines.

TRACEY KNAPP (issue 63) received her BFA from Syracuse University in 1998, where she was awarded the Raymond Carver Award for Best Group of Poems by an Undergraduate. *Match in a Bottle* (Kat Ran Press, 1997) which was awarded the Florida Fonteneda Society's Book of the Year, mentioned in *Antiquarian Monthly*, and carried by Josvatteller's Rare Books, Phillip Hill Books, and Veatchs Arts of the Book.

The results of our google search suggest that FREDERIC KOEPPEL (issue 63) lives in Memphis. Fred, was that you? Please call us. We worry.

Contributors

SANDRA KOHLER's (issue 65) *The Ceremonies of Longing* was selected by Cornelius Eady for the AWP Poetry Prize.

YUSEF KOMUNYAKAA's (issue 63) latest book of poetry is *Thieves of Paradise*. He teaches at Princeton University.

KELLY LEFAVE (issue 65) holds an MFA from the University of Massachusetts at Amherst. She lives in Salt Lake City where she is completing a doctoral program in poetry at the University of Utah.

In 1991 PHILIP LEVINE (issue 63) won the National Book Award with *What Work Is* (Knopf). In 1995 he won the Pulitzer Prize, also for poetry, with *The Simple Truth* (Knopf). In April 1999, Knopf published his new book, *The Mercy*.

YANG LIAN (issue 65) was sent to rural China in the 1970s as part of a governmental reeducation program, where he began to write. When he returned to Beijing he co-founded the landmark literary magazine *Jintian (Today)*. In 1983 his poetry was banned in China.

RICK LILJEGREN (issue 63) is the 1998 recipient of the Dorothy M. Hood Poetry Award presented by the Creative Writing department of Arizona State University. Rick currently lives in Scottsdale, Arizona where he teaches English.

ADA LIMÓN (issue 66) is originally from Sonoma, California, where she was raised in a community of artists and writers including her stepfather, Brady T. Brady, and her mother, Stacia Brady. She is a Winter Fellow at the Provincetown Fine Arts Work Center. Her work appears in the *Brooklyn Review*, *Blue Mesa Review*, and *Crab Orchard Review*. She currently teaches creative writing to second graders in the Bronx. She lives in Greenpoint, Brooklyn.

YANG LIPING's (issue 65) translations into Chinese include David Lodge's *The British Museum Is Burning Down*, Clive Cussler and Paul McCarthy's *Inca Gold*, John Berendt's *Midnight in the Garden of Good and Evil*, William J. Bennett's *The Book of Virtues*, and Dan Schiller's *Digital Capitalism*. Translations into English include *A Survey of Modern Chinese Drama*, Ding Pin's *A Catastrophe in the 20th Century*, and *A Collection of Deng Sanmu's Poetry, Paintings and Calligraphy*.

THOMAS DAVID LISK's work (issue 63) has appeared in many magazines and newspapers, including most recently *Boston Review*, the *New Review*, *Urbanus*, and *Apalachee Quarterly*. Apalachee Press published a collection of his poems, *A Short History of Pens Since the French Revolution*, in 1991. His poems have been twice nominated for Pushcart Prizes.

PRISCILLA LONG (issue 64) is the author of *Where the Sun Never Shines: A History of America's Bloody Coal Industry* (Paragon House, 1989). Her fiction and poetry have appeared in the *Southern Review*, *North Dakota Quarterly*, the *Seattle Review*, *Southern Humanities Review*, and other publications.

DEANNE LUNDIN (issue 63) has been published most recently in *Antioch Review*, the *Colorado Review*, and the *Kenyon Review*.

ANNE METTE LUNDOFTE (issue 65) has published essays in books and academic journals in Denmark and contributes reviews to the Danish national newspaper, *Politiken*. She is a doctoral candidate in the Comparative Literature Department at New York University, where she also teaches Danish in the Foreign Language Program.

Force Majeure is NIELS LYNGSØ's (issue 65) latest publication. His previous books of poetry are *STOF* and *Mask and Maskine*.

NIKKI MACDONALD (issue 63) is a graduate of the MFA program at Bennington College. Her poems have appeared in *Mudfish, Calliope,* and *Michigan Quarterly Review.* She lives in New York City.

ROSS MARTIN's (issue 67) first book, *The Cop Who Rides Alone,* was published in Fall 2001 by Zoo Press. His poems have appeared recently in *Agni, Boulevard, Bomb, Denver Quarterly, Kenyon Review, Poetry Daily, Slope, Witness,* and other publications. He has taught at Washington University in St. Louis, Rhode Island School of Design, and the New School University.

CANDACE MCCLELLAND (issue 64) is a writer, student and teacher at Miami University, Ohio.

JERRY MCGUIRE (issue 63) books include *Vulgar Exhibitions* and *The Flagpole Dancer.* He recieved first prize in the 2000 Sow's Ear Poetry Review Competition. He had us at hello.

WAYNE MILLER (issue 64) is working on his MFA at the University of Houston, where he serves as a poetry editor of Gulf Coast. He won a 2000 Ruth Lilly Fellowship from *Poetry* magazine, and his poems are forthcoming in the *Paris Review, Chelsea, Western Humanities Review,* and the *Texas Review.*

ANDER MONSON (issue 67) is from Michigan but lives in Tuscaloosa, Alabama. Recent work can be found in *Quarterly West, Many Mountains Moving,* the *Florida Review,* and elsewhere. He edits the *Black Warrior Review* and *Diagram.*

CARLEY MOORE (issues 63, 66) is a poet who lives in New York City. She teaches writing to freshmen at New York University and Bard College. Her work has appeared in *Fence.* She is currently at work on her dissertation "Writing Trouble: *Seventeen* Magazine and the Girl Writer."

CHRISTIAN NAGLE (issue 63) has previously published in *Paris Review, Partisan Review, Antioch Review, New England Review, Connecticut Review,* and other journals. He has work forthcoming in *Southwest XXXX* and *Cimarron.* He was the Grand Prize Winner of *Inkwell* Magazine's 1999 poetry competition.

DANIEL NESTER's poetry (issues 63, 67) has appeared in *Mississippi Review, Slope, Fine Madness, Minnesota Review, Water~Stone,* and *Cortland Review.* A longtime editor of *Painted Bride Quarterly,* he is now a contributing editor and is editor-in-chief of *La Petite Zine.* His first book *God Save My Queen* will be available Spring 2003 from Soft Skull.

KRISTY NIELSEN (issue 64) has published work in *Mid-American Review,* the *Madison Review, The Prose Poem,* and *Spoon River Poetry Review,* among other journals. She was born in Detroit and lives in the San Francisco Bay Area but has yet to experience an earthquake.

KATE NORTHROP's work (issue 66) has appeared in *Black Warrior, Third Coast, Poet Lore,* and other journals. She is an Assistant Professor of English / Creative Writing at West Chester University and an assistant editor at *American Poetry Review.*

GIL OTT (issue 63), Editor and Publisher of Singing Horse Press, is the author of twelve books of poetry, the most recent being *Traffic* (Chax, Tucson). A collection of essays on Ott's writing is forthcoming (Chax).

ETHAN PAQUIN's (issue 65) first book is *The Makeshift* (Stride, UK). He edits *Slope,* founded *Slope Editions* and his poetry appears in *Boston Review, Stand,* and *Conduit.*

GREGORY PARDLO (issues 65) has studied at Rutgers University, Camden and the University of Copenhagen, and he has recently completed an MFA in poetry at New York University. He is a member of the Cave Canem African American poet's workshop and has received fellowships from the *New York Times* and the MacDowell Colony. His poetry has appeared in *Callaloo, Hawaii Review,* and *Lyric.*

SIMON PERCHIK (issues 63, 66) is the author of numerous books, most recently *Hands Collected* (Pavement Saw, 2000), *Touching the Headstone* (Stride, 2000), and *The Autochthon Poems* (Split/Shift, 2001). His work has appeared widely, in journals such as *PBQ*, the *Partisan Review*, *Poetry*, *American Poetry Review*, and the *New Yorker*.

JAMES POLCHIN (issue 67) lives in New York City and teaches writing at Princeton University. He is completing his dissertation at New York University in American Studies.

JESSY RANDALL's poems (issue 66) have appeared in *Antietam Review*, *Mudfish*, and *Pif*. She has work forthcoming in *Explosive Magazine* and *Light*. She lives in Colorado Springs and is Curator of Special Collections at Colorado College.

M. REBECCA RANSOM (issue 63) holds an MA in Creative Writing from Hollins College and has received an Academy of American Poets Award.

KATHRYN RANTALA (issue 63) has published in the small presses for many years and is the author of *Missing Pieces*, a collection of "forensic" poems and prose. She is founder and coauthor of *Snow Monkey*, an eclectic Seattle literary magazine.

DONALD RIGGS (issue 63) is a Sagittarius with Mercury in its detriment, a lazy Jupiter, and Moon on the Midheaven.

MJ ROBINSON (issue 67), a PhD candidate in Media Ecology at New York University, writes about filmmakers, film schools, celebrity, and consumer culture.

JACQUES ROUBAUD's (issue 65) works in English translation include the novels *Our Beautiful Heroine*, *Hortense Is Abducted*, *Hortense in Exile*, *The Great Fire of London*, and *The Princess Hoppy*, as well as the poetry collections *Some Thing Black* and *The Plurality of Worlds of Lewis*.

Originally from Georgia, T. B. RUDY (issue 66) is a lecturer at Cornell University, where he earned his MFA. Recently he has also had poems appear in *Clackamas Literary Review* and *Poetry Midwest*.

ELIZABETH SCANLON (issue 67) is the associate editor of the *American Poetry Review* in Philadelphia.

JOANNA SCOTT (issue 65) is the author of *Indochina's Refugees: Oral Histories from Laos, Cambodia and Vietnam* and two novels, *Charlie and the Children*, a Vietnam war story, and *Pursuing Pauline*, a sexual farce. Her poems have appeared in *Ontario Review*, *Malahat*, and *Spoon River Poetry Review*. Her manuscript "New Jerusalem" won the 1998 Capricorn Award for Poetry.

MAUREEN SEATON's (issue 63) fourth solo book, *Little Ice Age*, was published by Invisible Cities Press, in 2001. *Furious Cooking* won the Iowa Prize and the Lambda Literary Award. Her chapbook with Denise Duhamel, *Oyl*, was published by Pearl Editions in 2000.

RICHARD SIEBURTH's translations (issue 65) include books by Hoelderlin, Benjamin, Leiris, and Michaux. His *Selected Writings of Gerard De Nerval* received the 2000 PEN-Book-of-the-Month Translation Prize.

SEAN SINGER's poems (issue 65) have appeared or are forthcoming in *Harvard Review*, *Pleiades*, *LIT*, *Callaloo*, *Slope*, and *La Petite Zine*. He lives in Cambridge, Massachusetts.

KAREN SKOLFIELD (issue 63) is a Pennsylvania native who now lives in New England. She works at the University of Amherst in the College of Engineering.

ADAM J. SORKIN (issue 65) has published thirteen books of literary translation. His transla-

Contributors

tion *Sea-Level Zero*, poems by Daniela Crasnaru (BOA, 1999), was supported by an Academy of American Poets grant. His collaborative translations have appeared in numerous literary magazines including the *New Yorker*, *APR*, *Poetry*, and *TriQuarterly*.

RUTH STONE's (issue 63) most recent collection, *Ordinary Words* (Paris P), won the 1999 National Book Critics Circle Award. She teaches Creative Writing at State University of New York, Binghamton.

JULIA STORY (issue 64) received her MA in English from the University of New Hampshire in 1999. She is currently an MFA candidate at Indiana University and resides in Bloomington, Indiana.

TIM SUERMONDT's poems (issue 63) have appeared in many magazines, including *Poetry*, *Southern Poetry Review*, *Indiana Review*, *River Styx*, *Northeast Corridor*, the *Cortland Review*, *Barrow Street*, and *Graffiti Rag*. He is the author of the chapbook *The Dangerous Women with Their Cellos* (1998). He is a headhunter of stockbrokers and lives in Jamaica, Queens.

JENNIFER SWENDER's (issue 64) "The Paperhanger" was recently chosen as the Second Place Winner in Glimmer Train's Very Short Fiction Award Contest. She currently holds a one-year writing residency at Fort Juniper, the Robert Francis house in Amherst, Massachusetts.

RICHARD TAYSON's (issue 63) first book of poems, *The Apprentice of Fever*, won the Wick Poetry Prize. Other awards include a Pushcart Prize and *Prarie Schooner*'s Bernice Slote Award. His work appears in *Paris Review*, *Kenyon Review*, and the anthologies *The World in Us* and *American Poetry: Next Generation*.

Recipient of the 2000–02 Stegner Fellowship, BRIAN TEARE (issue 65) received his MFA from Indiana University. A former poetry editor for Indiana Review, he has poetry and prose appearing or forthcoming in *Ploughshares*, *Bellingham Review*, *Sonora Review*, and *Phoebe*, among other journals.

PAUL THOMPSON (issue 67) is an Associate Professor of Film and Television at New York University's Tisch School of the Arts. He was resident dramatist with the Royal Shakespeare Company (1977) and with the National Theatre (1977–79). He has also written for BBC Television, BBC Radio, and for feature films.

RODNEY TORRESON's (issue 63) book of poetry about the New York Yankees, *The Ripening of Pinstripes*, was published by Story Line Press in 1998. A book of his rural poems was published by New Issues Press in 2001.

DAVID TRINIDAD's (issue 67) most recent book of poems, *Plasticville*, was published in 2000 by Turtle Point Press. His other books include *Answer Song* and *Hand over Heart: Poems 1981–1988*. He currently teaches poetry at Rutgers University, where he directs the Writers at Rutgers series, and he is a member of the core faculty in the MFA Writing Program at the New School. He has also taught at Princeton University.

JEFFREY TWITCHELL-WAAS (issue 65) has taught at universities in China, the United States, Taiwan, and presently is Dean of OFS College in Singapore. Translations include *Original: Chinese Language-Poetry Group* (Parataxis, 1994), and recently he has been compiling a biographical and bibliographical resource on contemporary Chinese poets for Duration Press (www.durationpress.com/international/china/index.htm).

KYOKO UCHIDA (issue 64) works as a translator and lives in Washington, DC. Her work has appeared in such journals as *Georgia Review*, *i*, and *Black Warrior Review*.

Contributors

KARLA VAN VLIET (issue 63) lives and writes in Bristol, Vermont.

SCOTT WALDEN (issue 63) divides his time between New York and Newfoundland, photographing and teaching philosophy in both locations.

JO-ANNE M. WATTS's short fiction (issue 66) has appeared in *Other Voices*, the *Crescent Review*, *South Carolina Review*, *Sou'wester*, *Mississippi Mud*, *Northeast Corridor*, *West Branch*,and *Writers' Forum*, among other publications. She has completed a novel entitled *Becoming Ketzel Peres* and is currently working on a comic novel about the atom bomb.

CHARLES HARPER WEBB's (issue 66) book of poems, *Liver*, won the 1999 Felix Pollak Prize and was published by the University of Wisconsin Press. A new book, *Tulip Farms and Leper Colonies*, was published in 2001 by BOA Editions. A 2001–02 Guggenheim fellow, he teaches at California State University, Long Beach.

ELLEN WEHLE (issue 66) is an editor at a Boston advertising agency. Her recent activities include readings at Nichols College and the Boston Poetry Festival and performing as Eve in *Paradise Lost*. Her work has appeared in *Seattle Review*, *Greensboro Review*, and *Southeast Review*, among other journals.

VICKI WEISSMAN (issue 67) lives in London. Her reviews and other writings have appeared in *American Book Review* and the *New York Times Book Review*.

JOE WENDEROTH's (issue 64) first two books of poems, *Disfortune* (1995) and *It Is If I Speak* (2000), were published by Wesleyan University Press. Shortline published a chapbook, *The Endearment* (1999). His *Letters to Wendy's* (Verse, 2000) is available in an edition along with a CD, read by actor James Urbaniak (*Henry Fool, Sweet and Lowdown*). He is an assistant professor of English at Southwest State University in Marshall, Minnesota.

LESLIE WILLIAMS (issue 63) lives in Chicago, Illinois. Her poems are forthcoming in *Sou'wester* and *Poet Lore*.

MICHELE WOLF (issue 63) is the author of *Conversations During Sleep* (Anhinga), winner of the Anhinga Prize for Poetry, and *The Keeper of Light*, winner of the Painted Bride Quarterly Poetry Chapbook Series. Her poems have also appeared in *Poetry*, the *Hudson Review*, *Boulevard*, *Painted Bride Quarterly*, and others. The recipient of an Anna Davidson Rosenberg Award for poems on the Jewish experience, she lives in New York City, where she works as a magazine writer and editor.

ANNE HARDING WOODWORTH's (issue 63) poetry has been published in numerous journals. Her book of poetry, *Guide to Greece and Back*, was published in Athens, where she lived for several years. Her poetic monologue, "Skin Play," won first prize in the Source Theatre's 12th Annual Ten-Minute Play Competition in Washington, DC, in 1997. She lives in Washington, and is chair of the Poetry Board at the Folger Shakespeare Library.

MATTHEW ZAPRUDER (issue 65) has recently published poems in *Harvard Review*, *Fence*, and the *Verse Younger American Poets Issue*. He has work upcoming in *Volt*. Poems from his translation of Eugen Jebeleanu's *Secret Weapon* have appeared in *Verse*, *Salt Hill*, *Fence*, *International Poetry Review*, and *Exquisite Corpse*.

Work by MAX ZIMMER (issue 66) has been awarded the Pushcart prize and has been included in the PEN New Writers Series. Originally from Utah, he lives in northwest New Jersey, where he is completing a novel, *Can't Feel My Way Home*, and a collection of published poetry and fiction called *Utah Died for Your Sins*.

Editor Marion Wrenn

Senior Editors Melisa Cahnmann, Tom Hartman, Daniel Nester, Gregory Pardlo

Associate Editors Scott Edward Anderson, Christopher Connelly, Patrick Goughary, Margaret Longbrake, Carley Moore, Robin Mookerjee Jason Toogood

Readers Toni Brown, Keetje Kuipers

Contributing Editors Kathleen Volk Miller, Major Jackson

Legal Counsel Robert Louis, Chad Rutkowski

Interns 2000–2001 Sandy Landgraf, Michele Robinson, Pamela Swanson, Kim Cobb, Scott Coon, Monica Fisher, Patty Gavras, Nicole O'Keefe, Kara Monagle, Ana Hartman.

Web Design First National Digital
additional HTML authoring by Daniel Nester, Christopher Connelly and Robin Mookerjee

ISSUE 66/67

Editor Marion Wrenn

Managing Editor Kathleen Volk Miller

Senior Editors Melisa Cahnmann, Gregory Pardlo

Associate Editors Kazim Ali, Toni Brown, Christopher Connelly, Patrick Goughary, Margaret Longbrake, Robin Mookerjee

Contributing Editors Scott Edward Anderson, Major Jackson, Tom Hartman, Daniel Nester

Founding Editors Louise Simons, R. Daniel Evans

Legal Counsel Robert Louis, Chad Rutkowski

Editorial Staff Kim Cobb, Monica Fisher, Patricia Gavras, Kara Monagle, Lisa Nikolidakis

Student Interns 2001–2002 Alicia DeMarco, Charlene Lawler, Erin McCool, Andrew Paull, Courtney Rohan, Naima Stone, Amy Thompson, Robin Waterhouse, Jennifer Whitman

Web Design First National Digital

Web Maintenance La-Beeba Jones

HTML Authoring Daniel Nester and Robin Mookerjee

Address
Painted Bride Quarterly
English Dept.
Armitage Hall
Rutgers University
Camden, NJ 08104

Lily:
out of the water
out of itself

The Nick Virgilio Poetry Project
Part of the Camden Online Poetry Project
www.nickvirgilio.rutgers.edu
311 N. Fifth Street
Camden, New Jersey 08102-1405

Off the Cuffs

Poetry by and about the Police
Edited by Jackie Sheeler
Introduction by Bob Holman
$15 | 1-887128-81-6

Off the Cuffs is a poetry anthology by and about the police, and it does what no one wants writing on cops to do: It tells both sides of the story. Then collection explores the intersections of humanity where police officers are not seen just as brutalizers or heroes, but as complicated human beings in a position that is sometimes terrifying, sometimes rewarding, and often questionable. It is the exploration of this dynamic point of understanding that makes *Off the Cuffs* unique.

Off the Cuffs features poetry by cops, criminals, and upstanding citizens alike, including work by Denise Duhamel, Allen Ginsberg, Colette Inez, W. S. Merwin, Muriel Rukeyser, Kevin Young, and dozens of others.

Heredity

A novel by Jenny Davidson
$15 | 1-887128-79-4
A *Gear* Magazine *Gear* 100 Buzz Pick for 2003!

Jenny Davidson's *Heredity* tells the story of Elizabeth Mann, a young American woman who hopes to escape her troubles by taking a travel-writing assigment to London. She quickly finds herself entangled in a mystery concerning an infamous eighteenth-century criminal named Jonathan Wild, and caught up as well in a love affair with an older man and fertility specialist named Gideon Streetcar. As her obsession grows, Elizabeth and Gideon concoct a plan whereby she can become pregnant with Wild's child, and she soon shows signs of pregnancy. A devious debut.

"A refreshingly taut, deadpan take on the old intertwining-narrative, hands-across-the-centuries thing, Jenny Davidson's *Heredity* reads like the novel of which A.S. Byatt's *Possession* was the baggy and sentimental first draft. It's also as dark as your hat: sex-and-death with a side order of extra death. A masterful and outrageously readable first novel."
—Bruno Maddox, author of *My Little Blue Dress*

Surviving the Moment of Impact

Poems by T. Cole Rachel
Introduction by Albert Goldbarth
$12 | 1-887128-86-7

"It is a fierce hymn of a nearly cannibalistic passion for the people he has loved against all odds."
—Edmund White

"Rachel's debut, *Surviving the Moment of Impact* is filled with the exuberant misery of youth; it is also sweet-hearted, funny, idealistic, and full of promise . . . . Only 28 years old, Rachel has already survived several impacts, it would seem from the poems here, which tell a beginning-of-life story that is sad without being maudlin, moving without being sappy."
—*Time Out New York*

Soft Skull Press | 71 Bond St., Brooklyn NY 11217 | softskull.com

GOD SAVE MY QUEEN *a tribute*
by DANIEL NESTER

ISBN: 1-887218-27-1 | Trade Paper | 140 pp. | 7x7 | $13.00 | Music/Memoir/Poetry

In *God Save My Queen* a short essay or riff accompanies, in order of album and track, every song record-ed by the British rock band Queen, in chronological order. Part memoir, part prose poetry, part rock book, Nester's first book is genre bending at its poignant and hilarious best. It will, it will, rock you.

Daniel Nester's work has appeared in *Open City, Nerve, Mississippi Review,* and *The Best American Poetry 2003.* He is the editor in chief of the online literary journal *Unpleasant Event Schedule* (www.unpleasanteventschedule.com), former editor in chief of *La Petite Zine,* and contributing editor of *Painted Bride Quarterly.*

"Daniel Nester is a transcendent trickster, a Gogol of Rock 'n' Roll. This book is not, like so much con-temporary literature, merely a realistic snapshot of life, but an ambitious effort to find in music the rhythms of life itself."   —Darin Strauss, author of *Chang and Eng* and *The Real McCoy*

"*God Save My Queen* is funny and sorrowful and strange, just like 'Bohemian Rhapsody' was before the buffoons stole it away, just like being young and alive was before we got old and alive. Nester has wrested it all back for us in this antic, tender book." —Sam Lipsyte, author of *The Subject Steve* and *Venus Drive*

"Nester has invented the perfect form for his obsession—poems inseparable from the songs they replay, liner notes to a never-ending epiphany."   —David Trinidad, author of *Plasticville*

"Nester's brilliant tour de force *God Save My Queen* wickedly exploits the romance of rock 'n' roll to explore the shifting contures and constraints of contemporary sexuality—not to mention the way he takes the pulse of that relentless back-beat of Time itself! ... Trust me; you've never seen anything like this ambitious and compelling book."   —David St. John, author of *Study for the World's Body*

SOFT SKULL PRESS | 71 BOND ST., BROOKLYN, NY 11217 | WWW.SOFTSKULL.COM

http://pbqarchive.rutgers.edu/

WE ARE GRATEFUL FOR THE SUPPORT
OF THE FOLLOWING INDIVIDUALS AND ORGANIZATIONS

N–3 Oceanic

Tim Shields

National Endowment for the Arts
Pennsylvania Council on the Arts
The Ford Foundation

Dr. Geoffrey Sill
Dean Margaret Marsh
Dean Daniel Hart
Roger Dennis, Provost of Rutgers University-Camden
The Rutgers-Camden English Department

The Camden Online Poetry Project

Michael Neff
Webdelsol

Dr. Robert Donley

Jeremy Fenn-Smith